Amazing Women
of the Civil War

Amazing Women of the Civil War

WEBB GARRISON

Rutledge Hill Press®
NASHVILLE, TENNESSEE

Published by Rutledge Hill Press,® Inc., 211 Seventh Avenue North, Nashville, Tennessee 37219-1823.
Distributed in Australia by The Five Mile Press Pty., Ltd., 22 Summit Road, Noble Park, Victoria 3174.
Distributed in Canada by H. B. Fenn & Company, Ltd., 34 Nixon Road, Bolton, Ontario L7E 1W2.
Distributed in New Zealand by Southern Publishers Group, 22 Burleigh Street, Grafton, Auckland.
Distributed in the United Kingdom by Verulam Publishing, Ltd., 152a Park Street Lane, Park Street, St. Albans, Hertfordshire AL2 2AU.

Cover design by Schwalb Creative Communications, Inc.
Typography by Roger A. DeLiso, Rutledge Hill Press,® Inc.

All photos are from the author's private collection, unless otherwise noted.

Library of Congress Cataloging-in-Publication Data

Garrison, Webb B.
     Amazing women of the Civil War / Webb Garrison.
          p.   c.m.
     Includes index.
     ISBN 1-55853-791-0 (pb)
     1. United States—History—Civil War, 1861–1865—Women Anecdotes.
2. Women—United States—Biography—Anecdotes.   I. Title.

E628.G37   1999
973.7'082 21—dc21   99-32580
                                                                      Rev

Printed in the United States of America
1 2 3 4 5 6 7 8 9—04 03 02 01 00 99

Contents

Part Four: Angels of Mercy

Part Five: Movers and Shakers

Introduction

The Civil War was fought largely—but not exclusively—by men. Long ago, someone came up with a ballpark figure of about three hundred women who actually fought in either blue or gray. Although that figure cannot be documented or confirmed, it is widely cited. The truth of the matter is that no one knows precisely how many females went into Rebel and Federal fighting forces because many of them were disguised as males and were extremely clever. What makes this number even less accurate is that the most clever of them were probably never discovered.

Even so, three hundred female soldiers, more or less, represent only a minute fraction of the total number of troops that clashed on one battlefield after another for the 1,400-day duration of the war. Although their roles as soldiers are fascinating and absorbing, these women were not, by any stretch of the imagination, important to the outcome of any single armed clash.

Civilian life during the Civil War, however, tells an entirely different story. Here, women were almost as involved in the crisis as the fighting men they saw go off to war. In the United States and the Confederacy during the years 1861 to 1865, there were very few passive spectators. Life at home was almost as fully transformed as life in the camps and on the fields, albeit not nearly so fraught with imminent danger.

A glance at this book's table of contents indicates that women played many roles during the Civil War. What's more, only a small fraction of the millions who were caught up in the war are represented in this volume. Women had an important role. They became intimately and personally involved in raising money, making army shirts, being nurses, and acting as volunteer spies on both sides. They helped shape the course of the intensifying struggle in which Americans slaughtered Americans by the tens of thousands.

The chronicles they left behind of the tiny fragments of the war in which they were involved have no clear counterparts. Though seemingly infinitesimal in the larger scope of the war, we owe female diarists and letter writers a tremendous debt for spotlighting events about which we'd know little or nothing if we were limited to traditional (masculine) sources.

Although they differed so widely in their wartime activities that no two women whose stories are included here are alike, all had one significant element in common. Each had memorable experiences. When we view these experiences and the war at large through their eyes, we realize that all women, on both sides of the conflict, were civilian casualties of one sort or another. The wealthy and powerful labored and suffered as much as the obscure and humble.

A special debt of gratitude is owed to Bill, Cheryl, Mary, and Webb Jr.—all of whom have the same surname. These Garrisons pitched into this project and worked very hard to gather and sort through source material—the quest for some of which was comparable to having teeth pulled without anesthesia. Dr. John Simon of Southern Illinois University graciously gave permission to use a rather long quotation from the only existing biography of Julia Dent Grant.

Here's hoping that a vicarious adventure into the lives of three dozen amazing women from the Civil War will give you a new outlook on this troubled time in American history—and more important, that you'll thoroughly enjoy getting to know these women as real people instead of just names in a reference book.

Amazing Women
of the Civil War

Part I
ALL'S FAIR IN LOVE AND WAR

1

Sarah Edmonds, aka Frank Thompson

Nurse and Spy

A bill granting a pension to Mrs. Sarah E. E. Seelye, alias Franklin Thompson — Be it enacted by the Senate and House of Representatives of the United States of America in Congress assembled; that the Secretary of the Interior is hereby authorized and directed to place on the pension roll the name of Sarah E. E. Seelye, alias Franklin Thompson, who was a late private in Company F, Second Regiment of Michigan Infantry Volunteers at the rate of $12 a month.

Passed in early July 1884, the above bill was signed into law after just a few days by President Chester A. Arthur. As a result, the nurse and spy who was known to comrades as Frank Thompson drew a pension of $144 per year for fourteen years as a Civil War veteran.

Born in New Brunswick, Canada, "Frank" began life as Sarah Emma Edmondson, fifth daughter of a farmer. Her father, Isaac, openly lamented that his son, Thomas, had no outdoor interests, so Sarah did her level best to fill a spot that her brother didn't seem willing to occupy. She became an expert rider and a skilled shot with a squirrel rifle; for a time, she went so far as to wear trousers to please her father. He acted as though she had done nothing for him, however, and was so brusk and harsh that in secret talk with her siblings she began referring to him as "the brutal father." There are no hints that Sarah was sexually abused by Isaac, but she despised him so thoroughly that she ran away at about age sixteen and dropped the last two letters from her surname.

Looking back on her life in later years, she said that the name change was the first step she had taken in a desperate search for independence and "an entirely new kind of life." Once on her own and earning a pittance in a millinery shop, she might have been forced into prostitution

Pvt. Franklin Thompson, 2nd Michigan Volunteer Regiment.—Michigan State Archives

had she not been struck with a brilliant idea. Since all jobs worth having went to men, she reasoned, why not become a man and get one of them?

She may have decided to take that drastic step as a result of having seen an advertisement placed by a book publisher in distant Boston, Massachusetts. According to a notice in a provincial newspaper, the L. P. Crown firm was in immediate need of one hundred men who were willing to hustle and who were "disposed to act as agents." For practical purposes, that meant the company was ready to put men to work as door-to-door salesmen and pay them a small percent commission of their sales. Men who would come to Boston to make application in person were certain to be the ones most likely to be hired.

Somewhere en route to Boston from a small Canadian town in late 1857 or early 1858, Sarah cut her hair short and donned male attire. When "Franklin Thompson" presented himself at the offices of L. P. Crown & Co., his eagerness to work won him a position, despite his slender build, youth, and lack of experience. Frank didn't do well as a Bible salesman, but his experience with Crown won him a better job with a larger publishing firm based in Hartford, Connecticut.

After about a year on the road, Frank had saved enough money to make a trip back to the north. He reached his mother's home and knocked on the door as the sun was setting. Always hospitable, Elisabeth Edmondson invited the young fellow from the United States to come in and stay for supper. While finishing the meal, she regaled the stranger with an account of how one of her daughters had disappeared "a little more than a year ago" and had not been heard from since. Long afterward, Frank keenly remembered that his free supper was "the hardest meal to swallow of any I ever ate." When he said he was full and sat back with his arms folded, Mrs. Edmondson turned to her youngest daughter and remarked, "Fanny, don't you think this young man looks a lot like your poor lost sister?"

Back in the United States and seldom passing a door without knocking and displaying books, Frank was transferred to Flint, Michigan, where he was soon a boarder at the table of Charles Pratt. His sales in the new territory picked up so rapidly that he decided he might like to spend the rest of his life going door to door.

That notion vanished almost overnight after news reached Flint that secessionists had fired on Fort Sumter. As soon as President Abraham Lincoln's call for volunteers was printed in the local newspaper, a recruitment center was hastily set up. Lots of young fellows, Frank among them, thought it would be great fun to spend ninety days in uniform in order to whip the slaveholders of the South. Some of them were accepted as volunteers, organized into Company F of the Second Regiment of Michigan Volunteers, and sent to a training center in a nearby city.

Frank had offered his services, but was told that at five feet six inches, he was too short—and too delicate, besides. Soon, however, Capt. William R. Morse was back in Flint with his recruits, under orders to bring Company F up to a regulation number of one hundred men in order to be accepted for Federal service. On May 17, an empty spot in the regiment was filled when Frank signed up for three months of service. Because he was small and agile, he was entered on the muster roll as a nurse with the rank of private. He enlisted during a period when all military nurses were male; pioneers like Clara Barton and

Far behind his regiment on the night after Bull Run, Frank Thompson found a horse and sped toward Washington.—Nurse and Spy

At Yorktown, disguised as a black man, Frank was put to work on Confederate defenses.—Nurse and Spy

Dorothea Dix hadn't yet succeeded in persuading officials at the U.S. War Department to use females.

When Company F reached its full enrollment, the recruits were assembled at the armory for farewell ceremonies and were given front page coverage in the *Wolverine Citizen*. Frank and his comrades reached Washington during the first week of June and were assigned quarters in one of the many camps that had sprung up. Since he was listed as a nurse, he was told to report to Dr. Alonzo Palmer. A nearby hospital had been hastily improvised by putting several oversize tents close together.

At first, Frank and his fellow nurses had nothing to do but play checkers. All of them were glad to have the monotony broken by the arrival of a volunteer who had a severe case of dysentery, known as "bloody flux." Soon, cots in part of one tent were full with patients. Two or three fellows had come down with mumps; another, who looked as though he wished he'd never heard of fighting secessionists, was diagnosed by Palmer with a severe case of typhoid fever.

In his spare time, of which he had plenty, Frank managed to get inside the unfinished Capitol of the United States. He was surprised to see a long line of men waiting at the door of the executive mansion. He learned that they were seeking to become officers and hoping that the president would put their names on the government payroll.

Suddenly, tedium vanished and sight-seeing came to an abrupt halt. Thousands of green soldiers were ordered in the general direction of Richmond, Virginia. With luck, some of them would get off a few shots at Rebels if the Union put up a fight before their 90-day volunteer status expired. Camp talk had it, though, that there probably wouldn't be a battle at all. President Lincoln had placed Gen. Irvin McDowell in command of Federal forces, and Rebels were likely to give up and bring their states back into the Union as soon as they saw that "Old Abe" meant business.

Washington socialites packed picnic lunches and made plans to see the "fun" when it appeared certain that converging forces would meet somewhere in the vicinity of Manassas, Virginia, on the third Sunday of July. To the consternation of political leaders, they found that the city didn't have enough carriages to accommodate all who wanted them. By the time folk discovered on Saturday night that they wouldn't be able to join the "gala" activities near Bull Run, the 2nd Michigan had moved out of Centreville to meet the enemy.

Frank found battle to be anything but a picnic, and he fervently wished that his regiment could have taken part in a victory instead of the ignominious defeat. After the retreat of McDowell's forces turned into a rout, Frank became separated from his comrades as a result of searching for a missing friend. It was very late when he climbed on a horse and urged it toward Washington at top speed.

Within days, the governor of Michigan appealed to men of the 2nd regiment to stay at the front instead of coming home. Practically all of them agreed to do so, making their regiment the first in which enlistments remained for three years instead of just three months. Sent on a foraging mission when Federal forces moved toward Yorktown, Frank spent several days hunting for food. Later, having stumbled upon a wounded Rebel in a deserted house, he brewed tea and cooked hoecake for the dying man.

While Federal forces were closing in on Yorktown, a phrenologist examined Frank's head. To the surprise of the private, he was told that the configuration of his skull indicated that he'd make an excellent spy. Word of this verdict reached officers, and the private was instructed to go into Confederate lines and gather as much information as possible. Having blackened exposed parts of his body and donned a woolly wig, the neophyte undercover agent headed toward Yorktown. Falling in with a gang of conscripts who were forced to labor on Rebel fortifications, Frank was put to work with them. He managed to elude sentries and return to his regiment "with blistered hands and a head full of hastily gathered information about Rebel positions and plans."

There were no sick or wounded men to be cared for at the time, so Frank became a mail carrier and served briefly as regimental postmaster. According to his detailed account of activities during 1862, he was an aide to Gen. Philip Kearny during the Seven Days' Battle. In June he was transferred to the staff of Gen. O. O. Howard, for whom he was a courier at Fair Oaks. The terrific slaughter there caused every field hospital to overflow long before all the casualties were removed from the field. Dozens of them were placed on the ground under what they jokingly called the hospital tree. Serving temporarily on detached duty as a spy, Frank was spared the agony of hearing men sobbing for breath and having to dress their fatal wounds.

At an unspecified time shortly before or after being at Antietam for the bloodiest day of the war, Frank later said he "posed" briefly as a female. In this "disguise," he penetrated Rebel lines several times and brought back valuable information. He was greatly distressed, however, when he discovered once while ministering to a casualty that the wounded soldier was also a female in disguise.

At Fredericksburg, the Canadian reported in an account of his activities as a nurse and a spy, that he had served as an aid to Gen. Winfield Scott Hancock. Soon after the tragic Federal loss at the Virginia city, the 2nd Michigan was sent to Louisville, Kentucky. As a result of this move, Frank was in the river city on the same evening that Southern-born Pauline Cushman performed her daring actions and also became a spy for the Union (see Chapter 14).

The loyalties of many Kentuckians, he soon discovered, were so badly divided that a fellow could get into serious trouble almost anywhere. While on another spy mission, he encountered a Confederate

While ministering to a dying soldier, Frank was amazed to discover that the casualty was a female.—Nurse and Spy

captain who tried to force him into a gray uniform against his will. Unable to escape by any other means, Frank shot and wounded the Rebel officer. Back with his comrades, Frank was soon heavily engaged in hand-to-hand fighting for the first time in his short military career.

Weakened by fatigue and a lack of proper food, the Canadian soldier in Federal uniform contracted malaria. Even though the spread of this disease was not understood even by the surgeon general at that time, Frank had seen enough cases to be positive that he was in the clutches of it. Malaria would leave him unable to cope without medical treatment. Hospitalization would have meant an examination of his body, so Frank deserted.

Fearful of arrest if he returned to his regiment, after having recovered from the chills and fever of malaria, Frank took another drastic step. Resuming female attire and identifying herself as the Sarah Edmonds of earlier days, the deserter from the 2nd Michigan spent most of the remainder of the war in St. Louis as a worker for the U.S. Sanitary Commission. She had started work earlier on a book of "experiences and observations" of the Civil War. Published in Hartford as *Nurse and Spy in the Union Army: Comprising the Adventures and Experiences of a Woman in Hospitals, Camps, and Battlefields,* the volume was successful beyond Sarah's wildest dreams. By the time it went out of print it had sold an estimated 175,000 copies. A success on this scale practically demanded another book; entitled *Unsexed; or The Female Soldier*, it described in detail the dual life of Sarah Edmonds and Frank Thompson.

Sarah became Mrs. Linus Seelye on April 27, 1867, and spent nearly two decades in obscurity. Because she never devulged the identity of her regiment in her published works, her decision to attend a reunion of the 2nd Michigan regiment led to the revelation that Pvt. Frank Thompson had been a young Canadian woman in disguise.

Many of the events described in *Nurse and Spy* are clearly the products of a vivid imagination. No soldier could have worked intimately with men like Kearny, Hancock, Howard, and McClellan without being named in dispatches, orders, or correspondence. How much of what Frank Thompson supposedly experienced is genuine and how much of it is false, it is impossible to determine.

This much is clear, however; of the several hundred females believed to have fought in the Civil War disguised as males, Sarah Edmonds is probably the most widely known. It is amply documented that she was placed on the pension rolls as a veteran and that she subsequently succeeded in getting "deserter" removed from the record of her alternate life as Frank Thompson.

As if these accomplishments were not enough, Sarah Edmonds Seelye was later mustered into the Grand Army of the Republic in April 1897. When she was accepted as a member of the George B. McClellan Post, Number 9, she became the only female member of the national veterans' organization. Hence, it was fitting that on Memorial Day 1901, the remains of Frank Thompson aka Sarah Emma Edmonds—or Sarah Emma Edmonds aka Frank Thompson (depending on how you look at it)—were interred in Washington Cemetery's plot of the Grand Army of the Republic in Houston. By explicit request of the deceased, the tombstone was inscribed with nothing but her real name and the designation "Army Nurse."

2

The Roswell Women

Vanished

On July 21, 1864, Indiana's *New Albany Ledger* carried a page one account of new arrivals in the region:

> A small detachment of the Southern Confederacy in the shape of two hundred and nineteen women and children, arrived in the city last evening on the Nashville train. They are all ardent admirers of Jeff Davis and the Southern cause. They were picked up "Way down in Georgia" by order of Major-General Sherman, and forwarded to this city to be sent north of the Ohio River to remain during the war.
>
> The population of Indiana is on a rapid increase, but we fear that the additions will not add much to the loyalty of the state. The officers in charge of the detachment report that a motley group of the disloyal citizens of Georgia, said to number fifteen hundred, of both sexes and of all ages, are now at Nashville, waiting transportation to the land of freedom and drafts beyond the flow of the Ohio. These people are mostly in a destitute condition, having no means to provide for themselves a support. Why they should be sent here to be transferred North is more than we can understand.

This story, slightly modified from one that appeared a day earlier in the *Louisville Journal*, omits an especially disparaging comment made about the newcomers to the land where freedom from slavery reigned, but men and their relatives dreaded each new draft for soldiers. Of the Georgia women and their children the *Louisville Journal* demanded, "Is it right to

Gen. Garrard celebrated the capture of Roswell by ordering a ration of whiskey for his men.

throw upon Indiana, because she happens to be 'North of the Ohio,' the burden of supporting this class of people?"

These and other newspaper accounts constitute the last clues to the disappearance of more than four hundred women and children who were seized by Federal forces in Roswell, Georgia. These unidentified civilians upon whom Federal wrath was vented simply vanished when they put their feet on the soil "north of the Ohio River," and their relatives never found out where they went, what happened to them, or where their bones lie today.

The only offense committed by these women and children: working in textile mills close to Atlanta. New York's *Commercial Advertiser* called word of the affair "a frightful disgrace" and urged readers to hope that the terse accounts of it would prove to be false. Their truthfulness, however, sheds light on a seldom-seen aspect of the life of Southern women during the war.

Coastal planter Roswell King had discovered in 1835 that Vickery Creek could be dammed in such a way as to provide abundant water power. He built a thirty-foot dam and waterfall with a wooden millrace; within three years, Roswell Mills was fully operational.

By 1850 King's operation required five bales of cotton a day for production of shirting, yarn, and osnaburgs—several kinds of coarse linen first made in Osnaburg, Germany. About one hundred and fifty women worked in the mills at that time, eleven hours a day, six days a week. The war brought new, imperative demands for cloth. No Georgia community was better prepared to meet that demand than Roswell—boasting two cotton mills and one woolen mill at the time. Many workers lived in sturdy, two-story apartment buildings.

With Federal forces pushing inexorably southward from their starting point at Chattanooga, July 4, 1864, saw vigorous action. Confederates tried to bar the entrance of the enemy from Ruff's Station, about five miles above Marietta, Georgia. Though the number of troops involved was small, the significance of the encounter was great. It showed that Rebels would fiercely contest the approach of Federal forces on the rail center of Atlanta.

C.S. Gen. Joseph E. Johnston had spent weeks fortifying high bluffs along the Chattahoochee River. They constituted the most formidable obstacle that lay in front of Federal forces. Even Union Gen. William T. Sherman knew that hasty frontal attacks would be futile. Until troops could be moved across the river in great numbers, there was no way he could strike directly at his next target.

Yankees had reasonably good geographical information. They knew that north of the city of Columbus, Georgia, there were very few bridges across the Chattahoochee. The best of them were sure to be burned by Rebels once they got their men and guns across the waterway. One of these bridges was located at Roswell and ran parallel to a long Atlantic and Western Railroad bridge. Since it had been built solely for use by wagons, this structure wasn't suitable for movement of troops and heavy field artillery. However, numerous ferries were believed to operate between the railroad bridge and Atlanta.

Because he was skirmishing near Chattanooga, Sherman sent Gens. James B. McPherson and John M. Schofield to locate the lower ferries. At the same time, he ordered Gen. Kenner Garrard to head for Roswell and its bridge. The cavalry leader asked what he should do on reaching

Numerous operators of spindles lived in this two-story "apartment building."

An unknown artist—who may or may not have been present when the women reached Marietta—sketched the buildings in which they stayed briefly.

Roswell, a village about which little was known. "Don't make a damned bit of difference," his commander stormed, "so you get out of here and go for the rebels."

Garrard's advance column reached Roswell on July 5, and the main body of his riders followed the next day. A small opposition force, falling back toward Atlanta, had burned the bridge over the Chattahoochee as they retreated. That was not a surprise; Sherman and his commanders had learned to adapt, preferring good fording places to bridges.

Roswell owed its very existence to one of these shallow fords. In days before white men gained control of the region, the old Native American Hightower Trail ran across the Chattahoochee River by means of this fording place. Yankees secured the ford, taking stock of the assets of the captured village. To Garrard's surprise, he found that despite its small size, Roswell was a major manufacturing center. Garrard and his men set all three mills on fire. That night he reported to his commander: One of the cotton mills, he said, was equipped with 216 looms. All three mills had been working at capacity, "making cloth, thread and rope for the rebels." Several thousand yards of cloth were confiscated. As yet, however, the Yankee cavalryman had only found time to inspect the ruins of one mill. He'd been momentarily puzzled by one of the mills, he reported. Though it looked much like other Roswell structures, he found a French flag flying over it. After consideration, he decided that the flag was a Rebel ruse. So he ignored the possibility of an international incident and ordered that it be torched along with the other buildings.

Sherman received Garrard's report "in the field near Chattahoochee" on July 7. He promptly replied that he "had no idea that the factories at Roswell remained in operation." He then gave his full approval to the burning of the factories, even though he had not ordered it.

Furthermore, use of the French flag at Roswell triggered an outburst of Sherman's famous temper. "You will arrest the owners and employees [of all the factories] and send them, under guard, charged with treason, to Marietta," he ordered. He then continued by saying:

> I will see as to any man in America hoisting the French flag and then devoting his labor and capital in supplying armies in open hostility to our government. Should you, under the impulse of anger, hang the wretch, I approve the act beforehand.

Sherman's long telegram to Garrard further ordered him to:

> Arrest all people, male and female, connected with those factories, no matter what the clamor, and let them foot it, under guard, to Marietta, whence I will send them by cars to the North. The poor women will make a howl. Let them take their children and clothing, provided they have the means of hauling or you can spare them.

Back in Roswell, Gen. Grenville Dodge was busy attempting to rebuild the Chattahoochee River bridge with lumber salvaged from the ruined factories. Celebrating the cordial telegram from his commander, Garrard ordered a ration of whiskey for each of his men—only the second time he'd provided it since hostilities began.

No one knows precisely how many women were to be treated as traitors and deported to the North. Most estimates range between 350 and 400 adults. One account says that two of the female workers were black.

During a period of about seventy-two hours, all of the Roswell women and some of their children were sent to Marietta, a few miles away. According to Garrard, they went in U.S. Army wagons. Dodge recalled years later, however, that the women climbed on the backs of horses behind cavalrymen and rode to Marietta without saddles. A correspondent for the *New York Tribune* said he personally saw "the 400 factory girls loaded into one hundred ten wagons" for what he believed to be a thirteen-mile journey.

Gen. George H. Thomas, stationed at Nashville, was at a loss as to what he should do with the Roswell women.

"Only think of it!" the newsman wrote. "Four hundred weeping and terrified Ellens, Susans, and Maggies transported in the seatless and springless army wagons, away from their lovers and brothers of the sunny South; and all this for the offense of weaving tent cloth and spinning stocking yarn!" Yankee Capt. David P. Conyngham, in a letter sent home, wrote simply that "it was feeling to witness how the women wept."

Official U.S. Army records plus letters of eyewitnesses make it clear that the women reached Marietta. Ted Upson of the 100th Indiana regiment wrote home that:

> We have some 400 young women in the old Seminary Building near town. They have been working in a factory making cloth for the Confederate government. Some of them are tough and it's a hard job to keep them straight and to keep the men away from them.

Harper's Weekly artist Theodore R. Davis, who sketched occupied Marietta, didn't say where the factory women were housed during their brief stay. Reporting to Sherman by telegram, Gen. George H. Thomas said that "the Roswell factory hands, 400 or 500 in number, have arrived. Most of them are women. I can only order them transportation to Nashville, where it seems hard to set them adrift. What had best be done with them?"

Sherman replied tersely, "I have ordered General [Joseph] Webster at Nashville to dispose of them. They will be sent to Indiana."

Women forcibly deported to the North made up only part of the stream of civilians using the mostly single-track railroad held by Yankee invaders. Col. D. C. McCallum, Chief of Federal Military Railroads, estimated that for a time one thousand refugees headed for Nashville each day. According to him, most who reached that city were turned away.

Even in the emotional climate of war, Union supporters and leaders questioned Sherman's actions with respect to the Roswell women. "The capture was a novel one in the history of wars," the *Cincinnati Commercial* informed its readers.

No formal justification of the deportation was ever offered by U.S. officials. Since the United States had not actually declared war on the Confederacy, a scholar would probably say that the factory workers couldn't possibly have been guilty of treason. More personal—and even more obscure—is the question of what happened to so many women and their children. Notice of them in official records ends at Nashville. Newspaper stories indicate that they were actually dispersed in Indiana. If this took place, their economic status and the troubled times meant that all ties with their former lives in Roswell were severed.

This nearly forgotten side incident of the Civil War was, at the time, only a minor incident. Armies were in collision, cities were being shelled and burned, and generals on both sides were being shot from the saddle. Thousands of men lay dead on battlefields, and tens of thousands were being subjected to the surgeon's saw for amputation of legs and arms. Under such circumstances, who had the time, inclination, or writing materials with which to record the movements of such an obscure group of refugees?

The Roswell Historical Society has only a smattering of information about the women who were sent North from that location. Neither the Georgia State Archives, the University of Georgia libraries, nor the Atlanta Historical Society has any significant information not already included in official records or the letters of soldiers. The Indiana State Library has a few brief newspaper accounts of arrivals in the state, but no information about subsequent events in which the women were involved.

All of this brings this inquiry to a close with one question: Is it possible, even in the turmoil of war, that an estimated four hundred American women forced to go "north of the Ohio River" could have been turned loose to fend for themselves and subsequently have vanished without a trace?

3

Six Vignettes

Surprise! Surprise!

The French Lady

Males aboard the side-wheel steamer *St. Nicholas*—members of the crew as well as passengers—tried to sneak covert glances at the heavily veiled lady who boarded not far from Federal Hill in Baltimore on June 28, 1861. Women tossed their heads and looked the other way; they pretended to have no interest in the colorful passenger who was listed as Madame La Force. It was impossible, however, to escape noticing that the French lady, as she was called by her shipmates, had an unusually large quantity of luggage—much of which was in large millinery trunks.

By the time the vessel reached Point Lookout, a possible sight for a Federal prison camp, the weather had become nasty. Rain caused most of the passengers to pay only slight attention when eight men boarded there. Speaking with a decidedly continental accent, the beguiling passenger explained that "rain hinted that it would be wise to retire for the night" before going below.

When the *St. Nicholas* was half an hour from the wharf and headed toward her next stopping point, Rebel Richard Thomas, wearing a Zouave uniform and armed with a cutlass and pistols, sprinted on deck. Without the heavy veil and hoopskirts, he didn't look a bit like the mysterious French woman he had pretended to be. He gestured to approximately two dozen of his followers, who had come aboard during the last forty-eight hours, and a few of them ripped open the trunks of the "French lady" and began distributing weapons to their comrades. Soon they had taken over the vessel, successfully completing the first step toward seizing the mighty USS *Pawnee*, believed to be moored on the Virginia side of the Potomac River.

Thomas, a former cadet at West Point with an urge for adventure, had spent time in California before going to Italy to fight pirates. He had taken on the pseudonym of Zarvona, which appears in many dispatches and reports. His daring escapade, which apparently had been approved by high-level Virginia leaders, might have succeeded had the *Pawnee* not been moved to a relatively inaccessible location much closer to Washington. Undaunted by failure, Zarvona, using the same technique, set out to capture the *Columbia* instead.

Unfortunately for him, seamen onboard from the *St. Nicholas* recognized him almost as soon as he came aboard. Aided by a Federal officer and a policeman from Baltimore, these sailors took over the ship and headed toward Maryland's Fort McHenry, where an entire company of soldiers swarmed aboard. Zarvona's uniform, weapons, and papers were found immediately, but the sailors found no trace of Zarvona . A 90-minute search revealed that Zarvona had slipped into a cabin and was curled up in the drawer of a piece of furniture.

The "French lady" later spent nearly a year imprisoned at Fort Lafayette in New York Harbor, then languished almost as long at Fort Delaware. There "one of the most colorful women of the Civil War" was released in April 1863 on one condition—that he leave the United States

A fellow passenger picks up the kerchief of Madame LaForce, aboard the steamer soon to be hijacked.—HARPER'S WEEKLY

and never come back. Zarvona solemnly made the required pledge of exile and went to France, where he spent the rest of his life. In his latter years he had the satisfaction of knowing that he was the only person in the Civil War whose impersonation of a member of the opposite sex spread his exploits across forty-four pages of the *Official Records*.

Mrs. Turchin

Ivan Vasilevitch Turchinoff of Don, Russia, fought in the Crimean War before coming to the United States in 1856 and Anglicizing his name. Working as a topographical engineer for the Illinois Central Railroad when war broke out, he immediately volunteered and was put in command of the 19th Illinois. Like many officers on both sides, Turchin took his wife with him into camp and seems to have depended on her for military as well as domestic advice.

Given command of a brigade without having been made a brigadier, Turchin led his men well at Bowling Green, Kentucky, and later during a famous raid on Huntsville, Alabama. They encountered stiff opposition in Athens, Alabama, and, after fending off attacks by Rebels, went on a looting spree. Tried by a court-martial over which James A. Garfield presided, the Russian was found guilty of misconduct; his dismissal from the military service was recommended.

While court was in session and before a verdict had been reached, Turchin's wife raced toward Washington, where she gained an audience with Abraham Lincoln. When the verdict concerning her husband reached Washington, she not only persuaded the president to set it aside, but also secured a commission for her husband in recognition of his service at Huntsville, by which he became a brigadier.

Known by his men as the "Russian Thunderbolt," Turchin fought well at Stones River, Chickamauga, Missionary Ridge, and Atlanta. In July 1864, constant bouts with illness led to his resignation. For ten days during one of his periods of illness, his wife had commanded his unit. Described as having "seemed almost imperial, riding side-saddle on a great horse," the Russian woman reputedly led her husband's regiment in at least one engagement. Even if that is the case, the Smithsonian Institution's recognition of Harriet Tubman as the only American woman to do so stands unchallenged—for Mrs. Turchin was the daughter of a regimental commander in the army of the czar of Russia, not an American woman.

Tainted Woman

As the only child of a merchant and farmer, Anna Blair had comforts that many of her era envied. After her mother's death, she and her father moved to Wisconsin; at age sixteen she married a man known only as Etheridge. Their union was brief, and after having secured what she believed to be a divorce, she was viewed askance in the village of what was then the West.

Anna went back to Detroit just as the Civil War was beginning, with regiments largely under state rather than national control. Michigan authorities seem to have welcomed women who offered their services as nurses. As a result, Anna became one of more than a dozen women who were attached to the 2nd Michigan regiment just days after the fall of Fort Sumter.

Anna Etheridge with her military medals.— MICHIGAN STATE ARCHIVES

Many of these volunteers were discharged after their 90-day enlistment expired, but some members of the regiment—Anna included—signed up for three years.

She was the only woman who was included in regimental rolls when her unit fought at Bull Run. On detached service for a period, so that she could work for the Hospital Transport Service, her ties with the Army of the Potomac were so strong that she told old comrades goodbye when they departed for the Western Theater. Having transferred to the 3rd Michigan so she could remain in the East, she was at or near Gettysburg, Cold Harbor, and numerous other battlefields.

At the war's end, the woman, who was considered tainted by some because she was divorced, married another veteran. The pair settled down in Washington. There, she had the joy of telling her children and grandchildren that during four years of hard living and bitter fighting, she was the only woman on whom the special Kearny Medal—named for Gen. Philip Kearny and awarded to those who served honorably under him—was bestowed.

Pvt. Albert D. Cashier

Because Illinois was hard pressed to fill its draft quota, recruitment officers asked few questions when Albert D. Cashier indicated his willingness to fight. When he was accepted early in August 1862, the Irish-born recruit was put into Company G of the 90th Illinois regiment.

Within a month, the regiment was mustered into Federal service and was soon assigned to the Army of the Tennessee. Much of 1863 was spent in the lengthy Vicksburg campaign, after which the soldiers from Illinois took part in the Red River expedition. The unit gave a notable performance at Brice's Cross Roads, Mississippi, before taking part in the Battle of Nashville. Having completed almost three years of service, the regiment was mustered out during the summer of 1865.

On returning to Belvidere, Cashier received a tremendous ovation from fellow townsfolk. Work was scarce there, however, so the combat veteran moved to Saynemin and found a job as a farmhand. In 1911, after working there for years, Cashier sustained a leg injury in an accident. On examining Cashier, the doctor discovered that his patient was actually female. At age sixty-six and suffering from severe arthritis, Cashier was sent to the Soldiers' and Sailors' Home in Quincy. This change apparently triggered mental as well as physical problems, and the Civil War veteran was committed to an asylum for the insane in 1913.

That's when authorities and newspaper reporters learned that Albert Cashier was really named Jennie Hodgers. The revelation was questioned when stories about the Union veteran broke in newspapers. Members of an examining board in Washington made a careful investigation and concluded that the Irish-born immigrant had kept her gender a secret for forty-two years, during part of which time she was paid an invalid soldier's pension of $70 a month. Had she been lucid at her death in 1915, Jennie could have held her head very high; records indicate that she was the only woman in blue or gray who served a full term of enlistment and was honorably discharged. What's more, her assumed name is included in the massive Illinois monument at Vicksburg.

Younger Brother

With the possible exception of western Tennessee, no section of the South was more politically divided in 1861 than was western North Carolina. Slightly more than half the natives were strongly opposed to secession. But many of their neighbors desperately wanted out of the Union and bragged that "any southerner worth his salt can lick half a dozen Yankees with one hand tied behind his back."

Traipsing around western North Carolina's towering Grandfather Mountain during childhood, Malinda Pritchard suffered hardships comparable to those of young Harriet Tubman. Though she and her family were never legally enslaved, their grinding poverty served as leg irons and handcuffs that prevented them from doing more than simply sustaining life, working from sun-up to sundown.

At age fourteen she was so rebellious that members of her family heaved a mighty sigh of relief when they learned she planned to marry Keith Blalock, ten years her senior. (Keith was not the bridegroom's real name; during adolescence he so admired a popular bare-knuckle boxer named Keith that he began using the athlete's name.)

Though most of his close relatives were Unionists, Keith decided to put on a gray uniform. When his bride learned of his plans, she whacked off

"Sam Blalock," the supposed younger brother of Keith, in later years.—The Southern Historical Collection, University of North Carolina at Chapel Hill

her hair, pulled on trousers large enough to conceal her figure, and joined the 26th North Carolina as Sam Blalock—younger brother of Keith. After a few weeks of service around Kinston, North Carolina, Keith became fed up with the life of a soldier. He found a thick patch of poison oak, took off most of his clothes, and rolled in it long enough to become "a sight to behold" when the poison took effect. A hasty examination by a regimental surgeon led to the conclusion that Blalock had a contagious disease of some sort, so he was discharged during the spring of 1862. In order to get a discharge also, "Sam" confessed that the two were not blood relatives and she was actually a female.

The pair, who had tried military life for only a few months, were not welcomed by the Unionist majority in their town when they returned. Consequently, they drifted into nearby Tennessee and joined a band of fighting men who had no formal allegiance to either side. Malinda, who had successfully posed as her husband's younger brother, was one of only a handful of females in the North or South who rode, fought, and plundered for many months as a member of a guerrilla group.

Young and Rather Pretty

A newspaper correspondent working part-time for the *Altoona* (Pennsylvania) *Register* wandered into remote Huntington County late in the spring of 1862. To his surprise, he found the hamlet of Broadtop City buzzing with excitement. Everyone there wanted to be first to tell this newly arrived writer about a newcomer in town who was mostly described as "young and rather pretty." She had just been discharged from Federal forces and had come to the village wearing an infantry uniform.

Major Belle Reynolds in civilian attire.

Residents told the man from Altoona that Mary Owens, whose parents had come to the United States from Wales, had involved herself in the Civil War when she announced that she planned to marry John Owens. After a secret marriage in Montour County, she and her husband enlisted in the same company—calling themselves John Owens and John Evans.

The pair camped and fought side by side for about eighteen months, until one day, Owens fell dead by the side of his disguised wife. According to the *Rebellion Record*, "This remarkable woman took part in three battles, and was wounded twice; first in the face above the right eye, and then in her arm, which required her to be taken to the hospital, where she confessed the deception." Unwilling to resume civilian life where she left it, the young widow chose a different community in which to make a new start. By the time word of her exploits reached the *Altoona Register*, the female veteran was widely hailed as "the heroine of the neighborhood."

Musketoon Bearer

Like Col. and Mrs. Turchin, Belle Reynolds went to war serving the same state in which Abraham Lincoln was living when he became president—Illinois. Her military service seems to have occurred entirely within units of state guardsmen. Though little is known about her activities, one unusual and unique fact has survived: She reputedly disdained the use of muskets and insisted on carrying a musketoon when serving in the 17th Illinois. The musketoon had a large bore and a short barrel, making it the Civil War equivalent of a sawed-off shotgun.

State guardsmen drilled, marched, and spent some of their weekends in camps. They were not, however, subject to the authority of Federal commanders. This, plus the fashion in which governors appointed most officers up to and through the rank of colonel, was a prime source of irritation to Gen. William T. Sherman and many others who were less vocal about their objections.

Though never going off to war, a number of women who were members of these state forces received commissions from their governors. Most of them became lieutenants, and a few became captains. Reynolds's claim to fame was being an Illinois state major.

The Famous and Fictitious Sue Mundy

Long before tabloids became popular in the United States, many a newspaper correspondent and editor exploited sensational stories to boost readership and circulation. George Prentice of the *Louisville Courier* often boasted to readers about his skill in finding and publicizing stories that other papers neglected or overlooked. That's why some of his pro-

fessional colleagues were suspicious when he ran a front-page account of a female "second in command" of a gang of cutthroats who often called themselves partisan rangers.

"By pure coincidence," Prentice said, the female guerrilla had the same name as that of a notorious Louisville madam— Sue Mundy. She and her band reportedly roamed throughout much of Kentucky and staged a spectacular bank robbery at Harrodsburg. Mundy, said Prentice, dressed as a male and often wore a full Confederate uniform. "She is a bold rider and a dashing leader who can be detected only by her comely form," he wrote.

Marcellus Clark, aka Sue Mundy.

According to the editor, the she-devil about whom he wrote had participated in murder, robbery, and partisan raids. His accounts of her exploits were highly embarrassing to Gen. Stephen G. Burbridge, commander of Federal forces in the state. Why on earth, suggested the editor, couldn't the head of a large body of soldiers put an end to the depredation of this young woman?

No one—least of all Burbridge—had a ready answer to that question. Soon, it was suggested that the Mundy gang had joined forces with the notorious William Quantrill, who was responsible for atrocities in Kansas. An intensified hunt failed to bag Sue, but a troop of cavalrymen was successful in capturing a young guerrilla known as Marcellus Clark.

When he confessed to most of the crimes of which "the female partisan" was accused, authorities began to see the light. Clark, who wore his hair very long, was young and slender. Descended from a prominent family, he was probably well known to Prentice. In a series of moves designed to embarrass Burbridge and his troops, the editor had deliberately deceived the public by inventing the fictional character Sue Mundy and attributing Clark's exploits to her.

Here the saga of one of Kentucky's most notorious female guerrillas should have ended, but it did not. Largely due to publicity from the reported deeds of Sue Mundy, Clark was brought to trial for crimes against the state. Public feeling ran so high that Clark, who never actually posed as a woman but was associated with the stories of Sue Mundy, lasted only three days, after which the leader of notorious robbers and killers was hanged.

4

Harriet Tubman

Conductor

An index finger pressed firmly against her lips, the "conductor" signaled silence. Fourteen shivering, terrified, and determined slaves hunkered down in the night air and obeyed the woman who risked her life for their freedom. Their breath visible in the cold Canadian air, they waited—anxious for the coming of the next person to guide them on the final leg of the journey.

Harriet Tubman made nineteen similar trips during the decade prior to the Civil War. Traveling along a clandestine trail that stretched from Dorchester County, Maryland, to St. Catharines, Ontario—a major branch of the Underground Railroad—she helped an estimated three hundred slaves reach freedom. Her first such journey was to escape slavery herself. Later, she served as an advisor to John Brown in his raid at Harper's Ferry. She then became a spy, nurse, cook, and grave digger for Union forces. She even led a military raid that made history.

Born as Araminta Ross to Harriet Greene (Old Rit) and Benjamin Ross (Old Ben) circa 1820 on a Maryland plantation owned by Edward Brodas and situated on Big Buckwater River in Dorchester County, Harriet served as a fieldhand, scrubwoman, cook, and house servant— wherever she was commanded to be. When she was five years old, Brodas sold her to the Cook family, where the mistress beat her repeatedly and often sent her barefoot and without proper clothing to set muskrat traps with Mr. Cook. Exposure to the elements resulted in a severe cough, which developed into bronchitis. Burning with fever, Harriet no longer had value, so the Cooks sent her back to Brodas, and Harriet's mother nursed her back to health.

At age seven the girl was sent to care for the child of another family— a job that proved disastrous. Many nights she slept shivering from cold, hungry and poorly clad, tucking her feet close to her body and positioning herself between the family's dogs and the warmth of the stove. Once she tried to steal a lump of sugar without being seen by the mistress (known as Miss Susan). Harriet was convinced Miss Susan had eyes in the back of her head, for the woman spun around just in time to see Harriet pop the lump of sugar into her mouth.

Miss Susan went into a screaming rage and savagely whipped the frightened girl. Harriet's meticulously choreographed twists and turns were accented by wails from a terrified baby and a frustrated, furious mistress. Harriet bolted through the door—heart pounding, lungs burning, and adrenaline providing a burst of energy that catapulted her over a fence to refuge in a pigsty. There she hid for five days, hidden from punishment and dining from the same menu as the swine. Eventually, Harriet gathered enough courage to return to the main house; Miss Susan sent her packing back to Brodas, claiming she "was not worth a sixpence."

The next six years found Harriet inside the main house, cleaning, cooking, and bored. She longed to be out in the fields and physically active. Finally, she was allowed to join the men in the fields, where she plowed and tended to apples, wheat, rye, and corn.

One eventful day in 1835 Harriet placed herself between an overseer and a runaway slave he was beating. Thwarted, the overseer heaved a two-pound lead weight at the runaway. It missed its target and struck Harriet in the head instead. Bleeding and with a concussion, she lay in a coma for a long time as her mother again nursed her back to health. She never fully recovered from her head injury. She suffered "sleeping fits," or narcolepsy, often falling asleep while walking across the fields where she worked with her father, Old Ben. Otherwise, she was exceptionally strong and could do the work of any man—like cutting down cypress, oak, and poplar trees, which were sold to a nearby shipyard.

Brodas, however, concerned that he now had a worthless slave indeed, decided to find a new owner for Harriet and two of her brothers. Oral accounts say that Harriet learned of Brodas's plan to sell her brothers, so she prayed that the Lord would "convert old master." When her petition had no effect, Harriet prayed, "Lord, if you're never going to change that man's heart, kill him, and take him out of the way so he won't do more mischief." Not long afterward, Brodas became quite ill and died. Harriet is said to have felt deeply guilty over the incident—a factor that may have influenced her drive to work so diligently and for so little reward on behalf of other slaves.

After Brodas's death, Harriet was hired out to John Stewart, a local builder. Stewart liked Harriet; he came to trust her, allowing her to hire herself out to other plantations when times were slack on his farm. For

Harriet Tubman, Underground Railroad conductor who was widely known as Moses.—
LIBRARY OF CONGRESS

the privilege, she paid Stewart the first $50 of her earnings each year. Harriet was allowed to keep the rest, enabling her to save a bit of money.

In 1844, Stewart gave Harriet permission to marry a free man, John Tubman, but this did not change her own status as a slave. Furthermore, any children they might have would become the property of the plantation owner.

Strangely, Harriet was at the time a legally free woman, but did not know it. The man who originally owned Old Rit willed her to one of his young relatives, stating that at age forty-five she was to be set free. The new owner died soon afterward, technically resulting in freedom for Old Rit and her children. But because Rit had been sold in spite of the will's provision and continued to live as a slave, a local lawyer told her that no judge would uphold the stipulation of the will.

Harriet craved freedom, so she persuaded two of her brothers to escape with her, but their fear of reprisal was more powerful than dreams of liberty. The boys made it only a short distance before turning back against Harriet's pleas to continue. She returned with them, curling up in bed next to her husband. Still, the hope that she would some day make a trip to freedom was so vibrant that it made her head throb.

She waited, and finally, one night in 1849, she quietly slipped from under her covers, leaving her husband's side, moving without notice onto the fields, where just the day before she had chopped and stacked timber. Soundlessly she crept, reaching a thicket sufficient to camouflage her trembling body. She waited and listened. Certain she was clear of peril and that her escape had not been observed, she sprang to her feet, running swiftly but cautiously along a trail that paralleled the main road back to the Maryland plantation that had been her home for nearly twenty-nine years. She clutched a small kerchief containing cornbread and salt pork. Her clothing was tied with a rope belt, and she wore around her head a brightly colored bandanna, which she began wearing at age eleven as a sign of growing up. From the trail near the plantation, Harriet began her barefoot journey to freedom.

Her father, Ben, had taught her about berries, plants, woods, and swamp survival. He told her to follow the North Star at night and during the day to look for the soft moss on the sides of trees. "That's always the north side," he told her. Fearing patrollers and slave catchers with dogs, she slipped into the muddy water of the Choptank River with the advice of a Quaker woman clear in her memory: "Follow the Choptank 40 miles to its beginning. Then follow the road to Camden, and look for a white house with green shutters. A conductor will help you there."

Hiding under potatoes or straw and in attics and adopting disguises became routine for Harriet. Helped by sympathizers, she went to two men known only as Trent and Garrett, who gave her the first pair of shoes she'd ever worn. She slipped past the slave catchers in Wilmington disguised as a fine lady. Then she went on, making her way to Philadelphia. Once, she suffered one of her sleeping fits—falling on the side of the road. She fell miraculously into the tall weeds, hiding her body sufficiently from slave catchers whose horses pounded past her, inches from her head. Awakened by the sound of the passing horses, Harriet gave thanks to God and continued her trip to Philadelphia.

Abolitionist and orator Frederick Douglass, a friend of Tubman, refused to take part in John Brown's grandiose scheme.

She had been given a slip of paper with PHILADELPHIA written neatly on it. She was told that a sign bearing those letters would spell her freedom. When she found that marker with the letters matching the paper in her hand, she knew she was free. Looking down at her own hands, tradition has it that she wondered if she had changed any, now that she was a free woman.

Nat Turner, leader of a bloody slave insurrection in Virginia, had inspired her dream to escape and her plan to help others out of bondage. She adopted the name Moses for use on her many journeys, having often sung with other slaves, "Go down, Moses, Way down in Egypt land / Tell old Pharaoh, Let my people go . . ."

Because of the Fugitive Slave Act of 1850, Harriet was forced into Canada. There she was visited by John Brown, whom she considered an instrument of God for bringing an end to slavery. After having battled proslavery forces in "Bleeding Kansas," he now planned to assemble a force of blacks and whites to attack at Harpers Ferry, Virginia (now West Virginia). Their plan was to seize arms and liberate slaves.

A skeptical Frederick Douglass considered Brown's grandiose plan to be both hazardous and unworkable and he had referred him to Harriet. J. W. Loguen, a black clergyman who was a friend of Harriet's, took Brown to St. Catharines, where Harriet was living at the time. Tubman later met Brown in Boston and advised him so effectively that he began to call her "General Tubman." Had it not been for a sudden illness, Harriet might have been at Brown's side during the bloody Harpers Ferry raid.

On October 16, 1859, with five blacks—three of them his own sons—and sixteen whites, Brown went into Virginia to seize its federal arsenal. Almost immediately, they were attacked. Twelve of Brown's twenty-one men—two of his sons included—were killed. Brown surrendered, was convicted, and was hanged along with six of his followers.

Horrified on hearing of these events, Harriet recalled a vivid dream she had while in Canada. Her dream had taken her into a wilderness where a snake with a white-bearded head rose out of the bushes. Then two other snakes with heads of younger men rose to join the bearded snake. They were subsequently attacked by men who struck down all

A typical prewar dwelling in Beaufort, South Carolina.—SOUTH CAROLINA STATE ARCHIVES

three. She wondered whether her dream had foretold the fate of Brown and his sons.

The following April, Tubman led a raid of her own in Troy, New York, where she rescued Charles Nalle from slave catchers. The Fugitive Slave Act specified that any slave caught even in a free state must be returned to his or her owner. Many Northerners—some of whom weren't even abolitionists—felt that the edict violated basic human rights. It is said of Harriet that she shouted, "Drown him [Nalle] rather than let them have him!" Her band of conspirators responded by whisking Nalle away from bondage to safety.

One of Tubman's most touching rescues involved a young woman and two of her children imprisoned in Cambridge, Maryland. William Still of the Philadelphia Vigilance Committee—a black man who was born free—informed Harriet that she must employ the help of the woman's husband, John Bowley. Tubman remembered that name as the man who had married her younger sister, now in prison.

The husband, also a free man, agreed to pose as an auctioneer's slave, using letters forged by a local Quaker. He instructed that the woman and her two children (his wife and children) be sent to the hotel where the auctioneer resided. Hiding in the attic of a Quaker family and slipping out at night by sailboat, Harriet and her sister, Mary, went to Philadelphia together. By this ruse, Bowley freed his wife and children.

Harriet went back to Maryland to get her brothers, taking them away on Christmas Day without their mother's knowledge. She later returned for her parents and purchased from William H. Seward a small piece of land in Auburn, New York. This became a permanent home for her parents, Old Rit and Old Ben, both of whom lived to be one hundred years old.

With the onset of war, Union troops advanced through Maryland. Large numbers of slaves left on abandoned plantations became known as contrabands. They were no longer enslaved, but they were not free either. Tubman responded to their plight in South Carolina. Plantation owners of the region feared Union troops and had fled, leaving slaves behind to overrun Union camps. Tubman reached Beaufort in March 1862 and helped feed and teach numerous contrabands in spite of language difficulties. Her own poor command of the English language plus the Gullah dialect spoken by these people made communication strained at best. Yet Harriet managed to organize many of the contrabands, keeping them on the outskirts of the Union camps and out of harm's way.

From Beaufort, Harriet went to a military hospital in Florida for a brief period. Men dying of dysentery were treated with one of Tubman's concoctions of roots and wild plants. The medicine helped some recover, but the formula was never recorded. Despite exposure to small-pox and malaria, Harriet never got sick—she believed that God would protect her until her time came.

She returned to Beaufort in December 1862 to help her friend Col. Thomas Higginson recruit and organize black soldiers at Camp Saxton, and when Federals needed information about the enemy in the spring of 1863, Harriet agreed to serve as a spy—a role that suited her because of her vast experience running up and down the Underground Railroad. Information she gathered was transmitted to Col. James Montgomery, an expert in guerrilla warfare. Harriet considered it a privilege to assist Montgomery because he had fought in Kansas with John Brown.

During the summer of 1863—about six months after Lincoln signed the Emancipation Proclamation—Gen. David Hunter, commander of Union forces in the region, called on Col. Montgomery and Harriet to carry out a special mission. They were asked to take several gunboats up the Combahee River, pulling up torpedo mines placed by the Rebels as they went. They were also instructed to destroy railroads and bridges, which supplied the Rebels, and to lead out slaves known to be held prisoner by Confederates.

On the night of June 2, 1863, "General" Tubman, along with Col. Montgomery, lead her first military expedition. One hundred and fifty black soldiers traveled up the river on three steam-powered gunboats. They destroyed immense amounts of cotton, plus a few dwellings of secessionists, and freed 756 black prisoners in the process, without a single life being lost. The only casualty was Tubman's skirt, which was caught in the mud and torn from her during her flight back to the gun-boats. (It is believed she was later sent bloomers by the ladies of the Soldiers' Aid Society of Boston, who praised the virtues of trousers over skirts.)

Tubman also witnessed the July 18 Union assault on Fort Wagner. Men of the Massachusetts 54th regiment—a black unit led by a twenty-six-year-old white man named Robert Gould Shaw—stormed the para-pet of Fort Wagner on Morris Island near Charleston. Shaw and half of his men were killed.

Harriet responded to a call to help bury the dead after the battle was lost, knowing that Shaw's body was surely among them. Sadly, she remembered serving him his dinner only the night before. Unfortunately, Shaw had been buried immediately with malice and forethought by the Confederates. When Shaw's father asked for his son's body to be returned, a Confederate officer replied, "We buried him with his niggers."

Tubman remained in the South for the next year, helping in various guerrilla activities. In 1864 she left Port Royal Military Hospital to return to Auburn, New York, in order to be with her parents for a while. She then traveled back to Washington to work as a nurse in the U.S. Sanitary Commission until the war ended. Trying to return home to Auburn, she suffered her first and only "battle wounds," minor scrapes and bruises, when an irate white conductor snatched her from amidst the passengers and hurled her into the baggage car.

The year 1890 was bittersweet: Congress finally agreed to pay her a pension of $20 a month, but that same year her husband died. With her small savings as collateral, she purchased some land at an auction in hopes of building a proper home for poor blacks. She later deeded acreage to an African Methodist Episcopal Zion church, which built the home of her dreams. Harriet Tubman, conductor, retired there. She died on March 10, 1913.

Few females who participated in the Civil War have received more honors and praise. Frederick Douglass said of her that "excepting John Brown, I know of no one who has willingly encountered more peril and hardships to serve our enslaved people." Gen. Rufus Saxon, commander of a brigade of contrabands, emphasized that "she made many

The military market at Beaufort, South Carolina, where some contrabands sold farm produce to soldiers.—THE SOLDIER IN OUR CIVIL WAR

a raid inside the enemy's lines, displaying remarkable courage, zeal and fidelity." Queen Victoria bestowed a silver medal on her, which arrived along with a letter of recognition and an invitation to visit England. The Smithsonian Institution honored Tubman in 1982 as "the only American woman ever to plan and lead a military raid."

5

Mary Walker, M.D.

Square Peg

"Why don't you wear proper clothing?" demanded Gen. William T. Sherman. "That clothing is neither one thing nor the other."

The U.S. Volunteers contract surgeon who momentarily expected to be assigned to Sherman's command tossed her curls defiantly. Without a word, Dr. Mary Walker stormed out of Sherman's improvised office. Despite the man's rudeness, she was eager to serve under him. Her transfer from the command of Gen. George H. Thomas was late in arrival, however. This woman—exactly five feet tall and one of only a handful of female physicians in the nation—did not take part in the March to the Sea.

Soon after her encounter with Sherman, Walker switched from tunic-over-trousers attire to the uniform worn by Federal surgeons. She never trimmed her curls or had her uniform altered to fit her figure, so her dress continued to be a subject of ridicule. A group of Confederates first got a good look at the enemy female during the spring of 1864. Describing the encounter, Capt. Benedict J. Semmes wrote of her, "We were all amused and disgusted at the sight of a thing that nothing but the debased and depraved Yankee nation could produce. [A woman] was dressed in the full uniform of a Federal surgeon. She was not good looking, and of course had tongue enough for a regiment of men."

Several biographers give Walker the benefit of the doubt and label her choice of clothing as a mere eccentricity. That conclusion may be accurate, but it is not fully descriptive. From girlhood, Mary Edwards Walker was a square peg in a round hole. No matter where she went or what she did, she never quite fit neatly and comfortably into her surrounding context—civilian or military. Her decision to wear trousers all of her adult life may have stemmed from her father's insistence, "Tight-

Dr. Mary Walker wearing the Medal of Honor that was given to her in lieu of a commission as a major.—LIBRARY OF CONGRESS

fitting clothes are not good for you; as long as you're under my roof, don't try to wear a corset." A would-be physician who lived in New York and who had turned to farming, Alvah Walker may have encouraged his daughter to get the M.D. degree which he had yearned for.

Mary took action instead of yearning—a typical course for her. Soon after she became an adult, she applied to Syracuse Medical College and became its only female student. Having saved her money for years, it was easy to pay the $195 tuition for three thirteen-week semesters, not all of which were consecutive. She was awarded her degree in 1855, just six years after British-born Elizabeth Blackwell became the first female physician in the United States.

It took only a few months for Mary to discover that a medical degree didn't guarantee its holder a practice. After filing in Columbus, Ohio, the fledgling physician returned to Oswego, New York, to marry former classmate Albert Miller. Most of the townfolk knew Mary, and some correctly predicted that her wedding would be "something to see." For this special occasion she donned a dress coat over her trousers, but flatly refused to take the customary vow of obedience. The couple tried to work together in nearby Rome, but the effort was comparable to hitching a horse and a cow together. After four years, Mary called it quits and moved into a separate office; Albert left town and headed for the West. A decade later, Mary went to Iowa, where it was easy to get a divorce, and officially removed her ex-husband from her life. Not that the legal formality made a lot of difference; on her wedding day she had refused to take her husband's name, so it wasn't even necessary to change her name when they separated.

In May 1860, Mary paid for a classified advertisement announcing the opening of her new office over the clothing store operated by the Messrs. Shelly. Editors of the *Rome Sentinel*, always glad to get advertising revenue, gave her write-up a column inch or two in their newspaper. Readers were advised that "those who prefer the skill of a female physician to that of a male, have now an excellent opportunity to make their choice."

Apparently, not many preferred a female physician, so Mary closed her office and went to Washington on learning of the surrender of Fort Sumter to secessionists. With civil war in the offing, she reasoned, the U.S. War Department would need every available physician and, hence, would be happy to put a woman in trousers on the payroll.

Once more, she found out how faulty her judgment was. Surgeon General Clement A. Finley accepted her application politely enough, but did nothing with it for days. After making a dozen trips to his office, she was told that a woman couldn't possibly serve in field hospitals around battlefields. She launched a formal appeal of Finley's verdict, but failed to get a hearing and gave up for the time being. Since she had nothing better to do, she decided to serve her country as a volunteer. To do so meant turning her back on her education; to aid the sick and wounded men, she'd have to serve as an unpaid nurse.

Her first post was in a hastily arranged hospital that occupied a building of the U.S. Patent Office. Mary soon found that she had no specific duties, but was expected to do whatever her supervisor, Dr. J. N. Green, wanted done at a given time. That meant she was for practical purposes working in a prototype of a twentieth-century MASH unit.

Some days she would escort convalescent soldiers to railroad depots or to some of the many camps that had sprung up around the capital. She often ran errands for Green and occasionally had the opportunity to wash and dress the wounds of new arrivals. These duties didn't even begin to exhaust her time, skills, or energy, so she devised ways to make herself even more useful.

Finding that numerous women had come to Washington to see sick or wounded members of their families and were living with the poorest of lodgings and food, she organized and administered a Women's Relief Association. Noticing that numerous convalescents sat around all day so bored that they spent much of their time sleeping, she launched a drive to put checkerboards in every hospital. Though she fell far short of reaching her goal, she had the satisfaction of seeing what she described as "a decided change for the better" in the hospitals which she personally provided with checker sets.

Gen. George H. Thomas, famous as the "Rock of Chickamauga," was the only commander to give Mary Walker a chance to serve as a surgeon.

Early in 1862, after several months of work and still a volunteer, Walker transferred to the Forest Hall Prison in Georgetown. As was the case in Washington, she found that her services were welcomed, but her gender was not. Fuming at "the stupidity of this male-dominated system," she went back to New York and earned another degree from the Hygeia Therapeutic College.

Now armed with two diplomas from medical schools that were nationally recognized, Walker returned to Washington in search of a military commission. Knowing Gen. George B. McClellan to be the son of a well-known surgeon, she expected to be received cordially by him. Instead, she was rebuffed by subordinates and never had an opportunity to talk in person with the the "Young Napoleon."

When Gen. Ambrose Burnside replaced McClellan in November 1862, she managed to see the new commander. Years later she remembered him as having been extremely cordial and seemingly "ready to use a well-trained surgeon, regardless of sex."

Immediately after Burnside began making the decisions for the Federal forces, Mary claimed to have been with the Army of the Potomac for an attack launched along the Fredericksburg–Richmond line. There is no record, however, that she was actually on the Fredericksburg battlefield, where thousands of men in blue became casualties, desperately in need of medical attention.

Had she not been severely restricted by her gender, some of Mary's views would still have made it hard for her to win a contract or a commission. According to the *New Yorker,* hundreds or thousands of needless amputations were performed in the wake of every major battle. Mary, the Syracuse and Hygeia graduate, told everyone who would listen that even seriously injured men could be brought back to health by a period of intensive therapy. "A damaged arm or leg is far better than a useless stump," Walker proclaimed. Therapy would have required time that military leaders felt their surgeons simply didn't have, and amputation was the traditional way of dealing with a mangled limb. As a result, nearly any field hospital could be detected from a distance by the stench of rotting arms and legs, which accumulated near surgical quarters.

Walker was getting close to the point of giving up all thoughts of a military career, despite the fact that medical personnel were badly needed in the Eastern Theater. Suddenly the North was rocked by the realization that brothers and sons would soon be fighting fiercely what was then called the West—meaning almost anywhere outside of Virginia and Maryland.

Mary apparently got the attention of U.S. Secretary of War Edwin M. Stanton when Washington newspapers publicized one of her ideas. With the enlistment of volunteers lagging badly and the Union desperately in need of more troops, she offered to recruit men with criminal backgrounds. They could be formed into "Walker's U.S. Patriots," she suggested. She'd see to it that they had medical care because she would personally act as their surgeon.

Stanton wanted nothing to do with a regiment of criminals, but he also wanted to get Mary out of the capital. As long as she was there, he told aides, "This woman will continue to stir up trouble." Largely to silence her, he sent the female physician to Tennessee with a recommendation that some suitable spot be found in which she could make herself useful. She arrived at her destination soon after lengthy casualty lists from the fiercely contested Battle of Chickamauga began to appear in newspapers. By the time the last of these lists appeared, average people in the horrified North knew that in the Western Theater about 58,000 more men in blue were dead, wounded, or missing in action.

Gen. George H. Thomas seems to have been in such desperate need that he didn't have time to worry about how well a woman could do her job. He accepted her as a contract surgeon—still a civilian, but working for the armed forces—at a salary of $80 a month. She got just what she expected from other medics—the cold shoulder. One veteran of many battles fumed and snorted that he had been sent "a medical monstrosity" and tried to see that the newcomer was assigned to menial tasks only. Though she almost certainly knew what names she was being called, the woman from New York tried to act as though she were among professional equals.

When her contract was about to expire, she wasn't sure that she could stay much longer with the Army of the Cumberland. The unexpected death of a surgeon at Lee and Gordon's Mill at the southern edge of Tennessee brought about a sudden change in her status. Thomas badly needed to fill the vacancy—and Walker was the only qualified successor who was on hand and available. Thomas took the radical step of naming the female civilian as an assistant surgeon of the 52nd Ohio regiment. At this point in her career, she took off the clothing she had designed earlier. Her new outfit was the uniform of a Federal surgeon, complete with a green sash indicating membership in the medical service.

Col. Dan McCook went out of his way to let Mary know he was glad to have her in his command, but some members of his medical staff protested vociferously. These men seem to have set themselves up as an examining board for the sole purpose of determining whether or not Walker was competent to deal with sick and wounded soldiers. It took only days for them to rule that she was incompetent and to advise that she be dismissed.

Though she did not offer her resignation and nothing was actually done about the proposal to dismiss her, colleagues made it clear that she was not wanted or needed. As a result, she began going into the countryside to care for civilians who were also in desperate need of medical help. All of the doctors who once practiced in the region were now in gray uniforms, and the only available medications consisted of herbs and home remedies.

She found entire families in which all the males, including the sixteen-year-olds, had gone off to war. Women and children often hid in thickets and swamps; some of them were seriously ill. Considerable evidence suggests that Walker soon began taking supplies from the Federal stores and using them to treat "enemy" civilians.

On April 10, 1864, on a mission of mercy, the Yankee physician stumbled upon an outpost of Rebels that had moved to the northern border of Georgia. After taking her prisoner, they didn't know what to do with her. Hence, she was sent up the line to Gen. D. H. Hill, who was well aware that Federals had recently stopped honoring an agreement under which all captured surgeons were immediately released. Angry at anyone and everyone who wore blue, Hill sent the prisoner to Richmond.

She was confined in Castle Thunder for about ninety days. Prison officials who were eager to get her off their hands arranged for her to be exchanged for a Confederate major who had been imprisoned in the North. With the Army of the Cumberland now deep inside Georgia and headed toward Savannah, it was impossible for her to rejoin her outfit. As a result, Mary took any assignment she could get. One of them took her to the Women's Prison Hospital at Louisville for a period. She was later sent to an orphanage in Nashville, where she was serving when peace was declared.

By the time she returned to Washington, John Wilkes Booth had succeeded in making Abraham Lincoln the first chief executive to be assassinated. Walker was the only woman who succeeded in being present when members of the Booth conspiracy were hanged, but that didn't help her when she tried to see President Andrew Johnson. He probably received and read some of her numerous petitions to be given a commission as a major, but he never responded favorably. She eventually received $423.26 in back pay, but never had the opportunity to don a surgeon's uniform with the rank of major.

Denied the thing she most wanted, the woman who never fit smoothly into any niche as a civilian or as a military surgeon badgered every high-level official whose name she knew. She made such a nuisance of herself that officials in the War Department offered her a Medal of Honor in lieu of the commission she craved. Bestowed in January 1866, the accompanying citation said that she had "rendered valuable service to the Government" and had been "earnest and untiring in a variety of ways."

Always dressed as a man in public, Mary entered the lecture circuit, pinning her medal near her shoulder. Constantly traveling, she talked to many an audience about the healthful aspects of wearing trousers, and she shared stories of her wartime experiences and the rights that were then denied to women. At one point, a professional booking agency signed her at $150 per week—but directed her to appear with puppet acts and sideshow freaks.

A 1901 interpretation by an artist of Walker at work in a field.—LIBRARY OF CONGRESS

Walker here is dressed for an appearance on the lecture circuit with her top hat and the first Medal of Honor conferred on a woman.—LIBRARY OF CONGRESS

She was still going strong in 1917 at the age of eighty-five. That's when a formal board of review, after having examined the records of 2,625 recipients of the Medal of Honor, made public its findings. Of these recipients, the report said, 911 were awarded the Medal of Honor for services that were not performed in the face of enemy fire. All 911 recipients were ordered to return their medals and were told that failure to act promptly would constitute a misdemeanor.

Legend has it that the messenger who told Dr. Mary Walker that she must hand her medal over to him was told, "You can have it over my dead body!" Ignoring threats of legal action, the first woman to serve as an assistant surgeon in U.S. military forces wore the first Medal of Honor bestowed on a woman for the rest of her days. She died in Washington at age eighty-six, the result of a fall on the Capitol steps. Records fail to indicate why she was visiting the building. Chances are good that she was there to ask for an increase in her veteran's pension—or to try to find just one more lawmaker who would support a movement to permit women to vote.

6

Kady Brownell

Daughter of the 1st Rhode Island

During the month it took to cross the Atlantic Ocean, one group of immigrants, hoping to find new lives in the New World, spent a great deal of time getting to know one another. Some of them became especially fond of a lithe Scottish girl, whom they knew only as Kady. She enlivened many a meal by singing a few Highland ballads, but said very little about her life. Beyond the fact that she was an "army brat" who was born in Africa's Caffraria and reared on British army posts, she volunteered hardly any information about herself. As the coastline of North America came into view and their little vessel neared Narragansett Bay, she blurted a confession to another woman who stood at the rail with her.

"Don't know why I'm here," she admitted. "I've never seen an American, and I'm not sure I'll like 'em."

Having heard that a new factory would soon open in Bristol, she reached the little city in time to apply for a job. Shaking his head, the fellow who was hiring hands muttered "men only," without so much as saying he was sorry. Kady, who prided herself on being muscular and healthy, would have liked to help manufacture rifles. Having spent her entire life in army camps, she was familiar with weapons and was a skilled shot. Barred by her gender from her first choice of occupation, she settled for work as a house maid.

At a little pub she visited two or three times a week, she became acquainted with Robert Brownell, another immigrant about her age whose grimy face and hands revealed him to be a workman of some sort. He lived in Providence but had come to the southern tip of the Rhode Island and Providence Plantations to help a fellow named Burnside get his factory started.

"I'd like to be working there," Kady mused. "Why do you call this a plantation? Aren't we in the state of Rhode Island?"

"Naw. You've come to the Rhode Island and Providence Plantations."

"You're sure?"

"Sure as shootin'. Haven't been here very long, myself. But I've been all over the place. Folks outside call it Rhode Island," he admitted with a grin. "I don't, since I'm inside it."

By the time Robert's job began to peter out, he had become enamored with Kady and wanted to take her back to Providence with him. She didn't bat an eye when he blurted out his hopes. She simply said, "Let's find somebody who can do a marriage."

In Providence, Robert took his bride to see the mansion that once belonged to William Coddington. "He was the governor a long time ago," the self-taught mechanic explained. From the capital, the new-lyweds spent their free time exploring the smallest state in the Union. Familiar with the immense distances on other continents, at first Kady didn't believe her husband when he told her that they had just stepped across the border on the Dayville Road and were standing in Connecticut.

"Rhode Island ain't but about forty miles wide," he explained.

Eager to know more about the tiny "plantation" where she expected to spend the rest of her life, Kady asked her new acquaintances a lot of questions. They just said, "Folks here have always been a little different."

Puzzled, she wanted to know why, but never got a satisfactory explanation. When she found out that the state flag and the state seal both displayed an anchor, she nodded with understanding. "That's because everybody came here in ships," Kady mused, "like me and Bob."

Though more than 150 years old when Kady first saw it, the Coddington mansion in Providence was still in good repair.—HARPER'S ENCYCLOPEDIA OF UNITED STATES HISTORY

Early in the winter of 1859–60, Providence buzzed with excited gossip. Folks said they got it from men who were in the know: They were sure that their next governor would be "a rich kid named Sprague."

Listening to talk one night about the young Sprague's age and lack of experience, Bob Brownell had all he could take. "Quit calling that fellow a kid," he protested. "They say he's older'n me, and I ain't a kid by a long shot. He's plenty old to make a good governor."

The rumor proved to be right. In April, 1860, twenty-nine-year-old William Sprague was sworn in as Rhode Island's fifty-ninth governor, only the tenth chief executive to be chosen since the adoption of the state constitution. (From 1663 until 1842, governors functioned under rules spelled out in a royal charter that was granted by King Charles II.)

Before taking office, Sprague confided to his intimates that one of these days he would be the richest man in the state. No one challenged that boast; it was generally known that he was already well on his way toward that goal. But he hadn't had time to warm the seat in his new office before secessionists at Charleston opened fire on the Federal garrison at Fort Sumter. As soon as Sprague learned that Maj. Robert Anderson had been forced to haul down the Star-Spangled Banner and surrender the vast old fortress, he banged his desk and shouted to no one in particular, "This means war!"

To the surprise of Rhode Islanders, the new president of the United States did not call for congressmen and senators to come together for an emergency session. Instead, he assumed extraordinary powers and made all the decisions, calling on the citizens of loyal states to come forth and crush what he called the "insurrection in the South."

Having anticipated that there would soon be a need for troops, Sprague decided to form a battery of light artillery. His announced plan to get into the struggle early enough to bring it to a quick end struck a responsive chord with Indiana-reared Ambrose E. Burnside. Although he was a West Point graduate, he had left the U.S. Army to become a tailor. His rifle factory in Bristol, Rhode Island, had failed to turn a profit, so he had put some of his energy into what he called "upgrading the state militia." Before the organization of the governor's battery of artillery was completed, Burnside was busy recruiting Rhode Island men to spend ninety days fighting for the Union.

Kady's husband took pains to be sure that his name was on the roster of early volunteers. Ashamed to say he never learned how to write properly, Bob asked a recruitment officer, "Put it down for me . . . Brownell. *Robert S. Brownell.*"

"You're now a member of the 1st Rhode Island Volunteer Regiment," said the recruiter. Since you're ahead of the pack, guess you might as well be a sergeant," he told him in a flourish at the end of "Brownell."

When Bob told Kady the news, she hugged him hard and didn't shed a tear. "I'm mighty proud to be a sergeant's wife," she said. "Who's the fellow that's behind organizing the regiment?"

"Don't know hardly anything about him," Bob confessed. "Some say his daddy once lived in South Carolina and owned a bunch of slaves. After the slaves were left behind, he grew up on a farm drained by the Ohio River. He's all for abolition. Guess he'll be our colonel for sure."

Bob's assumption was soon verified by a series of public announcements. At the head of the state's first regiment of volunteers, Col. Ambrose Burnside would soon take his men to Washington. There, they'd get ready to fight, if Rebels were in a notion to take a drubbing.

So many Rhode Islanders flocked to Burnside that he found himself facing a predicament. Regulations called for a regiment to be made up of ten companies of one hundred men each. He had already gone over the limit, and volunteers were still coming. Impulsively, Burnside let it be known that he'd form "an oversize regiment" made up of eleven companies.

When Kady heard the news, she turned to her husband and said, "Bob, I'm a-goin' with you."

Taken so aback that he couldn't find words with which to protest or argue, Brownell nodded. He didn't think a woman would be accepted, but he was wrong. Kady was soon listed on the muster roll of Company 11 in spite of the fact that lieutenants and captains didn't have any idea what to do with her. Having learned that a woman would follow him, Burnside handed down a surprising decision. Kady Brownell would serve as the regimental color-bearer, he ordered. That way, Kady could go along with Bob without having to carry a musket.

Even six months later, such an arrangement would have earned an instant veto from Washington. Veteran officers of the U.S. Army, many of whom had fought in Mexico, knew that color-bearers were conspicuous on a field of battle and likely to be targets of the enemy. If it was known in the capital that the Rhode Islanders were bringing a female color-bearer with them, nothing was done to prohibit her from coming.

Burnside soon found out that Kady knew a lot more about military life than most of the eleven hundred men he was preparing to take to the nation's capital. Inordinately pleased at including her in his command, he held an informal ceremony by which he made her "daughter of the regiment." This title, which had been used in Europe and Great Britain for several generations, was only honorary, but was highly coveted by wives and daughters of career officers.

Kady was too busy getting ready to pay much attention to her new title. She decided that a uniform like Bob's wouldn't be exactly right, so she devised her own. Pants protected her legs, but a short skirt over them revealed her gender to anyone who glanced at her. She wouldn't be allowed to carry a musket, so she found an old straight sword of the sort worn by many noncommissioned officers and strapped it to her side. Having practiced for hours bearing a flag on a staff, she was ready to help whip the Rebels. Since the term of the 1st regiment would last only three months, she expected to be back in Providence in time to finish her autumn chores before the start of winter.

Kady Brownell in army costume.— G. E. PERINE ENGRAVING

So many men living in tiny Rhode Island flocked to the colors that an entire brigade was formed—complete, of course, with Sprague's battery of artillery. When Bob and Kady and their comrades reached Washington, the little city was agog. Even among professional soldiers, few had ever seen a body of 3,200 marching men from a single state. When Sprague and Burnside decided to hold a review, dignitaries turned out by the score. Gen. Winfield Scott is said to have grumbled that the lines looked mighty ragged to him, but most viewers were aglow that so many Rhode Islanders had answered the president's call so promptly.

Abraham Lincoln, who almost certainly saw the review, was still derided as "the Illinois baboon" in much of the Northeast because of his long arms and legs. For days, he had agonized at the slow rate with which volunteers were trickling into the capital. Over and over, he asked, "When, oh when will they come?" Watching the huge brigade from Rhode Island, he must have seen that Burnside was as straight as a ramrod astride his horse and probably made a mental note that he was likely to need him soon as a general officer.

Soon Lincoln and his aides found themselves deluged. Large bodies of troops converged on the capital from Massachusetts, Pennsylvania, and New York. Even far-away Minnesota was represented by the first regiment raised in response to his urgent appeal. James H. Lane had brought a small band of men from strife-torn Kansas and insisted that they stay briefly in the executive mansion. Secessionist forces were likely to attack the capital at any hour, Lane believed, and he considered it imperative to give the president special protection.

Most officers and men of the Rhode Island brigade were sleeping in the Patent Office. The Treasury building was overflowing with the 5th regiment of Massachusetts Volunteers. Numerous men of the 71st New York regiment had written to their wives, telling them to address letters to the Navy Yard. Even a widely known commercial building, the Palace of Aladdin, was bulging with soldiers. Some of them wore blue uniforms, but others had blue shirts over gray trousers. Even though a special session of Congress was scheduled to begin on July 4, the Capitol was still crowded with 90-day men. When every conceivable building was jammed full, huts were thrown together and put in Franklin Square for use by members of the 12th New York regiment.

Behind his back, some envious professional politicians in Washington belittled Sprague by calling him "the boy governor." These men assured one another that a young fellow who was never seen without his spectacles wouldn't have been at Rhode Island's helm had it not been for his family's cotton mills. Usually seen in military attire topped by a yellow plume on his hat, the governor of Rhode Island didn't care a fig what Washington insiders thought of him. He was too busy to have been annoyed, even had he heard his new nickname. Lovely Kate Chase, daughter of the secretary of the Treasury, occupied most of his thoughts and practically all of his time. They were seen together day and night, and men from his state rightly calculated that they'd make a match of it before very long.

Thoughts of Kate temporarily left Sprague's mind when he learned that Gen. Irvin McDowell would soon order all of his forces toward a point where it was hoped that the Rebels might make a stand. By July 19, Burnside and his command were at the hamlet of Centreville. No

A Federal headquarters at Centreville.—Pictorial Field Book of the Civil War

one knew whether or not the tiny settlement got its name from its location, about halfway between Washington and Richmond. But McDowell, his generals, and their subordinates were all but certain that they would meet Rebel forces there within a few days and within a few miles.

Their educated guess was right on target. At nearby Blackburn's Ford, troops under C.S. Gen. James Longstreet clashed with Federal forces on July 18. Men wounded in this action reached Centreville about the same time that the 1st Rhode Island began to pitch camp. On July 21, the Confederate Congress confirmed Pierre Gustave Toutant Beauregard of Louisiana as a full general. He didn't learn about this action until later, for forces under his command were in the field close to Manassas.

Kady Brownell, who probably witnessed battles in Africa and India, became a participant instead of a spectator shortly before or after 1 P.M. that day. Wearing a red sash with big tassels and letting her long hair flow freely over her shoulders and back, the color-bearer of the 1st Rhode Island advanced boldly with her men.

Sharpshooters of the regiment held a spot to the left of the line as Burnside's force proceeded without pause. When they reached a stand of pines, they had to fight their way through underbrush and became exposed to Rebel fire. Men in gray who spotted the colors borne by the only woman known for sure to have been on the field that day tried repeatedly to break the Rhode Island line to dash for the flag. They failed each time, but the number of casualties in the regiment began to mount rapidly.

Frank Moore, who gained lasting fame by compiling and editing the twelve-volume *Rebellion Record*, was lavish in his praise of this female soldier, who had been in the United States only a few years. According to him, Kady "remained in line, guarding the colors," when men around her began to fall back in the heat of a general engagement. "There she stood," according to Moore, "unmoved and dauntless, under the withering heat, and amid the roar, and blood, and dust of that terrible July day. Shells went screaming over her with the howl of an avenging demon, and the air was thick and hot with deadly singing of the minié balls."

About 4 P.M., Union lines abruptly disintegrated at many points. Knowing the battle was lost, Burnside and his regiment turned and started back toward Centreville. According to Moore, their panic was so great that they forgot all about orders to rally on their colors and retreat in order. Kady reputedly stood her ground until screaming Rebels were within a few hundred yards of her. Moore wrote:

> Just then a soldier in a Pennsylvania regiment, who was running past, seized her by the hand, and said, "Come, sis; there's no use to stay here just to be killed; let's get into the woods."

At Bull Run, brutal hand-to-hand fighting turned the Rebel victory into a rout.

She started down a slope with him towards a pine thicket. They had hardly run twenty steps, when a cannon ball struck him full on the head, and in an instant he was sinking beside her, a shapeless and mutilated corpse. His shattered skull rested a moment on her shoulder, and streams of blood ran over her uniform.

She kept on to the woods, where she found some of the company, and before long chanced upon an ambulance, into which she jumped; but the balls were flying too thick through the cover. She sprang out, and soon after found a stray horse, on which she jumped, and rode to Centreville.

Bob was missing, so she climbed on the horse she had found and set out to search for him. On the way to the battlefield, she met Burnside, who told her that Bob had come through the battle without a scratch. He had been delayed by finding his way past a band of Rebels, but would soon be with her.

Since the term of enlistment of Kady and the other members of the regiment was about to expire, they returned to Providence. By then, Burnside was no longer a colonel of militia. Lincoln had made him a brigadier of volunteers and already had a special assignment in mind for him. Kady and most men who had formed the 1st Rhode Island regiment reenlisted in the new 5th Rhode Island.

Kady had lost her status as color-bearer because of Federal regulations and went with the 5th Rhode Island to North Carolina as "daughter of the regiment" when Burnside's expedition was launched. In early March 1862, the Federal force was deployed close to New Bern. Located at the confluence of the Neuse and Trent Rivers, this colonial town was once a provincial capital. Confederates were desperate to hold the place at whatever cost. Federal forces were eager to capture it. A victory, small or large, would inspire many Northerners who were beginning to lose heart, since one Confederate win had followed on the heels of another.

Possibly, but not positively, as a result of their excessive zeal, men of the 5th Rhode Island advanced toward the enemy without having notified other Federal troops of what they expected to do. Spotters wearing blue caught sight of the movement and from a distance took their comrades to be Rebels. Their mistake was natural and understandable; uniforms had not yet become standardized, despite several tragedies caused by this very problem at Bull Run.

Those who were there later said that Kady Brownell seemed to have been the only member of the Burnside force who realized what was about to happen. While their comrades prepared to open on them with both musket and artillery fire, the woman raced to the head of the advancing body and waved a bonnet so vigorously that her movements were understood. By her actions, she single-handedly prevented a case of friendly fire.

Persuaded by officers to go to the rear after the near-tragic incident, Kady turned her attention to care of the wounded. She was bent over a wounded corporal when Bob was brought from the field, badly injured in the thigh by a minié ball.

"Thank God," his uniformed wife exclaimed after a hasty examination. "The big artery wasn't cut. Now I've got to get you properly bandaged."

A surgeon who examined the wound shook his head in resignation. No healing could begin, he told Kady, until shattered fragments of the bone worked their way to the surface. That would take at least two weeks, he said, and it might take three. All Kady could do for Bob was bring him coffee and soup and try to soothe his injury with water from the Neuse River. A month after he fell in battle, he was strong enough to stand a voyage that took him and his wife back to Providence. However, after eighteen months as a semi-invalid, he was still not strong enough to march, so he and Kady were discharged by Burnside.

Tradition holds that Gen. Burnside personally presented Kady Brownell with the colors she had carried at Bull Run. The commander, who had become a major general as a result of his victory in North Carolina, also handed a sergeant's sword to the woman who had served under him. As a special tribute, Burnside had seen to it that "Kady Brownell" was carved into the scabbard of the blade.

In addition, Kady had retrieved "an excellent rifle" from one of the battlefields. She would have liked to put it with her other trophies, but according to Moore, decided that it was needed in the ever-widening conflict that was raging in her adopted country. Hence, she presented the rifle to a Rhode Islander headed for battle and never saw it again.

Though Bob and Kady Brownell probably never knew it, Kady was in a class almost by herself. Her father, a long-dead professional soldier, would have been extremely proud if he had known of her dramatic exploits far to the west of Scotland. Most of the estimated three hundred or so other women who fought in the Civil War donned male attire. In some cases, their gender was not discovered until long after the hostilities came to an end. But Kady Brownell had signed up and fought as a good soldier in two battles during which she was unmistakably a woman.

Part II
Army Wives

7

Mary Custis Lee

Loser

Moving slowly and painfully, a women, seemingly bent with pain, went to the front door of her residence at White House, Virginia. Using a hammer and a few small nails, she fastened to the door a notice that read:

> Northern soldiers who profess to reverence [George] Washington, forbear to desecrate the home of his first married life, the property of his wife, now owned by her descendants.

Mary Custis Lee, wife of Gen. Robert E. Lee, the commander of the Army of Northern Virginia, was preparing to abandon her home for the second time since the start of the hostilities. She had reason to believe that Yankees would soon occupy the hamlet in force, but was not aware that they had already planned to erect a huge supply depot there. However, her husband's name was enough to cause her to be treated with a strange mixture of respect and bitter hatred.

Furthermore, she made no effort to conceal her animosity toward Federal officers, whom she regarded as "foreigners who are trampling upon the sacred soil of the Old Dominion like lords and conquerors."

Though her life after 1861 was anything but sheltered, she had grown up utterly sheltered at Arlington Mansion (near Washington) as the pampered daughter of George Washington Parke Custis, the grandson of Martha Washington by her first husband. Idolizing the man who was both his step-grandfather and the father of his country, Custis built Arlington as a shrine to George Washington. Most of his adult life was spent hunting down, purchasing, and taking to Arlington whatever memorabilia of Washington he could find. By the time

Mary was grown, the collection was of mammoth size. It included a great deal of silverware, some splendid paintings, and numerous cut glass bowls and pitchers—even a few of the mildewed tents that served as his quarters when he was fighting the British, and the bed in which he died.

When the Custis will was read, assembled relatives learned that Mary had been given a life interest in Arlington, which her eldest son Custis was to take over at her passing. White House, one of the finest properties of the Custis family, went to William Henry Fitzhugh ("Rooney"), and Robert E. Lee Jr., known simply as Rob, received the less extensive and less valuable Romancock plantation. To the elder Robert E. Lee, the crusty lord of Arlington Mansion and Plantation left one building lot in Square 21, Washington, D.C.

It took only a few weeks to learn that it really didn't make any difference which Custis heir got what—for the deceased had left behind a mountain of debts. Robert E. Lee, who served as the estate's executor, soon arrived at a round sum estimate according to which he owed $10,000 to $12,000, which couldn't possibly be paid. Because Custis's will directed that his approximately two hundred slaves be freed at his death, these tangible properties could not be used to erase the debt that hung over the entire Custis estate.

Arlington Mansion, built by Mary's father in 1802, was grandly splendid when new. Admirers learned that its immense Doric columns were reputedly modeled after those of the Theseum in Athens. During decades of neglect, the place became decidedly shabby, however. It was visited late in 1861 or early in 1862 by U.S. Sanitary Commission founder George Templeton Strong of New York. Shaking his head in dismay as he was led from one part of the mansion to another, the reformer described it as "an odd mixture of magnificence and meanness, like the castle of some illustrious, shabby, insolvent old Irish family."

Steps leading to the portico had been built of wood, so it was not strange that over sixty years they had become dangerously rotten. Lacking a schedule of regular repair, the great Doric columns needed a lot of attention. Still, Mary was passionately fond of the palace-like structure in which she was born and reared. After becoming the wife of professional soldier Robert E. Lee, she took every opportunity to spent a few weeks or even months at Arlington.

Naturally, Arlington Mansion was where her wedding took place on Thursday evening, June 30, 1831. By Custis standards, the ceremony was "a small affair, at which the bride had only twelve attendants." Sidney Smith Lee, older brother of the bridegroom, who had left home

Mary Custis Lee at the time of her wedding.—WASHINGTON AND LEE UNIVERSITY

Arlington Mansion.—U.S. ARMY MILITARY HISTORY INSTITUTE

at age eighteen in order to become an ensign in the U.S. Navy, was Robert's best man. Most of the other members of his party were junior officers of the U.S. Army, who happened to be stationed conveniently nearby at Fort Monroe. Just two years out of West Point and still a second lieutenant, Robert probably didn't warn Mary that the life of an army wife often involved lengthy periods of separation from her husband.

Surveying the evidence from a distance of many decades, it is hard to avoid the conclusion that the dashing and handsome young military engineer had his eye on Arlington and the reputed Custis fortune when he asked Mary to become his wife. No one who ever knew Mary Custis called her beautiful, and very few found her charming. She had a strong temper and a sharp tongue, so she didn't have to fight off courtiers as she moved from late adolescence into early womanhood.

But if ever there were a ladies' man during the second quarter of the nineteenth century, that man was Robert Edward Lee. Dashing in manner and extremely handsome, even after age fifty, the military officer practically had to fight off his feminine admirers. When he achieved fame as a Confederate strategist, matters got worse in this respect. Respectable and otherwise sedate ladies yearned for a moment's touch of his hand—or better yet, a few strands of his hair.

Largely due to the hero worship that Lee inspired in Pulitzer Prize–winning author Douglas Southall Freeman, he was long viewed as the ideal Southern gentleman, as well as the greatest military leader of modern times. Emory M. Thomas in his 1995 biography of Lee boldly asserts that the man over whom many a woman swooned was never unfaithful to his wife. However, he emphasizes that Robert and Mary were often apart for months, even years, during which time they were hundreds or thousands of miles away from one another. Hence, it is impossible to avoid wondering how anyone could have known whether Lee, who was admittedly enamored of lovely young women, never cheated on Mary.

For fifteen years, she almost always became pregnant during one of Lee's brief visits to her. A paragon of virtue he may have been, but a tolerant and understanding husband he clearly was not. Many of his letters to his wife, whom he occasionally addressed as Molly, must have cut her to the quick. After receiving so many of his written scoldings, she must have dreaded opening his letters, instead of joyfully anticipating their arrival. She may have become tolerant of the fact that he failed to remember such things as the recent death of a grandchild and consistently put family matters very low on his list of concerns.

Robert and Mary hadn't been married even two years before he wrote to mutual friends that she seemed to be addicted to laziness. This attitude probably stemmed, he surmised—perhaps correctly—from the fact that she grew up attended by a retinue of slaves. According to the young offi-

Romancock Manor in King William County, Virginia.—WASHINGTON AND LEE UNIVERSITY

Robert E. Lee Jr., who at age eighteen joined his father's army as a private.—
VIRGINIA HISTORICAL SOCIETY

cer, his quarters would have been kept in apple-pie order if he had taken "a nice Yankee wife" instead of a Virginia heiress.

Writing from a distance, he told his wife in no uncertain terms that she should *never* expect an officer and a gentleman to hurry home at her behest when he had duties to perform. When his eldest son Custis was five years old, his faraway father wrote—apparently seriously— that he'd consign care of the family for the upcoming summer to him. On reporting to one of his assignments, the folk who lived there appeared astonished to learn that he had a wife at all, since he'd been inquiring about hiring a servant.

Mary's health created another set of marital problems. She was strong enough to conceive and bear children, one after another. They came in fairly rapid succession: George Washington Custis on September 16, 1832; Mary on July 12, 1835; William Henry ("Rooney") on May 30, 1837; Annie Carter on June 18, 1839; Eleanor Agnes on February 27, 1841; Robert Edward Jr. on October 27, 1843; and Mildred Childe on February 10, 1846. But during the fifteen years in which she spent the bulk of her time in pregnancy or the aftereffects of childbirth, the arthritis she suffered as a newlywed became increasingly severe.

She tried lengthy visits to mineral springs and other "healing waters," but found only temporary relief. Toward the close of the twenty-one months that Robert spent in Texas just before the outbreak of the Civil War, he confided to a relative that he doubted she would ever be well enough to go from one army base to another with him. By 1860 she was an invalid who had progressed from crutches to a wheelchair.

Her distance from the site of her husband's battles did not provide Mary with a trauma-free life. On the contrary, in addition to her husband's lengthy absences, his harping criticism of her, and his liking for pretty young women, she had to endure major personal losses and frequent changes of residence.

What the medical verdict would be today if she could spend a week at the Mayo Clinic for a thorough examination is anybody's guess. Her problems may have been wholly physical—or the mental agony and the series of losses she endured in silence may have exacerbated or induced some of her maladies. Probably without realizing the full import of his words, as early as the middle of the 1830s, Robert wrote of his wife that her "nervous system" seemed to be badly damaged.

Whatever the cause of Mary Custis Lee's arthritis, ague, colds, and other maladies, she was in no condition to follow the wartime example of Julia Dent Grant, even had she ardently wanted to do so. Unlike the wife of the man who became the top military leader of the Union, the wife of the commander of the Army of the Potomac never visited her husband in the field.

Arlington, filled with relics of George Washington, was located so close to the Federal capital that it was in danger within a month after the war began. Fearing the arrival of blue-clad officers and men, Mary hastily left her home in favor of her father's Ravensworth Plantation. When it appeared that enemy forces might move in that direction, she and some of the children hurriedly departed for Kinloch Plantation.

By the time she reached Kinloch, she had learned that Federal troops under Gen. Irvin McDowell had occupied Arlington. Deeply concerned about the mansion and some of the many slaves who lived close to it, she sent a scathing letter to McDowell in which she raged at the insult of having to sue for permission to go into her own home. He responded with courtesy and told her that regardless of what she might have heard, she could come to Arlington any time she wished.

Mary did not respond to that invitation, but she did arrange for Mrs. Selina Gray and her family to continue living in a slave cabin on the property. Correctly assuming that later commanders would be less considerate than McDowell, she soon found that many of the Washington relics had been removed and taken to the Union capital. Mrs. Gray, who had been born on the estate in 1833, served as the unofficial "caretaker" of Arlington until her death soon after the turn of the next century.

In time, Federal officials assessed taxes on Arlington and refused to accept payment from anyone except the owner. As a result, the mansion

Robert E. Lee astride his horse, Traveler, to whom he was sometimes more openly affectionate than to his wife.—Washington and Lee University

and its surrounding grounds were seized for nonpayment of taxes and were soon put to a use of which George Washington Parke Custis and his daughter had never dreamed. Gen. Montgomery Meigs, the Federal quartermaster, was authorized by the U.S. secretary of war to find a new place for a cemetery because those in the capital and in Alexandria were brimful with dead soldiers.

Meigs, who once served under Lee, but now passionately hated all supporters of secession, quickly selected Arlington as the site of a new military burial place. Undocumented tradition has it that the first burial on the estate was that of an unidentified Confederate whose body went into the ground on May 13, 1864. Meigs directed subordinates to have the bodies of men killed in battles near Washington buried near the front door of the mansion. He became enraged when he inspected the place in August 1864 and found that early burials had taken place in remote spots.

According to contemporary accounts in Richmond newspapers, Meigs quickly "made Arlington no longer habitable." He personally supervised transportation of twenty-six coffins to the estate and watched as they were interred in and around the rose garden that had once been a source of delight to Mary. At the center of that spot, Meigs later had the bones of 1,100 unknown dead Union soldiers buried. Though the Federal officer didn't know it, he had launched a train of events that produced the Tomb of the Unknown Soldier—highly important in its symbolism to later generations of Americans.

Finally, turning her back on Arlington at age fifty, the woman who until then thought she had a life interest in the estate went to White House. It was there that she penned the unsigned and audacious note that was nailed to the door when she fled from there. Leaving the plantation that belonged to her son, she took refuge at Marlbourne Plantation, one of several owned by of one of Virginia's most notorious secessionists, Edmund Ruffin.

From the Ruffin estate, Mary and her daughters moved to Leigh Street in Richmond—against the advice and wishes of Robert. Still another move—this time within the Confederate capital—took them to a much larger residence on East Franklin Street. Robert paid occasional visits to the new family home, but always slept in a private bedroom, never with his wife.

Lee's surrender at Appomattox and the Federal occupation of Richmond led Mary to understand for the first time why Robert had not wanted her to take refuge in the capital. Troops under Gen. Godfrey Weitzel occupied the city, and many fires set by departing Confederates were still raging. All accounts indicate that Federal troops, among whom were numerous black units, did their best to save part of the city and as many of its inhabitants as possible. One account asserts that an officer in a blue uniform responded to the urgent pleas of a young woman, who said her mother was bedridden and would surely burn to death unless rescued. The woman who was unable to flee from the fast-approaching flames was Mary Custis Lee. When rescued and identified, she seems to have had a Federal ambulance put at her disposal so she could seek another refuge.

She and Robert were reunited after peace came, and she went with him to Lexington after the ex-soldier became president of Washington College. Though Lee had been stripped of his U.S. citizenship, the two continued to live there in genteel poverty until death claimed him five years later. Decades of poor health and years as an invalid had failed to subdue Mary. Richmond badly wanted her husband's body, but she put her foot down and insisted that he be buried in the chapel of the little college.

A contemporary writer who described Mary's passing a bit later said that the woman who lost everything she had and was separated from her husband during most of their married life "was laid beside him" in death. In the 1870s, the resting place of the former mistress of Arlington and wife of the ex-commander of the Army of Northern Virginia was described as a vault covered with dark-grained wood and marked by "two plain white marble slabs, inscribed with the names and dates of birth and death—nothing more."

8

Julia Dent Grant

Defender

Banging on the door of her husband's stateroom, the wife of Gen. U. S. Grant awakened him well before his customary hour. Still not fully alert, he asked what in the world was taking place.

"Ulys," she responded, using her intimate name for him rarely heard in public, "one of your men is scheduled to go before a firing squad three hours from now, and I think you ought to stop the execution."

"There have been other executions that didn't get your steam up," responded the commander of the Army and Department of the Tennessee.

"Some of those men were probably not worth saving," she replied. "This time it's different; I know it is! You just have to call a halt!"

"Tell me more," Grant said.

"Soon after first light a young woman with a child in her arms got aboard our steamer. She found me and said she had to see you right away. I told her you were asleep, but that I would give you a message in a little while."

Far from satisfied, and realizing that she could not proceed as she had planned, the young mother babbled a nearly incoherent story punctuated with sobs. Pointing to the child in her arms, she explained that her first baby had been born about seven months ago and her husband had never seen it. Knowing it was a great risk for her husband to be away from his regiment for a few days without permission, the child's mother still insisted that he come see their baby. Her written persuasion had proved effective; her husband did as she urged and spent a few hours at home. On the way back to camp he was picked up by scouts, arrested as a deserter, and sentenced to the standard punishment for this offense—death.

He was technically guilty of desertion, Julia admitted, but she stressed that the mother's plea created extenuating circumstances. Few husbands could have resisted under similar circumstances, she told her

At least once, Grant yielded to his wife, against his better judgment, and pardoned a deserter.

husband. Grant, who had listened patiently, shook his head and said he couldn't interfere with military justice. The man who needed to hear the desolate mother's plea was Gen. Marsena R. Patrick—who was nowhere near the steamer. Julia nodded that she understood the necessity of following protocol, then she opened the door of her husband's cabin, revealing the mother and child about whom they had been talking. Without an invitation, the stranger entered the stateroom and babbled her story as well as she could to the general.

Grant gestured to his wife to bring him writing materials. He hastily scribbled a note commuting the execution scheduled for noon then told Julia that he was sure he had done the wrong thing. Writing her memoirs years later, Julia Dent Grant remembered that he grimaced and said that she and the unidentified young mother had probably saved the hide of a worthless bounty jumper. Julia never believed that was the case and she never regretted having persuaded her husband to act upon her instincts.

Most of Julia's interference consisted of challenging the views of those who seemed to be casting aspersions on her husband. She vehemently denied that he had a drinking problem—a view shared by Bruce Catton—despite the fact that Gen. John A. Rawlins, her husband's chief of staff, helped give that story almost universal credence. She blithely overlooked or completely forgot events of the dreary years during which it seemed that her husband could succeed in only one endeavor—making a mess of his life, her life, and the lives of their children.

Their start as a semi-engaged couple was auspicious enough. The decidedly plain daughter of a prosperous Missouri plantation owner caught the eye of twenty-two-year-old 2nd Lt. Grant of the U.S. Army, and they were soon deeply in love. The recent West Point graduate wrote at length to his "Dear Julia" from Camp Necessity, Louisiana, late in August 1844. He ended his letter as "Most Truly and Devotedly Your Lover ULYSSES." In a hastily scribbled postscript, he indicated that he felt it was about time to begin informing her father that they were more than casual friends. Scores of his letters to her were included with his *Memoirs* in a volume published by the Library of America in 1990. They are filled with abiding love that never diminished, even during periods of long separation.

Both of them took in stride a matter that to some would have caused anger, heartache, or both. Born in the Ohio settlement of Point Pleasant, Grant was named Hiram Ulysses. When he reported to West Point to start his military training, an officer carelessly listed the new cadet as Ulysses Simpson Grant. With the middle name that didn't belong to him abbreviated to a single capital letter without a period, the future general became known as "Sam" to many of his fellow cadets. In an early Civil War battle at Fort Donelson, Tennessee, he signed a demand for unconditional surrender as "U. S. Grant." That incident led to his being widely known as "Unconditional Surrender" Grant, despite the fact that he repeatedly pointed out that he had a middle "S" in his name "that didn't mean a thing."

During the Mexican War, Sam Grant fought with distinction at Cerro Gordo, Molino del Rey, and Chapultepec. When the war ended, he and Julia spent a period at Sackets Harbor, New York, before he was assigned to the Pacific Northwest—thousands of miles away from his bride, whom he had married on August 22, 1848, and their first son. Virtually all biographers insist that his fondness for alcohol during this separa-

Artist's conception of Grant leaving home to take charge of troops that were being assembled by the governor of Illinois.—LIBRARY OF CONGRESS

Back in uniform, the officer known to some of his men as Sam displayed an enormous beard that Julia soon persuaded him to trim.—LIBRARY OF CONGRESS [SKETCH FROM HARPER'S WEEKLY]

tion triggered his resignation from the U.S. Army on July 31, 1854—the same day he received his commission as captain.

Many of Grant's troubles were related to money. While returning from Mexico, $1,000 was stolen from a fellow officer's trunk; though a court of inquiry absolved Julia's sweetheart of having taken it, he was held responsible for its repayment. While on the Columbia River near Portland in the Oregon Territory, he tried to bolster his finances by selling wood, renting horses, and farming a 100-acre tract in partnership with other officers. A flood destroyed much of the crop. Earlier, a California con artist had relieved him of about $2,000. A business venture with a sutler cost him an additional $800, and he reached Julia at her father's White Haven mansion flat broke.

Still having not resolved the issue of the stolen money belonging to the army and no longer on salary, he began, in desperation, to clear sixty acres of land given to Julia by her father; for several years he had no income except what he derived from selling wood on the streets of St. Louis. Julia seems to have been able to keep the family afloat financially, for she still owned three slaves. Jule, her nurse and nanny, later accompanied her on many of her trips to see her husband during the Civil War.

By 1855 Ulysses and Julia were living in a house that belonged to her brother. Not satisfied with this arrangement, the former army officer built a six-room house that he called Hardscrabble. No residence ever had a more appropriate name. Early in 1857 Grant was forced to ask his father, a prosperous merchant, for a $500 loan so he could buy seeds and a few farm implements. On December 23 of that same year, desperate for money with which to buy a few Christmas gifts, he offered his prized gold watch to a pawn broker and parted with it for $22.

Things looked much better at the beginning of 1858. Julia's father decided to move to St. Louis, and he rented Ulysses his White Haven mansion plus two hundred acres of cleared land. But just as it had in the

Pacific Northwest, weather knocked his dreams of a profitable farming year into a cocked hat. He was forced to auction off his farm animals and equipment and return to selling wood. When one of Julia's cousins offered him a job as a rent collector in St. Louis, he quickly accepted, but soon found he couldn't make a living at it. He'd already failed to get an appointment as a engineer on the payroll of St. Louis County, so in desperation, he persuaded his father to make him a clerk in a leather goods store operated by his younger brothers.

This job took him, Julia, and their growing family to Galena, Illinois. They had been occupants of a rented house only a few months when South Carolina launched "the secession parade," followed by a prolonged artillery duel at Charleston. Lys—or Lyss as Julia often wrote his name—suddenly hankered to get back into uniform and draw a monthly salary. He wrote a summary of his military training and experience and dispatched it to the adjutant general in Washington, along with an offer to return to the ranks immediately.

Grant never heard from that application to serve the Union; while waiting for a reply, he visited his parents, who had moved to Covington, Kentucky. Since the town was very close to Louisville, he spent two days trying to see Gen. George B. McClellan and to offer his services to the army, but McClellan didn't even give him two minutes of his time. It looked as though he might be a leather goods clerk for the rest of his life.

The City Point, Virginia, headquarters cabin where Julia spent most of the winter of 1864–65.—Pictorial Field Book of the Civil War

Governor Richard Yates of Illinois rescued Ulysses from oblivion by offering him command of a regiment of volunteers. He accepted eagerly and gratefully and soon was at the head of the 21st Illinois regiment. Congressman Elihi Washburne, in whose district Galena lay, took an interest in the colonel and began pulling strings in Washington. On August 5, 1861, Washburne's political clout afforded Grant a commission as a brigadier—a promotion that was the stepping stone toward a meteoric rise to power and fame.

Julia's 333-page volume of memoirs largely ignores or glosses over the long period in which it seemed as though the West Point graduate would end his life as a stumblebum. No woman was ever more fiercely defensive of her husband and his reputation. Gen. Rawlins, a prewar attorney in Galena, served as aide to her husband for most of the Civil War, and she never minced words in condemning him for "lies he spread about the General's drinking." The notion that she was with him as much of the time as possible during the war in order to keep him away from the bottle is widespread. Though it is deeply embedded in the literature, Julia's account of the war years dismisses this matter as fruit of the imagination.

Whatever the reasons for their involvement, few general officers on either side had such frequent and prolonged companionship with their family members as did Grant. When his regiment was ordered from Illinois to Missouri, he sent word to Julia that their son, Fred, would soon be headed toward Galena. She instantly wrote back: "Do not send him home; Alexander [the Great] was not older when he accompanied [his father] Philip [of Macedon to war]. Do keep him with you." Though Fred didn't get to go to Missouri in 1861, he stayed with his father during much of the Civil War.

Julia went to her husband whenever she could, and stayed as long as possible—alternating between his headquarters, St. Louis, and their home in New Jersey. At Corinth, Mississippi, they occupied "a handsome and very comfortable country house, situated in a magnificent oak grove of great extent." A wide path around the house was sprinkled and raked twice a day. "It was the delight of Nellie and Jess [their children] to make footprints with their little rosy feet in this freshly-raked earth." She stayed at Corinth until a few days before a two-week struggle began on April 29, 1862.

After a brief stay in St. Louis, she joined Ulysses at Jackson, Tennessee, where their home was "a straggling old country house, part log, part frame, with a long, low piazza fronting south." From Jackson, Julia and her husband visited their friend James B. McPherson at nearby Bolivar.

Their arrival coincided with a dispatch from Washington notifiying McPherson that he had just been confirmed as a brigadier. Julia took out a needle and a little gold thimble, then "firmly fastened McPherson's first stars for him on his brave, broad, handsome shoulders." On that joyful day, it did not occur to anyone that McPherson would fall at Atlanta and become the only commander of a Federal army to die in a Civil War battle.

Her friends advised Julia to have her photographs taken in profile so that her eyes wouldn't show.—FROM A SAMUEL SARTAIN ENGRAVING

After a brief stay in St. Louis, Julia went to Holly Springs, where she came perilously close to being captured by Rebels under Gen. Earl Van Dorn. Having left Holly Springs just before fighting men in gray arrived there, she went to Memphis and spent the summer with her husband.

Grant was so obsessed with the challenge of taking Vicksburg that he tried several futile experiments, one of which involved attempting to dig an immense canal. His wife consoled him each time he admitted failure— then encouraged him to try something else. After months of discouragement, he decided to try to send gunboats down the Mississippi River so they could be used to transport troops from the west to the east bank of the great waterway. Julia was by his side on a river boat during some of the most dramatic hours of the entire war. She saw vessels under the command of Cmdr. David D. Porter run the gamut at the Confederate-held river city and gave her husband a wordless hug when it seemed evident that heavy fire from bluffs above would not stop the flotilla. After the July 4, 1863, surrender of Vicksburg, Julia went there and wondered aloud how the women and children of the city had endured a siege so lengthy that they were happy to get horse meat to eat before it ended.

After several months in Louisville, the Missouri native went to Nashville, which had been captured. It was probably during her stay in the Tennessee capital that Jule, her slave who had served as nurse for her children, left her. Disconsolate for a while, the woman who had been reared in luxury finally consoled herself by remembering that

Ulysses and his parents had always been strongly opposed to slavery. She, however, could hardly imagine life without slaves and held hers as long as she could. Both sets of parents had opposed the marriage. The Dents thought their daughter could do better than a "poor soldier boy" who couldn't provide her the life to which she was accustomed. Jesse Grant, who once owned slaves had freed them before moving to Illinois. Having become an ardent abolitionist, he didn't want his son to marry a slave owner.

In St. Louis once more and keenly aware that her husband was now the only lieutenant general since George Washington, she decided it was time to act on some previous advice. She consulted Dr. Charles A. Pope, who had often urged her to undergo a simple operation to correct her misaligned eyes. Earlier, she had failed to muster the courage to let him use his scalpel on her face, but with a husband who was now famous, she decided it behooved her "to try to look as well as possible" instead of continuing to be "so very, very plain."

Pope shook his head sadly when he learned the reason for her visit. It was too late, he told her; the surgery would have been successful only if they had performed it when she was much younger. Confiding to Grant about the experience, Julia expressed her regret. As she remembered the incident long afterward, he embraced her and declared that her eyes belonged to him. He might not like her "half so well with any other eyes," he told her tenderly.

Still having eyes that many described as crossed, Julia spent most of the winter of 1864–65 with her husband at his City Point, Virginia, headquarters. He hoped to capture Petersburg quickly, but the city was stoutly defended. His wife was on hand when a huge cache of gun powder exploded close to his headquarters. Possibly an act of sabotage, this became one of the biggest and most mysterious explosions of the war. Fortunately, no member of the family was injured. She also saw Abraham Lincoln and his wife here briefly—just long enough to form a poor opinion of the Kentucky-born First Lady.

At the war's end, and with her husband still at the front, Julia made her first visit to Washington alone and attended a gala reception given by President and Mrs. Lincoln. She was present at the triumphant two-day Grand Review of Federal armies that celebrated the unconditional surrender of their enemies, and this time had occasion to see Mrs. Lincoln with some frequency.

Julia considered the president's wife extremely possessive of him and jealous of any other woman to whom he showed any attention. Her dislike of the Kentucky native was so great that she persuaded her husband to decline an invitation to go to Ford's Theatre the night Lincoln was assassinated. At his wife's urging, Grant told the chief executive that he was sorry, but he had urgent business at his home in New Jersey and must leave before the scheduled party.

If Julia had any regrets about preventing her husband from being on hand to guard Lincoln on Good Friday 1865, she kept very quiet about them. Had investigative reporters been flourishing in that era, one of them would no doubt have

Julia, her husband, and her children, as painted by William Cogswell in 1867.—THE SMITHSONIAN INSTITUTION

queried her about this matter. A careful look at her long and eventful career and her personal account of it in her memoirs gives at least a clue of how she would have responded to questions about Ford's Theatre. Had she been true to form, as she nearly always was, Julia Dent Grant probably would have told the inquirer that her whole purpose was to protect the good name of her husband, and that required all of the time and energy she could devote.

Eliza Anderson

Taker

"**P**eter Hart! He can do it!" Until this exclamation ended, Eliza Anderson was not aware that she was speaking to herself. Sitting bolt upright in her bed at about 3 A.M., she was in a strange, half-conscious state. Had she been dreaming, or simply sleeping soundly? It hardly mattered, she quickly decided. Regardless of where it came from, she now had the answer to the question that had been troubling her since she heard of her husband's dangerous plight.

Writing to her from hundreds of miles to the south just after taking over Fort Sumter, Maj. Robert Anderson said in part:

> Thanks be to God, I give them with my whole heart for His having given me the will, and shown me the way to take my command to this fort. I can now breathe freely. The whole force of South Carolina would not venture to attack us. Our crossing was accomplished between six and eight o'clock [on the evening of December 26, 1860]. I am satisfied that there was no suspicion of what we were going to do. I have no doubt that the news of what I have done will be telegraphed to New York this night.

The professional soldier's estimate of his exploit's news value was correct. New York papers were full of accounts of it even before this letter reached his wife. However, the journalists were unanimous in warning their readers to expect news that Anderson and his handful of men were under siege.

To the frail wife who had awakened in pitch darkness on January 3, 1861, it seemed like hours before the first dim signals of the dawn came.

Unable to wait any longer, she went to the nurse who looked after her children.

"You must get up immediately," she directed. "I know it's early, and I'm sorry to disturb you. But you must run a very important errand for me as soon as you can get dressed. I need a city directory. Some of the shops that sell newspapers open at five o'clock. One of them will surely have it."

Within an hour, Mrs. Anderson was poring over the pages of a battered directory to New York City, where she was living at the time. "Hart. Hart," she said to the listening nurse who sat close to her. "There are more of them here than I would have imagined. Bring me paper and a pencil, please."

Mrs. Eliza Clinch Anderson.—LOSSING, PICTORIAL FIELD BOOK OF THE CIVIL WAR

Excited and confident that she would soon find the man whose name had popped into her brain a few hours earlier, she jotted down the street address of every Hart in the city. The nurse went for a carriage, helped her into it, and offered to accompany her.

"Thank you, no. You must stay here to look after the children. I will be back as soon as I can," she said.

At twilight, she briefly wondered how many sets of stairs she had climbed and how many doors she had knocked on. She had failed to find Peter Hart, a soldier and friend who had been with the Andersons at three or four U.S. Army posts during the decade following the Mexican War. But there were six or eight more names and addresses on her list. She would resume her search early the next day.

Shortly before 8:30 A.M., with only two or three more Harts left to check, she was given a clue. The Mrs. Hart whom she had just questioned shook her head to indicate that her husband was not named Peter. Visibly agitated, Eliza turned wearily away, but the stranger called, "Wait a minute. I may be able to help you after all. I think I have heard [my husband] say a man with his name is now a member of the

Ex-sergeant Peter Hart.

police establishment. This man was once a soldier; I hope he's the one you're looking for."

At police headquarters, Eliza Anderson began questioning the superintendent as soon as she was ushered into his office. He immediately expressed sympathetic understanding and reached for a gray book.

"Peter's here," he explained, "but I'll have to look up his address. He lives some distance away, just outside the city. I can send a message to him, if you like."

"Thank you! That will be wonderful." Scribbling her name and address on a sheet of paper, she said simply, "Please come at once. This is urgent."

Two hours later, a burly New York City policeman, accompanied by his wife, appeared at the door of Mrs. Anderson's apartment. "I need your husband's help," she explained to Margaret Hart.

"He'll do his level best, Mistress."

"Major Anderson is at Fort Sumter, close to Charleston, South Carolina," she explained. "He is in a desperate and dangerous situation. If he ever needed someone close to him that he can trust, that time is now. I want you to go with me to Charleston and then remain with the major and see that no harm comes to him." Hart shot a quick glance at his wife, who nodded silently.

"I'll go, Madam. When do we leave?"

"Be here tomorrow morning at six o'clock, and I'll be ready. Thank you from the bottom of my heart! Thank you, my faithful Margaret!"

The ex-sergeant and Eliza found seats on a southbound train and left New York on Thursday evening, January 5. None of Eliza Anderson's friends knew that she was leaving, and her nurse was under strict orders to answer no questions about her absence.

Many passengers climbed out of their cars at various stations, so by the time the train reached Cape Fear, North Carolina, Eliza was the only woman on it. Men who took seats in her car were mostly rough-looking farmers who talked loudly about their own plans. Several of them were headed to Charleston to join the state military forces, whose leader was expected to launch an attack on Fort Sumter soon. A particularly talkative braggart told his acquaintances what he'd do when he "got his hands on that Yankee who pulled down Sergeant Jasper's flagpole and set it on fire." Eliza Anderson had no idea of what he was talking about, but sensed that he was angry and dangerous.

Their train reached its destination late in the evening, so she asked a station attendant to call a carriage for her. Instead of acting on her request, he demanded to know where she came from and where she wanted to go. When she explained that she and her companion had come from New York, he blurted that he couldn't possibly get a carriage at that hour.

"Then give me a piece of paper so I can write a note to Governor Pickens. If you can't get me a carriage, he will send me one."

Her quick and decisive action was not boastful. Her husband and Governor Francis Pickens had known each other for years and were genuinely fond of one another. Though Pickens was the chief executive of the independent Republic of South Carolina, he could be depended on to accommodate the wife of his longtime friend.

Mention of Pickens was enough to suddenly change the mind of the station attendant. "You don't have to bother the governor," he responded. "I'll try to get a carriage for you."

Within minutes Eliza Anderson and Peter Hart were on their way to the distinguished old Mills House, where she had reason to believe that one of her brothers might be staying. Ushered into the gas-lit parlor nearly filled with men who were smoking cigars and talking loudly, she asked to see Bayard Clinch.

He soon appeared behind a bell boy, and the sister and brother embraced for a long moment. Before he could ask her what on earth she was doing there, Eliza threw a question at him.

Maj. Robert Anderson, whose devotion to duty led to civil war.—NATIONAL CYCLOPEDIA OF AMERICAN BIOGRAPHY

"Some of these men are angry at my husband. They keep talking about a flagstaff. What does it mean?"

Her brother reminded Eliza that during the American Revolution, a British fleet launched an attack on Fort Moultrie. One of their cannon balls clipped the flagstaff of the fortress held by Continental soldiers, and to observers it looked as though the little garrison had surrendered. At that dramatic moment, Sgt. Jasper jumped from behind his defensive shield of palmetto logs, seized the fallen flag, and restored it to its place. The incident was hailed throughout the colonies, and Jasper was honored by having a Georgia county named in his honor. Her husband had ordered that very flagstaff cut down and stripped of its emblem only a few days earlier. Patriots in general, and South Carolinians in particular, were outraged at such treatment of what they considered to be a sacred emblem.

Thanking her brother for the explanation, Eliza told him that she now knew what the "bear of a man meant by things he said on the train." After having secured a room for her and another for Peter Hart, Bayard, who had not seen his sister in many months, went to her room. They talked until very late.

He interrupted when Eliza started to explain her mission. Instinctively, he knew what she was doing as soon as he learned that she was in the city. Though his own loyalty was with the South, he volunteered to get a pass so she could visit her husband. He also offered to go with her, and she accepted gratefully.

For the better part of an hour they talked about their childhood. Their father, Duncan L. Clinch, was a native of North Carolina, who gloried in the fact that Eliza's grandfather had fought in the War of 1812.

The evacuation of Fort Moultrie by Maj. Anderson and his men.—
The Soldier in Our Civil War

During the First Seminole War, Duncan Clinch won regional renown for having ordered the execution of 270 Native Americans and runaway slaves. For this exploit he was universally addressed as "General," despite the fact that colonel was his highest regular rank. On leaving the army in 1836, he bought a plantation in Camden County, Georgia. At their father's spacious Lamont Hall, Eliza, Bayard, their four brothers, and two sisters were reared. As children, they had only a fuzzy understanding of the distinctions between owners and slaves, but always had one or two at their beck and call.

Memories of their father and his second wife, the mother of all eight children, triggered a comment from Bayard. He gravely told his sister that she was likely to catch sight of an armed steamer called the *General Clinch*. The vessel that commemorated their father, he informed her, was a Rebel gunboat that was likely to fire on Fort Sumter. She nodded understandingly and asked no questions, fully aware also that two or three of her brothers were likely to be soldiers challenging her husband's occupation of the fort.

Eliza did venture to wonder why her husband had been sent to take command of Federal installations in Charleston. Bayard shook his head in bewilderment, but said that he had heard some gossip that might explain the assignment. John B. Floyd of Virginia had been the U.S. secretary of war until December 29. Rumor had it that he sent Maj. Anderson to the hottest spot in North America because he was a native of Kentucky and the husband of a slave-owning Georgian. According to this story, Floyd—a Confederate who was forced out of office a few days before Eliza began hunting for Peter Hart—believed that for the sake of his family, Anderson would have to support the secessionist movement launched by South Carolina.

If the story that reached Charleston was accurate, it revealed how poor Floyd's judgment was. Despite his extremely strong Southern ties, Robert Anderson never wavered in his determination to do his duty as he saw it. A West Point graduate in the class of 1825, his assignment to the 3rd Artillery as a second lieutenant meant that he had a splendid record as a cadet. West Pointers who ranked toward the lower half of their class invariably went into the infantry.

Along with his father-in-law, he fought in the Second Seminole War during 1835–37, then went to the Mexican War as an aide to Gen. Winfield Scott. He was dispatched by Floyd to Fort Moultrie late in November 1860. Judging that installation to be indefensible, Anderson made secret plans to withdraw from it and take possession of Fort Sumter.

Erected on an artificial island and furnished with numerous big guns that had never been fired, this five-sided installation was built to serve as a barrier to European warships. When political tensions eased with the youthful United States, work on the fort ground to a virtual standstill. No garrison had ever been sent to occupy Fort Sumter, and after her secession, South Carolina claimed it as her own. Warmongers in the North vowed that it would never become a Rebel fortress. In this climate Eliza's husband spiked the guns of Fort Moultrie and headed toward Fort Sumter. Soldiers busy splintering the wooden carriages of guns probably knocked down the flagstaff to which so much sentiment was attached.

Eliza knew that her husband had only a handful of soldiers in his command. Virtually everyone in the South and the North expected newly occupied Fort Sumter to become a bone of contention between already-hostile regions. That's why she felt impelled to bring help for her husband in the form of his ex-sergeant. If every other man in his command should abandon her husband, she knew that Peter Hart would be faithful to the death.

Governor Pickens acceded readily to Bayard Clinch's request that his sister be permitted to visit her husband briefly at a spot that was already off-limits to both civilians and soldiers. He balked at the notion of allowing Hart to accompany her, however, especially in view of Hart's military experience. There was danger that he might be a formidable foe when secessionists decided to move against the fort. Under Eliza's entreaties, the governor hemmed and hawed before making up his mind.

She pointed out that the independent nation of South Carolina, already making plans to send emissaries to Great Britain and to Europe, couldn't possibly be threatened by one man. Pickens relented and wrote a pass for Hart, with the stipulation that he must solemnly promise not to take up arms against South Carolinians under any circumstances. Pointing toward a large leather pouch, the chief executive of the self-declared republic made a gesture of goodwill.

"You know lots of letters for soldiers have been held up," he said to Bayard. "They're all there. Take 'em to the fort when you go."

Perched in a rowboat and headed toward the immense fortification that had been taken over by her husband, it seemed to Eliza that the distance of about a mile would never be covered. As their tiny vessel came close to the walls, a watchman challenged them. Bayard shouted that Mrs. Anderson had come to visit her husband, so they were soon escorted over rocks to the wharf, where the commandant of Fort Sumter met and embraced his wife.

"I have brought you Peter Hart!" she exclaimed. "The nurse is with the children, and they are well. I can stay only an hour or two. I must leave with the tide."

Nodding silently, Anderson gently led Eliza into his quarters, which were spacious and comfortable by the standards of army posts. She sipped a cup of tea and ate a bit of bread, unaware that it was the last available in the fortress.

Bayard's circle of friends had been in-

Maj. Anderson's quarters, Fort Sumter.—Lossing, Pictorial Field Book of the Civil War

formed that Eliza had come to tell her husband goodbye, knowing she might never see him again. A group of them met her when the return trip of the rowboat ended at the city's Battery. They offered her lodging and said they had plenty of food, so she could stay as long as she wished.

Shaking her head, Maj. Anderson's frail wife explained that she could not stay. The only available train that evening would be headed to Washington, and she planned to be on it. Charleston seemed to be a lovely city, she noted. But her husband might soon be under attack, and she could not bear to witness that.

Bayard arranged for a bed to be placed in her car, and Eliza started for the capital on schedule. By the time she reached Washington, however, she was unconscious, so she was taken to Willard's Hotel. Suffering from total exhaustion, she remained at Willard's for two days, then returned to her children in New York.

Peter Hart, she convinced herself, would make a difference. He would be loyal and true, no matter what might happen. She almost felt that his presence in the forbidding fortress meant that Maj. Anderson would have a guardian angel constantly looking over his shoulder.

So many records were destroyed that it is impossible to know whether or not Hart actually kept his pledge not to defend Fort Sumter.

However, it would have made no difference whether he fought or dutifully stood aside when the long artillery duel between Federal and secessionist soldiers began very early on April 12. Food supplies were so low that Anderson and his men were forced to give up in just a few days. Weak from hunger but otherwise in good condition, Robert conducted surrender ceremonies and then went to a waiting Federal vessel that took him to New York, to Eliza and the children, and to a wildly enthusiastic ovation from thousands of strangers.

Peter Hart's arrival at the beleaguered fortress in Charleston Harbor made no difference in the outcome of the struggle in which it was central. It had no impact whatever on the subsequent course of the most deadly civil war of the western world. Yet the noted historian Benson J. Lossing was deeply impressed with the determination and courage of Eliza Anderson.

Of her, he wrote, "She alone did what the Government would not, or dared not to do. She did not send, but took" an invaluable aide to her husband in the form of New York policeman Peter Hart.

CHAPTER

10

Princess Agnes

Charmer

H er shapely figure was very apparent in spite of her Federal uniform. Complete with captain's stripes, gold buttons, and braids, the outfit had been tailored especially for the young woman. Her oval face, chestnut eyes, fine features, and wavy dark hair were accented by a winsome smile as she greeted soldiers within the camp. Union officer Prince Felix Salm-Salm of Prussia could not tear his eyes away from the sight of the beautiful woman. His eyes followed her as she strolled confidently through the camp accompanied by a well-groomed nutmeg sorrel that trotted obediently behind her, their steps synchronized like familiar old friends. Felix drew in a breath and sighed to an aide that he must secure an introduction. Little did he know that this vision of beauty would be his constant companion for years and would one day save his life.

Salm-Salm was shaken from his moment of contemplation by his commander, for whom he served as chief-of-staff. "Lovely, isn't she?" Gen. Louis Blenker interrupted in German. Salm-Salm had no reply. "She's a mystery," continued Blenker, "some say she comes from Cuba. Others believe she's the daughter of a Canadian soldier or a circus performer or an actress. No one knows." Felix pondered Blenker's comments and requested a formal introduction. Blenker obliged, changing forever the life of a royal soldier.

A few short months later, in August 1862, Felix Salm-Salm, the thirty-four-year-old son of Prussian Prince Felix Constantin Alexander Johann Nepomuk Salm-Salm, and the twenty-one-year-old Agnes Elizabeth Winona Leclerq Joy were married. Attending guests stood outside Saint Patrick's Church in Washington, enamored of the handsome couple. Felix spoke only German, which Agnes could neither speak nor understand. They managed to become man and wife, each knowing only a few words in Spanish. Onlookers applauded when the two foreigners exchanged the nuptial kiss. One commentator on the life of the royal soldier of fortune and his wife informed readers that the prince was thirteen years older than his wife, but by the strangest of coincidence, both had been born on Christmas Day.

Their strikingly different backgrounds didn't seem to affect the love and devotion Agnes demonstrated for Felix, who had grown up as an indulged and spoiled child of royal blood. He was the youngest son of the reigning prince of Westphalia. Having chosen a military career, Salm-Salm's first commission was as a cavalry officer in the Prussian Army. His 1848 performance in the Schleswig-Holstein War was fairly spectacular. For his display of bravery, during which he was wounded seven times, he was awarded the sword of honor by future Kaiser Wilhelm I.

But his celebrity faded early in 1861 when Salm-Salm transferred to the Austrian Army in Vienna. His inability to control his extravagances led to financial ruin. Squandering vast sums of money, he fell hopelessly into debt. Saved from debtor's prison by the swift action of his father, the soldier of fortune went far to the west and gained a personal audience with Abraham Lincoln.

Unable to speak English, the Prussian was accompanied to the Executive Mansion by Baron von Gerholt zur Leyen, his country's minister to Washington and interpreter for the prince. Von Gerholt enjoyed the essence of Lincoln's comments before translating them into German for young Felix. Lincoln joked that he would not hold it against the young prince that he was royalty. His commission would assure that Rebels would know no difference, the president said. Assigned initially to Gen. Louis Blenker as his chief-of-staff, Salm-Salm saw little action or excitement, except for meeting his future bride.

Agnes Leclercq was believed to have been raised by the loving, invalid wife of an American cabinet minister in Philadelphia, who had spotted the child in Paris, adopted her, and brought her home to the United States. Hard to resist, even as a child, Agnes and her foster mother were involved in one adventure after another. The high-spirited girl won over the Americans, gaining for herself security and a fine education.

In 1857, at age sixteen, Agnes became bored with needlepoint, which she hated. Her love of books, physical challenges, and horses caused her to fantasize about becoming a circus performer. Her parents protested when she announced she would begin a career as a circus horse rider, but Agnes always had a way of getting what she wanted.

Adept at horseback riding, she studied exhaustively to achieve balance atop a galloping steed. She could never master this skill, however, and was forced to focus her attention on the slack wire. At an outdoor performance in Chicago in 1858, billed as "The Great Ascensionist," Agnes gave an eager audience their money's worth. All eyes in the crowd were riveted on her as she mounted the thin wire. Clad in pink and silver muslin, holding a balance pole, she moved her tiny feet carefully upward.

Horrified onlookers gasped as a gust of wind caught her. She was perilously high, but good fortune followed her, as a burly fellow performer had stationed himself below, strategically positioned to catch her as she tumbled from the wire. The crowd gasped, but jumped to their feet in delight as Agnes, undaunted by the fall, strode back to the wire to attempt the climb again. Her tiny feet slid inch by inch up the wire to the

Prince Felix Salm-Salm, who attached a monocle to his uniform, was one of a handful of Europeans with royal titles who took part in the Civil War.—U.S. ARMY MILITARY HISTORY INSTITUTE

top of the flagstaff, where she gave a modest bow, then returned to the bottom. The crowd roared with delight.

Grand rounds by the circus took her act to Western and Southwestern states, but in the summer of 1858, a local sheriff closed the circus and brought Agnes's career on the slack wire to an end. She moved between New York and Havana, Cuba, for the next two years. Cavorting as a high-spirited and unique individual, Agnes made friends and created purposeful relationships. It is rumored she was married in Havana, possibly twice, but confirmation of this has never been substantiated.

With the start of the Civil War, Agnes decided that Washington was the place to be. Fascinated by the certainty of sectional conflict, Agnes wanted to be amid the officers and influential people responsible for decisions about the war effort. Even as a young woman she recognized the benefits of knowing the right people. She wrote in her diary, "As I had to carry out certain purposes, I came in contact with all leading politicians, and heard and observed a great deal." She made it her business to know everybody. She moved from one influential circle to the next, leaving her card as a reminder that a clever and capable young woman had come calling.

In Washington her behavior gained her the name of "The Young Bohemienne." She was loved by men and hated by women, whose scornful glares were never able to quell her daredevil spirit. Two constant companions, known simply as Miss Blank and "army woman," were a model of gaiety as they laughed and cavorted about the streets of the capital.

When Agnes was not plotting mischief with her two friends, she often went to the campgrounds on the Potomac to visit with soldiers. She would throw a slender leg over the broad body of her favorite horse and ride—not sidesaddle, but straddling the steed—as proficiently as any man. On one of these ventures—to Blenker's famous XI Corp—she was seen by and introduced to Prince Salm-Salm.

Although Agnes was well known among members of society, she was not truly accepted into their elite circles until she had married and became Princess Agnes. She shed most of her military garb, retaining only the gold buttons—probably a protest at having to wear feminine attire—which brought stares from ladies and gentlemen alike.

Agnes was almost never subdued in her behavior; she was clever and thoughtful enough in her moves to obtain what she wanted. She knew exactly how to manipulate the moment—disregarding protocol—to achieve success. One of her first challenges as wife of Prince Felix was with New York Governor Edwin D. Morgan. Rumor had it that her husband would soon be out of a job because of Blenker's 1862 failure at the Battle of Cross Keys, so Agnes formulated a plan. She sought help from her friend Senator Ira Harris, who accompanied her on a visit to the governor.

Harris warned her that Morgan was notorious for disliking assertive women. True to form, he scowled at his visitor when she inquired about a possible commission for her husband in a German regiment. The governor growled that nothing was available, only reluctantly calling for his secretary to confirm this fact. Morgan's nervous military secretary fumbled the journals and reported that several commissions were indeed open—one being that of a colonel in Blenker's 8th New York. Her persistence and compelling words softened the governor; Harris later said he'd never seen anything like it. Clutched in her hands, Agnes carried the papers—fresh with Morgan's signature—that granted her husband another commission.

Salm-Salm, who had been left behind in the hotel room, was relieved and delighted to learn of his wife's remarkable success. As he unfolded his commission, he reached for his resourceful wife and embraced her in a display of gratitude, love, and admiration. The men of the 8th, eager to please their new commander and his wife, gave them an elaborate welcome, complete with morning serenades. A cake was sculpted out of mud and decorated with leaves, colored sand, and stones meant to look like fruit. Both Agnes and Felix were touched by the efforts of these men.

German regiments were known for such extravagances. Gen. George B. McClellan was a frequent visitor to the German camps, where he knew he would enjoy gaiety and possibly have a few moments with the lovely Princess Salm-Salm. In her diary, *Ten Years of My Life*, Agnes tells of festivities in her husband's camps, writing, "As we had to do nothing but amuse ourselves, and kill the time agreeably, scarcely a day passed without some excursion, pleasure party, dinner or ball; and for the entertainment of the soldiers care was taken like wise." She told of an occasion when Gen. Daniel E. Sickles linked together more than a dozen tents to create an "immense tent decorated inside and outside with flags, garland, flowers and Chinese lamps which offered a fairy-like aspect." As chef for this festival, the famous Delmonico from New York came prepared to serve only the "choicest provisions and delicacies."

Aquia Creek, Virginia, where the princess transformed a hospital tent into "a salon with canvas walls," was noted as the site of an early naval battle.

At Aquia Creek, Virginia, during the winter of 1862–63, the princess learned from these festive experiences that a hospital tent and the grounds around it could be transformed into a surreal picture. Employing carpenters, upholsters, masons, and other skilled members of the regiment, wooden floors were built over which carpet was laid. Lavish damask, prominent with crisp white and bright red colors, were arranged in rows of festoons, with flags inserted between each decorative wreath or swag.

In the salon, as Agnes called it, sofas stuffed with straw and carefully covered in the rich damask had been crafted by her private army. Numerous men were at her disposal to create a wonderland, a place uncommon to most battlefields. Perhaps it was boredom that inspired Agnes to undertake this transformation of the camp—there was no action, and her husband's commission was about to expire. Seated on the elegant sofa next to his princess, Salm-Salm once again pondered the future.

The prince soon asked Morgan if he could command a new regiment—if he could recruit enough men to form it. Morgan agreed, but the task proved to be easier said than done. The Salm-Salms opened a recruiting office in New York City, but the draft riots caused chaos. Hardly an able-bodied male was available to recruit. It seemed to Salm-Salm that he would surely be unemployed; as always, however, apparent disaster served to inspire Agnes.

Her creative talents flourished in the face of adversity. Traveling to Washington, the colonel's wife contacted the provost marshal of the army and convinced him to transfer men to the newly formed 68th regiment of volunteers. Afterward, while still in Washington, she wangled her way into a dance with Governor Richard Yates of Illinois. While twirling about the floor, the music surrounding them, Agnes persuaded Yates to transfer one hundred troops from Illinois to the 68th—along with a captain's commission for herself. Amazed by her abilities, her husband spent another year in command of the 68th New York.

Caring for the sick and wounded in the hospital at Bridgeport, Tennessee, Agnes gained recognition from Yates and was afforded a great deal of freedom from her husband. Always faithful—at least by historical accounts—she thought nothing of the possible scandal resulting from her numerous 1863–64 visits to Gen. James Blair Steedman in Chattanooga. One such trip included a horseback ride to Lookout Mountain. On the following morning an elaborate breakfast—called a *bon vivant* by the princess—was attended by Steedman and Gen. Gordon Granger, who also received visits from Princess Agnes at Stevenson.

Princess Agnes Salm-Salm captivated Atlanta during her husband's sevice as military governor of the city.—THE ATLANTA CENTURY

Perhaps her many excursions were in preparation for her next appeal on behalf of her husband—who remained on an island in the Tennessee River with his troops.

The 68th New York proved as uneventful as his previous command; except for an encounter during the Battle of Nashville, he had no opportunity to demonstrate his skills as a soldier. His wife, however, continued to bring excitement into his daily routine by means of her escapades.

One of them was a memorable encounter with Mary Todd Lincoln, who despised Agnes, often referring to her as "Mrs. Salm" and refusing to acknowledge her royal status or correct title. Sometime in 1863, just before the Battle of Chancellorsville, Agnes took part in an official procession. Decked in her usual gay attire, complete with tall hat and flowing blue gauze veil, Agnes confused the order of carriages in the procession. She and a few of her vivacious female friends bolted ahead of Mrs. Lincoln's carriage, cutting in front of her. Their horses's derrières surely provided the prevailing view for Mrs. Lincoln that day.

Furious, the First Lady demanded of Gen. Joseph Hooker that the women be reminded of their manners. Weary of the pettiness, he ordered every woman out of the camp. "This of course includes Mrs. Lincoln," Salm-Salm asserted demurely.

Moments such as these only fostered more cavalier antics from Agnes. Oral tradition has it that she once bet an officer a basket of champagne that she could place a kiss on the lips of President Lincoln. While he was seated, waiting stiffly to be served, she altered the mood of the room by bounding up to the chief executive, swooping down over his shoulder, and planting a kiss directly on his mouth. Lincoln regained his composure and tried to give a reserved smile. It was too late, however; the princess had inspired other female guests to repeat her performance. Before long, all the women at the luncheon had kissed the president. This brought rounds of laughter from all, and Agnes claimed her champagne. Fortunately for her, and probably for the president as well, Mrs. Lincoln was not present at this luncheon.

The Salm-Salms spent some time in Atlanta, where he was military governor. Later, he was named military governor of North Carolina, a post he held until the war ended. Turning down a civil position in the U.S. government, Salm-Salm agreed to serve in Mexico as chief of the Foreign Legion and military advisor to Austrian Archduke Maximilian.

Backed by European powers, Maximilian had been given the throne of Mexico by the nation's ruling aristocracy. His reign was becoming unstable, however. By her husband's side, Agnes arrived at the capital

just as French Marshal Bazaine was pulling out his contingent. Max-
ilian and his staff were attacked and forced into Queretaro. Even to
Princess Agnes, ingenious in the face of tough situations, this one
seemed hopeless. Knowing Maximilian was dreaming that aid was
forthcoming, she encouraged him to surrender Queretaro—give up and
leave the country on condition that the insurgents would spare his life
and the lives of his officers.

According to her account of the matter, Agnes left the safety of her
quarters and marched confidently into the headquarters of Gen. Por-
phyra Diaz to offer this proposal. Diaz sent her to Escobedo. Her
numerous trips were of no avail; Maximilian and Prince Salm-Salm
were captured by Juarista forces, imprisoned, and sentenced to death.

Princess Agnes wrote that the crisis impelled her to give her finest
performance ever. She had contrived a plan of escape for the two men
by urging a guard at the prison, known only as Palacios, to assist in the
plan. The guard was offered two notes, valued at $100,000 each, in
exchange for which he was to see that the deposed ruler and Salm-Salm
escaped without harm. As a sign that the plan was in action, Palacios
was to give Maximilian his signate ring. Though he was a poor and caring man who badly needed the money, at the last minute the guard
declined to take part in the plot. Patriotism and lack of understanding
of the French language probably contributed to his decision.

Agnes was devastated. She knew she must somehow get another
audience with Mexico's chief executive, President Benito Juarez. She
later credited William H. Seward with helping arrange the needed meeting. When the massive doors were opened, Juarez was startled to see "a
determined dark-haired beauty who fell to her knees at his feet" and
cried to him that "if blood must flow, take my life, the life of a useless
woman, and spare that of a man who may do so much good in another
country!"

Deeply moved by her passion, Juarez sorrowfully told her, "By law I
am bound." But he reluctantly agreed to Salm-Salm's release on condition that he leave Mexico immediately. Shaking his head sadly, however,
he told the supplicant that Maximilian would be executed by firing
squad on the morrow.

Agnes kissed Juarez's hand, thanking him for sparing her husband's
life, but became overwhelmed with grief at catching a glimpse of
Empress Carlotta, with whom she had become a friend. Carlotta was
there as Maximilian's wife and mother to their two children to beg for
his life. Agnes could do nothing; she and Felix fled Mexico, saddened by
the death of Maximilian.

Salm-Salm died in the 1870 Franco-Prussian Battle of Gravelotte less than two years after their return to Prussia. In a French newspaper, an ad placed by his widow offered five thousand francs for the recovery of her husband's body. Choosing Karlsruhe, Germany, as her home, Agnes never remarried. She dedicated herself to healing. She died quietly, remembering her handsome, kind-hearted prince who shared her passion for war. The adventuress-acrobat-princess may have been the only foreign-born Civil War woman whose death was noted in the *New York Times*.

CHAPTER

11

Lucy Hayes

Scout

"**G**ive me the telegram first," Lucy said.

"Now, now, Lucy Ware, it can't be all that important. Finish reading the clipping from the *Enquirer* and then turn to the telegram," Lucy's uncle urged.

"No! I already know what has been heard in Cincinnati. The list of fatalities must run down the column for three inches. Rutherford's name heads the second paragraph. But the telegram is directed to me; it may have fresh news."

Her uncle feared that the message from the U.S. Department of War would confirm and maybe amplify the Cincinnati newspaper's report about the October 19, 1864, battle of Cedar Creek, Virginia. He hesitated to hand it to the thirty-four-year-old woman whom he regarded as "almost a daughter." Yet Lucy showed no intention of changing her mind, so he reluctantly handed her the personal dispatch.

"I don't know what to think," the wife of Col. Rutherford B. Hayes confessed after having read the telegram twice. "This is from a captain with whose name I'm not familiar. It was dispatched nearly two days ago, but you know how long it takes to get a telegram to a civilian. According to it, Rutherford had a bad fall and injured an ankle, but he's otherwise all right."

"What's the date line of the newspaper account?"

"I don't know; it was cut off."

"Then you have no idea which of the reports is right. He could have been injured first and then killed while lying on the field."

"Either way, he's seriously hurt or dead. I must find him—or his body. I'll nurse him if he's injured, and see that he has a proper burial if he is dead."

"Just what are you proposing to do, young lady?" her uncle inquired.

VOL. XIII.---NO. 4080.

VICTORY!

Another Great Battle in the Valley.

Longstreet Whipped by Sheridan.

VICTORY WRESTED FROM DEFEAT.

The Rebel Attack at First Successful.

Timely Arrival of Gen. Sheridan.

THE REBELS THEN UTTERLY DEFEATED.

Forty-three Pieces of Artillery Captured.

Many Prisoners and a Large Number of Wagons Taken.

Gen. Bidwell Killed, and Gens. Wright, Ricketts and Grover Wounded.

New York Times *headlines of Friday, October 21, scanned by Lucy in Baltimore, did not give her a single clue as to her husband's fate.*

"I will pack a few things and leave for Baltimore on the first train. I've been there often, and many of the officers know me. They'll arrange transportation so I can find my husband—alive or dead."

"That's foolish. No woman has any business going into a battle zone. Besides, your baby needs you here; he's been showing some signs of weakness, you know."

"The housemaid is perfectly capable of looking after my little George; I expect to be gone only four or five days at most."

Slipping from the bed in which she had been reading when the contradictory messages arrived, Lucy Hayes, formerly Lucy Ware Webb, dressed and moved swiftly. At 1:15 P.M., she left Chillicothe, Ohio, on her way to Maryland.

Having often been with her husband in one of his camps, Lucy was in the habit of saying a prayer of thanksgiving for every night that passed without bad news. Rutherford had been in battle a number of times and had sustained a serious injury at South Mountain two years earlier. At least three times, he had been in danger of being killed or captured when his horse took an enemy's ball or the fragment of a shell. It was entirely possible that his luck had run out during the clash at Cedar Creek.

From the Baltimore train station, Lucy hurried to Fort Dix. She didn't have to go into detail about why she was in urgent need of an ambulance and a driver; word of Hayes's death had reached the Federal installation before her arrival. Barely two days after receiving the conflicting reports concerning her husband, she was headed toward Winchester, Virginia.

When she reached the town, which had served as a base for Federal operations at Cedar Creek, she stopped at the two-story Logan House to ask for word of her husband. Although the big residence had served as headquarters for Gen. Philip Sheridan only a few days earlier, no one knew anything about her husband's fate. A man, whose name she did not learn, offered her a somewhat casual answer to her question.

"He may still be lying where he fell; there were lots of casualties on both sides, and some of the dead haven't been moved yet."

"In Ohio, newspapers listed the names of some of our officers who were known to have been killed in action, but they did not give estimates of casualties—at least, not before I left in order to come here."

"The battle you Yankees call Cedar Creek was plenty bloody. Around here, most of us call it Belle Grove, but the name don't make any difference to the dead. Folks say that Gen. Philip Sheridan lost nearly 6,000 men—some dead, some wounded, and a whole lot of 'em missin'. They say three of his generals were hit, but nobody around here knows their names. They sure don't know nothin' about blue-coat colonels."

"How do I get to the battlefield?"

"Lady, just follow the Valley Pike from here. There was fightin' all over the place, and you can't miss it."

Pausing as though he was a bit pleased to convey bad news to a woman from "way up in Ohio," the unidentified informant added, "If you don't see anything right away, you'll smell it. They started burning horses day before yesterday."

Lucy's heart pounded at the mention of horses; her husband was a skilled rider, but he'd already had three mounts shot from under him. If his animal had fallen while Rebels were advancing against his division, he could have been trapped in the saddle and helpless to make his escape before some of them reached him.

Following the Valley Turnpike toward Middletown, Virginia, Lucy encountered several bedraggled bands of Federal stragglers. No one knew anything about Col. Hayes; most of them didn't even know he was in the battle. Skirting a hill that was covered with dense underbrush, Lucy proceeded southward as fast as her horse would take her. She had spent time in numerous camps and had seen a few battlefields after the action was over. But nothing in her experience had prepared her for what she found near the banks of a rivulet around which fierce fighting had swirled for six or eight hours a few days earlier.

Lucy Ware Webb Hayes.
—John Sartain engraving

Ready finders were still picking through the debris left behind; most of them carried baskets, but a few dragged what looked like big crocus bags that were half full. Lucy didn't have to ask what these scavengers were after; shoes and rifles were worth money regardless of their condition. Civilians were always ready to shell out for souvenirs, so ready finders had a market for nearly everything they gleaned.

Spokes of wheels, fragments of caissons, plus bits and pieces of blue and gray uniforms littered the ground as far as Lucy could see. An occasional canteen or cartridge box that had been overlooked by the scavengers protruded above the surface. Three or four squads of soldiers were busy felling small trees to get fuel for the pyres on which dead horses had been dumped. Long before she reached her destination, the woman from the Buckeye State had been forced to hold a kerchief to her nose and mouth in a futile attempt to ward off the stench of death.

Only one of the fellows burning horses nodded when the woman climbed out of her ambulance and asked if anyone had word about Col. Rutherford B. Hayes.

"I heard he got it when the Johnnies made their first attack," he informed her. "Seems a minié ball took down his horse when he was tryin' to cross a gully. Never heard anything about what happened to him after Little Phil [Sheridan] got here and rallied the boys."

Glad to have a break from swinging his ax, the Federal soldier put his hands on his hips and leaned backward, easing his aching muscles. "You won't find nothin' around here, lady. Best place to ask is the Belle Grove house. You'll find it about a mile from here, on the pike to Strasburg. That big house is close to Three-Top Mountain," he volunteered. "They say a Rebel general named Gordon rode up the mountain before the surprise attack started an' got a good look at our camp so he could decide which way to send his men."

Following the soldier's directions, Lucy found the desolate ruins of what must have been the Belle Grove house, but no one was in sight. She resumed her journey and soon found that stragglers were established in what was left of Hottle's Mill. Although initially suspicious that the woman would turn them in, two or three of them warmed up a bit when she explained her mission.

"Tell you the truth, lady, we don't know nothin' about the battle except what we heard since," one of them explained. "When we saw them long gray lines headed toward us at a trot, most of us got out while the gettin' was good. Lots of our officers and men bought it fairly early, and they say some of 'em are still lyin' in the brush where they fell. Fella you're lookin' for might be just about anywhere."

Lucy was unable to restrain her emotions. Perhaps feeling a tad sorry for her, her informant offered a suggestion: "If you'll take a turn toward the north, you'll likely run into one of the Stickleys. They're big farmers in the valley an' they get around a lot. Just ask for Dan or Annie or Henry half a mile up the road."

However, not a single Stickley was to be found. With the sun dropping fast, the wife of the missing colonel decided she'd better spend the night in her ambulance. At first light the next morning, she realized that she was in sight of the Valley Turnpike, which she had followed from Winchester. Turning onto the turnpike, she soon found the charred ruins of a big farm house that she judged might have belonged to one of the Stickleys.

While pausing to take a quick look at the utter destruction of the civilian home, she was spotted by a Virginian walking from the direction of Middletown. He stopped, said that he had been a hand at Burnt Mills "until it really got burnt," and asked if he could be of help. When she explained what seemed to be her impossible mission, he gave her the most valuable clue she had received yet.

"They say prisoners taken by Rebels were sent to Richmond," he explained. "But lots of the dead an' wounded Yanks went thataway." Pointing in the general direction of Washington, about sixty miles southeast of the battlefield, he made his meaning clear despite the woman's lack of knowledge about regional geography.

"Thank you! Thank you! If my husband was sent to the capital, I know I can find him—or his body. They keep careful records in Washington, you know."

Her ambulance driver, who had been extremely patient thus far, reminded her that if they went to Washington, he could leave her there and get back to his base. He'd be expected to turn in his rig in three or four more days.

Slightly more than halfway to her new destination, the second day after leaving Cedar Creek, Lucy signaled for her driver to stop. "Do you think we're headed into another battle?" she asked. "I have heard enough artillery to know that guns are being fired somewhere up ahead."

"Couldn't say," responded the private. "Could be a skirmish, I guess, but we're getting close to Washington. More'n likely it's the salute that Grant ordered fired to celebrate Little Phil's big win at Cedar Creek."

In the capital, Lucy got no answer to her questions about Rutherford. Nurses at one of the hospitals volunteered, however, that "Colonel Hayes was mentioned in a lot of the dispatches." This news did not help her in the search, but the woman from Chillicothe had been around military men long enough to know that the information was significant. If Rutherford was still alive and on the road to recovery, he'd stand a good chance to be made a brigadier as a reward for his service at Cedar Creek.

She called at only three or four hospitals before she realized that her husband wasn't likely to be in the capital after all. Its hospitals had been packed with wounded and sick soldiers long before the first casualties arrived from Cedar Creek. A few probably went to the Union Hotel Hospital in nearby Georgetown, a surgeon told her. There was an outside chance that he could have found a bed in this small facility, but it was much more likely that he was somewhere near the Maryland state line. Quite a few temporary hospitals there had received men from Cedar Creek, but it would be days or weeks before records were brought up to date so that a specific individual could be located.

Using a carriage rented in the capital, Lucy, expecting to learn at any moment that she was a widow, went from one hastily requisitioned business or residence to another. Each of the temporary hospitals she visited was full, and many of their occupants had been at Cedar Creek. By this time she had become accustomed to seeing heads shake. Lucy was not surprised that no one seemed to know much about anything— least of all a colonel who had led a division of the Army of Western Virginia more than a week earlier.

Realizing that her options were quickly running out, the woman who was "on a scout for a missing husband" suddenly found out that Col. Hayes was somewhere close by. "He might be on Gibson's Island," said a surgeon from Columbus, Ohio, who was familiar with her husband's name from a notorious trial in which Rutherford received a lot of publicity.

Following the suggestions of the surgeon, whom she had encountered by chance, Lucy Hayes found her husband injured, but not technically *wounded*. After a long and silent embrace, she managed simultaneously to smile and to sob. "I left Chillicothe two weeks ago, as soon as I heard about Cedar Creek," she explained. "My uncle didn't want me to go, but I told him I'd either find you in a hospital and help to nurse you—or I would find your body and give it a proper burial."

After having assured her that she was right to launch her search, Rutherford told her why he was hospitalized. A huge body of Rebels, most of whom behaved like veterans of earlier combat, had attacked Federal forces in a predawn fog. In a turn of events that he never quite understood, he had ridden between his own line and that of the enemy.

President Rutherford B. Hayes.—Brady Studio portrait, Library of Congress

Suddenly realizing the extreme danger to which he was exposed, he spurred his horse toward a big patch of undergrowth that bordered a ravine. Just as he thought he had reached safety, his horse was hit by a ball that killed it instantly. When the big animal's full weight pinned him to the ground, Hayes felt his right ankle give way. No bones were broken, but he suffered a sprain so severe that he knew he couldn't walk until he'd had time to recuperate. After having been shunted from one facility to another, he had landed on Gibson's Island, where his determined wife finally caught up with him.

Lucy fervently hoped that the injury would lead to her husband's discharge, but it did not. He remained in uniform until June 1865, after which he resumed his law practice and entered politics, eventually

Lucy Hayes loved children, elaborately painted china, and her husband—but not necessarily in that order.

becoming America's nineteenth president. Later in life, he was much sought after as a platform speaker in his own and other states. Hence, he told many audiences that he might not be standing before them had not "a remarkably brave and determined wife mounted a one-woman scout for her husband's corpse—only to find him alive and kicking."

As an afterthought, he added, "Any way you look at it, Cedar Creek was unique. It may have been the only full-scale battle of the Civil War that involved the active participation of two Buckeyes who were destined to achieve a modicum of political success. One of them was your speaker, who was colonel of the 23rd Ohio regiment. The other was Major William McKinley of the same regiment. McKinley and I had a lot in common—but only one of us got lost in the shuffle after the battle of Cedar Creek and was found by a female scout."

Part III
Couriers, Spies, and Subversives

12

Elizabeth Van Lew

Crazy Like a Fox

A prisoner of war wearing a tattered blue uniform was visibly bewildered. He knew no one in Richmond and had already been interrogated by the Confederates. He was being detained in a makeshift prison with a sign on it saying "L. Libby & Son, Ship Chandlers." At the moment, he was wondering why anyone would be coming to see him, but he had been told that he had a visitor. Was something terrible about to happen to him?

He was relieved when he saw her—a small, sharp-nosed woman in her mid-forties with bright blue eyes, carrying food and a book. By means of only a few words and gestures, the woman communicated to him that she wanted to know what he could tell her about Confederate strengths and positions. By underlining words in the book, he could put together a message which she could walk out with and not be challenged.

She may have gotten what she wanted on that trip or she may have had to return for it, but one thing is certain: She *did* get the information. Elizabeth Van Lew—or Crazy Bet, as she was known by many—was to become one of the most effective Union operatives behind Rebel lines.

Born in 1818, she was educated in Pennsylvania by Quakers. Having been reared with nine slaves in her own household, her childhood may have established her abhorrence of slavery. Her father, John Van Lew, was a wealthy hardware merchant who died when she was still a young lady. Some accounts place his death as early as 1843 and others as late as 1851. That left her, her mother, and her brother, John, to attend to the estate. Elizabeth and her mother freed their slaves in 1851; however, most stayed with the household and some later helped her in her wartime espionage activities. One freed slave, a child when she gained her freedom, was Mary Elizabeth Bowser. Van Lew saw intellectual promise in the young girl and sent her to Philadelphia to be educated.

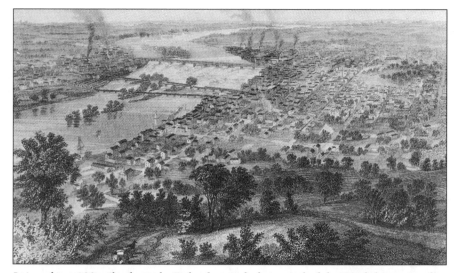

Lying about 100 miles from the Federal capital, the capital of the Confederacy was little damaged as late as December 1863.—LIBRARY OF CONGRESS

When the war started, Bowser returned to the Van Lew household and assumed the role of household servant. Elizabeth was able to secure a place for her on the domestic staff of the Confederate White House. There Bowser could listen to dinner conversations and perhaps read a paper or note. Negroes typically were not literate, so Confederate President Jefferson Davis and his aides did not attempt to hide anything from her. The important information that Bowser gathered was passed on to Van Lew or to Thomas McNiven—a bakery owner who was a central figure in the Richmond spy ring. Whenever McNiven made deliveries to the mansion in which Davis and his family lived, Bowser passed information along to him.

Neighbors and associates knew Crazy Bet was an outspoken abolitionist. They did not know that long before the war started the Van Lew mansion was part of the Underground Railroad, hiding and smuggling fugitive slaves northward. Though wealthy enough to be a member of Richmond's elite society, she chose exclusion over keeping her opinions to herself. With the outbreak of the war, she openly supported the Union, but few paid any attention to the things she said. Acquaintances regarded her as a lonely old spinster who was eccentric, but harmless. She fostered this point of view by wearing mismatched clothing, muttering to herself as she walked about the city, and letting her hair become tangled. She let acquaintances know that she had furnished a bedroom for Gen. George B. McClellan to use after his Peninsular Campaign, and folk who listened to her smiled knowingly at one another. As the fighting wore on, however, many citizens of the city began to regard her with contempt.

Her mansion sat atop Richmond's Church Hill, near the buildings that became Libby Prison. Union officers were held there under extremely bad conditions. Each of the three buildings known simply as East, West, and Middle was 110 by 44 feet in size and four stories tall in the fashion of tenements or lofts. Capt. Luther Libby had previously leased the west building for his ship chandlers' business, and the sign on it gave Libby Prison its name. After the Battle of Bull Run, C. S. Gen. John H. Winder gave Libby only forty-eight hours to vacate his building.

Learning of the conditions in Libby Prison, Elizabeth asked the commandant for permission to give food, medicine, and humanitarian aid to the prisoners. Lt. David H. Todd, half-brother to Mary Todd Lincoln, denied her request. Unwilling to give up when Todd turned her down, Van Lew approached Christopher Memminger, Confederate secretary of the treasury. She knew him only casually, but she believed he would take the concept of charity seriously. Hence, she asked him to appeal to the prison authorities so she could minister to "the boys." Memminger wrote a note to the provost marshal, who then gave her a pass to the prison.

Elizabeth became a frequent visitor to Libby Prison, supplying "her boys" with food, clothing, bedding, medicine, and reading material. Her brother John's prosperous hardware business provided the money

This lithograph of Libby Prison is based on a sketch by a member of Co. A, 24th Wisconsin regiment.

for this activity. New arrivals at the prison secretly supplied her with information on Confederate troops, which she transmitted to Union headquarters.

In addition to personally getting information from prisoners, she relied on others in whom she had confidence. Mary Bowser was in the Confederate White House, but she had other well-placed informants as well. One of them was in the War Department and another was in the Navy Department.

By early 1864, Gen. Benjamin F. Butler was receiving regular reports from Van Lew, whom he called "my corespondent in Richmond." Early in the war "Crazy Bet" had learned an ancient cipher using a two-digit number for each letter of the alphabet. She encoded her messages to Butler and other Federal leaders and wrote with an ink that became visible only when dipped in milk. A message of more than 300 words would have required at least 3,000 strokes of her pen.

Elizabeth Van Lew and her associates were not the only Union spies in Richmond. Other key players in the Unionist underground included Samuel Ruth and his associate, F. W. E. Lohman. Ruth was in the Richmond office of the Richmond, Fredericksburg and Petersburg Railroad and used his position to slow down shipments of supplies to Confederate soldiers as early as 1862. By early 1864, Ruth's team of couriers was the main conduit by which Van Lew's information went out of the Confederate capital. In addition to espionage activities, Ruth and Lohman helped Federal fugitives and Confederate deserters escape from Richmond.

On January 23, 1865, Samuel Ruth was arrested for consorting with the enemy. He was released nine days later when he convinced authorities that his accusers were just trying to get even with him for not giving them free passage on the RF&P rail line. Lohman, however, was jailed from January until April 2, when Confederate forces left Richmond.

In June 1864, when Gen. U. S. Grant's armies arrived in front of Richmond, Col. George H. Sharpe took charge of coordinating the efforts of the Van Lew and Ruth groups. Five depots, or drop points for communications, were designated by Sharpe. Some of these depots were east of the Chickahominy River. Couriers would get the messages to the depots, and Sharpe's scouts would retrieve them. Two-way communication was in place, however, so that Sharpe could specify what intelligence was needed.

Richmond was desperate for food, so travel to farming country for provisions was normal and natural. Van Lew often asked a servant to hide a message in his shoe in order to get it to a rendezvous point. Tradition says that on at least one occasion Crazy Bet concealed a message in an empty eggshell that was surrounded by good eggs in order to get it to Union headquarters. There is no record that any message sent by Van Lew to Federal leaders was ever intercepted.

Though never suspected of treason, Elizabeth and her mother became objects of scorn by the community. An article appearing in a Richmond newspaper singled out the two women as undesirables. "Whilst every true woman in this community has been busy making articles for our troops, or administering to our sick," readers were told, "these two women have been spending their opulent means in aiding and giving comfort to the miscreants who have invaded our sacred soil."

Acquaintances of Elizabeth Van Lew described the woman who was 5'3" tall as being "bird like."

Harassment reached such a level that Elizabeth feared for her safety. An appeal directly to Jefferson Davis produced no results, but she succeeded in convincing a commandant of Libby Prison to board his family in the Van Lew mansion and give her a degree of protection.

Espionage and her services to prisoners of war were not the only activities on Elizabeth Van Lew's agenda. She also helped escaped prisoners get out of Richmond. The most notable escape from Libby Prison took place on February 9, 1864, and was engineered by Col. Thomas E. Rose. A fifty-three-foot tunnel was dug from a room in the basement of Libby Prison to the other side of the street. This engineering feat was accomplished in seventeen days with just a pocket knife, chisels, a wooden spittoon, a rope, and some cloth. Before the tunnel was discovered, 109 Federal officers had escaped. Several were hidden in the Van Lew Mansion behind secret panels covering hiding places.

Among the escapees was Col. A. D. Streight, whose mule-powered raid into Georgia was foiled by Emma Sansom (see Chapter 15). Van Lew was able to help Streight get out of the city; however, only fifty-nine men involved in the prison break made it to Union lines. Many were recaptured, and two drowned. Rose, the tunnel's engineer, was among the forty-eight who were recaptured.

Col. Ulric Dahlgren, son of Rear Adm. John A. Dahlgren, was killed while leading a bold 1864 raid on Richmond. A note of controversial origin was found on his person, directing him to try to kill Jefferson Davis and his cabinet and to sack and burn Richmond. The corpse was viewed with repugnance by Confederates, and his body was trashed. A finger was cut off in order to remove a ring; his wooden leg was confiscated, and he was buried in Oakwood Cemetery in the section allocated to Federal dead.

A formal plea from his father to Jefferson Davis for the return of Ulric's body resulted in an attempted disinterment. Surprised workmen reported that the body was gone. Elizabeth Van Lew's cohorts had already exhumed the corpse and were holding it somewhere outside of Richmond for its eventual safe return to Dahlgren's father. One tradition asserts that Dahlgren's remains lay for a time in a wagon hidden among peach trees until Van Lew found a safer place for it. Not until after the war ended was the colonel's body sent to Pennsylvania in a metal coffin.

On one occasion a grand jury issued warrants for both Elizabeth and her mother, charging both with trafficking in greenbacks. This frightened the elder Van Lew so badly that she became ill. Nothing was ever proven, however, and the case was eventually dropped.

In February 1865 the Secret Service operating out of Washington enlisted the aid of an Englishman named Pole, not knowing that he was a double agent. As directed, he arranged to meet with several Union sympathizers—Van Lew included—in and around Richmond. Her papers (in the New York Public Library) reveal the apprehension she felt at the impending encounter. Fortunately, before he had an opportunity to meet with her, he exposed his mission by turning over other Unionists with whom he had talked to Confederate headquarters.

As the war drew to a close, Grant received flowers from Van Lew on a regular basis. He was aware of her efforts to preserve the Union and was determined to protect her and her family from reprisals. On the day that Richmond fell, Grant ordered Gen. Godfrey Weitzel to place a guard around the Van Lew Mansion to guarantee the safety of its occupants. Elizabeth, however, was not at home; she had reportedly gone to the burned Confederate White House in order to sift through ashes in search of documents that might be useful to Grant and his staff. As soon as she returned from her quest, she and a servant managed to raise the Stars and Stripes, smuggled into the city for this occasion, over her residence.

By the time the war ended, the Van Lews had spent their entire fortune in an effort to aid the Union. John's hardware business no longer existed—it had gone under in 1864. Both John and Elizabeth sought employment, but all of Richmond knew that they had in fact been much more than just Union sympathizers, and no one wanted them as workers. Sharpe did what he could to get a grant for the family that had sacrificed so much for the preservation of the Union. An unknown sum went to them, but it was not enough for them to continue in their accustomed lifestyle. Much later, one of the prisoners whom she had helped in Libby Prison, Lt. Col. Paul Revere of Boston, collected a purse and gave it to her as a token of personal gratitude.

Very early in his first term as president of the United States, Ulysses S. Grant made Elizabeth Van Lew postmaster of Richmond, and he reappointed her to that position four years later. When Rutherford B. Hayes took office, she was replaced. Moving to Washington, she took a clerical position with the post office. She returned to Richmond when Grover Cleveland took office as president.

Her latter years in Richmond were lonely because she was ostracized by the community. Few people would have anything to do with her, so her niece became her only companion. Her extensive journal includes the notation, "No one will walk with us on the street; no one will go with us anywhere, and it grows worse and worse as the years roll on." Strangely, she failed to realize why she was rejected. Another entry in her journal reads, "A person cannot be called a spy for serving their country within its recognized borders. Am I now to be branded a spy by my own country for which I was willing to lay down my life? God

The Van Lew mansion, headquarters of "the Richmond spy ring" that operated successfully throughout the war.

knows there is no vocation more ennobling, more honorable, and even the disgraceful word cannot stain my record."

Her niece's death in 1899 may have contributed to Elizabeth's own demise a year later. Legend says that she spent her last months with no companions except her forty cats. In 1911 many Richmond residents rejoiced in the demolition of the Van Lew Mansion on Church Hill.

A rough-cut tombstone in Shockoe Cemetery survives her. Its inscription reads:

Elizabeth L. Van Lew
1818–1900
She risked everything that is dear to man—friends, fortune, comfort, health, life itself—all for the one absorbing desire of her heart—that slavery might be abolished and the union preserved.

Below the epitaph another inscription informs viewers:

This boulder from Boston's Capitol Hill is a tribute from her Massachusetts Friends.

CHAPTER

13

Belle Boyd

La Belle Rebelle

In an era when life expectancy hovered around sixty years, two northern women, Julia Ward Howe and Harriet Beecher Stowe, achieved lasting fame when older than forty years. They were on the shady side of life when they made their great achievements. By contrast, one Confederate woman achieved lasting fame and was considered to be a great heroine by age twenty. Belle Boyd's career as a courier and spy began when she was only seventeen. Before it came to an abrupt halt three years later, she was known throughout the United States, the Confederate States, and Great Britain as "Cleopatra of the Confederacy." To readers of *Le Monde* and other French-language publications, she was *La Belle Rebelle*.

Her early years gave no hint that she would be making newspaper headlines. Born in 1844 in Martinsburg, Virginia (now West Virginia), she lived in affluence. Her father, a prosperous store owner, saw to it that she mastered French, the classics, and music at Mount Washington Female College in Baltimore. When Belle completed her four-year program of study, her parents took her to Washington for her debut to be properly introduced to the capital's society.

Though her academic record was above average, she never loved books. Horses were her real passion; before she made her debut, she was widely recognized as the best female rider in Virginia. When war broke out, she was back in Martinsburg, where residents described her as being "ablaze with secessionist views."

Located in the lush Shenandoah Valley, the village in which she grew up lay in the path of contesting armies. While still a teenager, she launched a career as a spy for Confederate leaders, specifically Gen. Thomas J. "Stonewall" Jackson. Precisely how much she contributed to Confederate victories in the valley is a matter of debate, for numerous experts regard her autobiographical tales as being greatly embellished. Some scholars, however, insist that Belle's accounts of her exploits ring true for the most part.

During her late adolescence and early womanhood, her appearance seems to have been largely shaped by the eyes of her beholders. One account describes her as having been tall, sandy-haired, and "so blue-eyed that she was an instant favorite" in Washington society. One admirer, however, lamented that Miss Boyd was not beautiful because her nose was too long and was set in a dour face. In London, a friend of Charles Dickens and William Makepeace Thackeray called her "disturbingly attractive." To him, her eyes seemed to be gray-blue, and her somewhat irregular face suggested "joyous recklessness." Still another contemporary description insists she was a tall and slender blonde whose most striking feature was "an abundance of curly hair."

On July 3, 1861, soon after her return to Martinsburg, the place was occupied by blue-clad Pennsylvanians under the command of Gen. Robert Patterson. He and his men hadn't been in the village even twenty-four hours before a scout informed Patterson that one of his men had been killed by "the Boyd girl."

Most or all of their neighbors knew that the Boyds frequently displayed a Confederate emblem at their home. Someone must have revealed this to the Federal soldiers, because one of them set out to replace the "secessh banner" with Old Glory. Reputedly relying heavily on alcohol-induced courage, he forced his way into the Boyd residence and shouted, "The Star-Spangled Banner will soon fly from your rooftop!"

A year or so later, few civilian Rebels would have dared to challenge such action. However, with military activity having been confined to a few minor skirmishes by Independence Day 1861, willingness to resist "Yankee oppression" was still very strong. Belle's mother is said to have told the intruder that she'd rather die than see the Federal flag raised over her home. He cursed her and gestured for her to move aside. Belle shot the soldier with a pistol, and he—having taken only a single step—dropped to the floor in agony.

Since the wound was mortal, Belle could have been charged with murder before a military tribunal. However, Patterson brushed aside suggestions offered by his aides for a speedy trial. Since "the spirited little colleen" was defending her own home, he ruled, she had acted within her rights. Officers who were ready to establish a board of inquiry were told to forget such a course of action. They had much more important things to do than inquire into why a teenager was such a good shot, he said.

Now a village celebrity, the girl who had gotten away with murder flirted outrageously with some of the men from the Keystone State. From them she learned, piece by piece, that Patterson was there in order to prevent Rebels under Gen. Joseph E. Johnston from moving southward.

Most of the 75,000 or so volunteers who had responded to an April call issued by Abraham Lincoln were 90-day enlistments. After having been under Federal command for ninety days, their obligations would expire and they would be free to go home. This crucial factor plus the May move of the Confederate capital to Richmond, dictated the course of Federal strategy. Daily head-

Belle Boyd in Martinsburg.—THE CONFEDERATE MUSEUM

lines in Horace Greeley's *New York Tribune* trumpeted "ON TO RICHMOND!" Lincoln needed no prodding; he had already decided that his army must seize the Rebel capital very soon. Since Jefferson Davis and his advisors would anticipate such a move, it was logical to believe that opposing armies would meet about halfway between the two capitals. Rebels under Gen. P. G. T. Beauregard were poised to move in the general direction of Manassas Junction. Hence, Washington felt it imperative that Patterson should prevent Johnston's force from joining the larger body of gray-clad soldiers based well to the south of the Shenandoah Valley.

Belle had been introduced to Beauregard in Washington and practically swooned at the thought of his handsome face and urbane charm. She seems to have taken it on herself to feed all information she got about Patterson and his plans to the Creole general, relying on outspoken Rebels to transmit what she learned to his headquarters. There is no evidence, however, that these messages were important or that he even received them.

Some clues suggest that the girl, not yet eighteen years old, chose to become a spy as a result of hearing tales about Betty Duvall. Though older than Belle, Betty was still universally described as being young.

Irish-born Gen. Robert Patterson.—
<small>LESLIE'S ILLUSTRATED WEEKLY</small>

She had often successfully disguised herself as a farm woman driving a wooden cart in order to penetrate Federal lines. Said to have changed into riding clothes at Fairfax Courthouse, Duvall was the courier who took messages from Mrs. Rose O'Neal Greenhow of Washington (see Chapter 17) to Beauregard. Though the importance of Greenhow's news is generally discounted today, when Belle was hearing it in 1861, it was widely credited as having been an important factor in the Rebel victory at Bull Run.

If Belle Boyd could have had her wishes fulfilled, she'd have donned a gray uniform and joined her father in the ranks of the 2nd Virginia Infantry, a regiment that later formed part of the famous Stonewall Brigade. Never realizing that she could dress as a male and get into the fight, she devoted her time and energy to being a nurse for wounded Rebels and to raising money with which to buy supplies for them and their comrades.

Col. Turner Ashby, a Rebel cavalry leader and a successful spy, is believed to have given Belle advice, plus an occasional assignment. Some accounts insist that in the aftermath of Bull Run, she fed a constant stream of valuable information to Beauregard, Jackson, J. E. B. Stuart, and other Confederate commanders. There is no documentary evidence to support this story, however.

But there is not a shred of doubt that some Federal officers became suspicious of Belle, for she was arrested early in 1862 and sent to Baltimore as a prisoner. There she turned on her charm for Gen. John A. Dix, the top-ranking officer of volunteers. Dix, like Patterson, may have taken pity on her youth, or she may have been fortunate enough to be involved in an early exchange of prisoners. Whatever the case, after a short stay in the port city, she spent a few days in Richmond and then returned to Martinsburg.

Her mother never forgot having seen her daughter shoot a soldier, so she urged her to leave town when there were signs of trouble brewing again. An uncle in Front Royal took her in without full knowledge of her recent activities. She had been in her new home only a few weeks when an unexpected challenge presented itself. Belle responded in so magnificent a fashion that commentators say that May 23, 1862, constituted "Belle Boyd's finest hour."

Headed in the general direction of a large Federal force at Strasburg, Jackson was joined by Gen. Richard S. Ewell and about nine thousand men. Though Front Royal was held by a force of only about a thousand men, Col. J. R. Kenly's advantageous positions suggested a Rebel victory could be costly in terms of casualties. Belle is described as having lifted her skirts very high in order to race through the streets when she learned that a Rebel force was approaching. Richard Taylor, a son of President Zachary Taylor, was in command of the body. His female informant gave him a detailed report of where the enemies were located. "They plan to make a stand, then burn their stores and move toward another Federal body, burning bridges as they go," she told him. Convinced that the girl knew what she was talking about, Taylor launched an attack before the arrival of his commander. Taylor's early move took his opponents by surprise. When the main Confederate body arrived, Federal resistance soon melted, and men in blue were ordered to withdraw. Hit hard by Rebel forces during their move, the majority of them were captured, and Kenly was seriously wounded. Front Royal constituted Stonewall Jackson's first significant battlefield victory, and he was elated beyond measure. Tradition, supported by Boyd's memoirs, says that the grateful Rebel leader made Belle an honorary captain that very night.

Her period of glory lasted only a few days, however. Shortly afterward, Federal troops reoccupied Front Royal, and a telegram arrived from Edwin M. Stanton, the U.S. secretary of war. That message led to Belle's arrest, after which she was immediately sent to the Old Capitol Prison in Washington. One newspaper exulted, "The Secesh Cleopatra Is Caged At Last!"

Reporters for nationally circulated newspapers rushed to get their own stories about "the beautiful adolescent spy." The correspondent of the *New York Herald* spent less than twenty minutes with Belle, then sent a brief dispatch in which he described her as "an accomplished prostitute." His rival from the *New York Tribune* was startled to find the girl "wearing a Rebel soldier's belt around her waist." And after having described her chin as beautiful, he wrote that beneath it dangled a gold chain that displayed a palmetto tree—the emblem of South Carolina, which led the secession parade. To complete the visual effect, she wore a strip of velvet across her forehead. The band was adorned, the newspaper man wrote, "with the seven stars of the Confederacy [one each for the seven original Confederate states]."

After having launched her prison stay as though she were a foreign dignitary on a visit to Washington, Belle turned to her journal. Instead of lamenting her fate, she wrote that she lay down in a tranquil frame of mind. She closed what she called her "first day in a dungeon" by reciting to herself the poem that includes the lines, "Stone walls do not a prison make / Nor iron bars a cage."

She was soon interrogated by William P. Wood, superintendent of the prison. Wood failed to get satisfactory answers to his questions, and she was then confronted by Lafayette C. Baker. A professional espionage agent, Baker later claimed to have been the founder of the U.S. Secret Service. Apparently, he was satisfied with her answers to his questions, for after a short while he ordered her to be exchanged again. This time, she was sent to the tip of the Virginia peninsula, where Fort Monroe had been built. From the fort she went north to Richmond, where she stayed long enough to receive new instructions from some leading Confederate officials.

Resuming her activities as soon as she returned to the Shenandoah Valley, she operated without hindrance for a period. Then, the Union victory at Gettysburg and the subsequent retreat of the Army of Northern Virginia left her stranded in what had become for the moment solidly held Union territory. Placed under parole that forbade her to leave her home, Boyd kept a low profile, but was arrested late in August "on suspicion" under the suspension of *habeas corpus*. She was sent to Washington again, but this time landed in Carroll Prison.

It was the worst possible season to be cooped up in an airless cell near the heart of the capital. She contracted typhoid fever, but seemed to recover rapidly under treatment. About the time that authorities planned to send her to a nearby jail for a term at hard labor, she again became deathly ill. At least, that's what the physician who examined her concluded. Whether she had another bout with typhoid or successfully feigned such an attack remains debatable. Whatever the case, her jail sentence was commuted, and she was banished from Federal soil. According to her account of the matter, she was told that she would face a death sentence if caught in Federal territory again.

Somehow, she managed to wangle permission to pass through Richmond on her way to the Deep South. Much evidence supports her story that she gained an audience with Jefferson Davis while there and offered to do for the Confederacy anything within her power. He reputedly entrusted her with documents consigned to Rebel agents in England, warning her that crossing the Atlantic Ocean in a blockade runner could be dangerous.

The Washington debutante from Virginia.—Matthew Brady Studio, Library of Congress

Never having known the meaning of fear, the Virginia native who had not yet celebrated her twenty-first birthday managed to reach Wilmington, North Carolina. There she booked passage on the *Greyhound* and was aboard when the fast little vessel slipped from her berth on May 8, 1864. Exultation at having escaped Federal clutches lasted only a few hours, however. Only one day later, the USS *Connecticut* captured the blockade runner and put the vessel in the charge of a prize crew led by Ensign Samuel W. Hardinge.

Obedient to orders, Hardinge set sail for Boston to deliver the *Greyhound* to a prize court and deliver his prisoners to Federal authorities. Long before the Boston Navy Yard was sighted, however, Hardinge lost his heart to his young prisoner. "His very movement," she later wrote, "was so much that of a refined gentleman that my Southern proclivities, strong as they were, yielded to the impulses of my heart." Her husband-to-be managed to persuade authorities that since she was under sentence of banishment, they could not imprison her in Fort Warren, but would have to send her to Canada instead.

Hardinge soon joined his exiled Virginia sweetheart in Canada, and they became man and wife. Married bliss ended after only a few months, however, when Sam died suddenly. His bereaved widow had a brief career on the stage in England, and she wrote and published *Belle Boyd in Camp and Prison*. She was frequently recognized on the streets of London. Back in the United States, not long after the end of the war, she managed to win small parts in stage plays. She later turned to giving "readings" about her dramatic life.

Accounts of her later life are very obscure. The widow Hardinge married at least two other men, losing both of them so quickly that, despite one marriage ending in divorce, some commentators have speculated that she knew how to handle poison. According to the *National Cyclopedia of American Biography*, the matron who called Martinsburg home was briefly married to outlaw Cole Younger and then to a pair of native American warriors—one at a time.

On Sunday, June 10, 1900, she wrote a brief note to her daughter from Kilbourn, Wisconsin (Wisconsin Dells today). She was greatly pained, she said, that it was impossible for her to send a substantial sum of money. Her brief letter concluded with the comment that "I have been able to play only one night, so I am sending you all I have over expenses, $2."

The one night of "play" to which she referred was a reading sponsored by the local post of the Grand Army of the Republic. Hours after dispatching $2 to her daughter, Belle Boyd Hardinge Hammond High died. Union veterans paid for her funeral and laid her to rest under a simple marker that read:

BELLE BOYD
Confederate Spy
Born in Virginia
Died in Wisconsin

14

Major Pauline Cushman

Turnskirt

C.S. Gen. Nathan Bedford Forrest barely glanced up from the cards he was shuffling. One look from him told Pauline Cushman that he was only interested in her as a prisoner. "I'm really glad to see you," the cavalryman in gray said. "I've been looking for you for a long time; but I've got this last shuffle, and I intend to hold you." Staring at Pauline with eyes that were universally described as fierce and implacable, he mused: "You've been here before, I take it—Know all the roads—don't you? And all the bridle paths, and even the hog paths—don't you?"

"Sir, every word you utter is as false as your own traitorous heart!" Cushman exclaimed. "I've never been here before, and I should like to send a bullet through the man who is mean enough to make the charge."

"Yes," Forrest nodded, "and I'd send one through you, if I could."

If Cushman's detailed first-person account of the events of these few months in 1863 is accurate, she was held briefly by men under noted cavalryman and raider Gen. John Hunt Morgan. Morgan seemed to have responded to her feminine charms, but Forrest's gaze was not so much on her as it was through her. Though he was sitting at a makeshift table during their brief interview, it was as though Forrest's mind was ranging through the countryside in search of a vulnerable body of Federal soldiers.

Until Forrest leaned back and ordered guards to keep a close watch on her, Cushman was worrried that she would be executed on the spot as a spy. Though keenly aware that she was in Tennessee of her own volition, the Creole woman may have briefly wished that she had followed a different path during the preceding tumultuous years.

Born in New Orleans in 1833, her brilliantly dark complexion was inherited from her French mother and her Spanish father. Though she was not beautiful by standards of the period, Pauline noticed very early that many men turned around to take a second look after passing her on the street.

After a brief period of financial panic wiped out everything her father had, he hastily took his family to Grand Rapids, Michigan, where he became an Indian trader. Pauline soon decided that she didn't like living at the edge of the big woods and much preferred the French Quarter of her native city. She would have gone back, had her father not warned her that she could be arrested and jailed for his debts. Even more than the isolation in Michigan, she wanted to get away from a young brave named Laughing Breeze. One of the Native Americans with whom Pauline's father traded, he dogged her steps at every opportunity. When she turned eighteen, she informed her parents that she'd "had enough of living in the sticks." She was hesitant to return to New Orleans, so she struck out for New York City to try to find a job as an actress.

In the city, she soon landed nonspeaking parts, walking across the stage several times a week without saying a word. These bit parts barely covered her rent and the cheapest food she could find. So discouraged that she was ready to go back to Grand Rapids, Pauline was barely off the stage one night when a cigar-smoking gentleman signaled to her. Thomas Placide, manager of a New Orleans theatrical company, was delighted to learn that she had spent her early years in the Crescent City. Though he didn't tell Pauline, he was positive that her "sultry good looks" would be an asset to his "Varieties," so he hired her on the spot and took her back to New Orleans.

At about age twenty-one, Cushman accepted a different kind of proposal from another New Orleans performer—a marriage proposal. But almost as soon she became Mrs. Charles Dickinson, she began wondering why she had married him. She gave birth to one baby after another, but none of them lived more than a few days. Diphtheria, then rampant, was judged to be the cause of most of these deaths. Saddled with a husband who was making less money than she, and barely getting out of her bed from one birth before becoming pregnant again, Pauline became despondent. She couldn't think of anyone or anything that could rescue her from her wretchedness.

Few in New Orleans expected the sudden eruption of the Civil War. It had been taken for granted that the North and England couldn't possibly get along without the vast amount of cotton that left the city's port. That notion proved to be without foundation, but the war soon relieved Pauline of Charles. He signed up with fighting men in gray as a musician and marched off, leaving his pregnant wife to fend for herself.

Before the baby arrived, word came that the child would be an orphan. Dysentery had gotten the better of Charles, and he had been buried near a Confederate field hospital.

Pauline might have spent the rest of her life in New Orleans, never seeing her name in newspaper headlines, if the baby had lived. Plenty chubby and healthy-looking, the child, however, lasted only about a week. Suddenly footloose and fancy free, she reassumed her maiden name because she didn't think a widow would have much of a chance on the stage. After a brief stint in Cleveland, she took passage on a paddle-

Gen. Nathan B. Forrest looked through Pauline Cushman rather than at her.—HARPER'S ILLUS- TRATED HISTORY OF THE CIVIL WAR

wheel steamer and went down the Ohio River to Louisville. It was easy to land a role in *The Seven Sisters* at Wood's Theatre, but the pay wasn't much to brag about. She got by, but barely.

Suddenly, for the first time in her life, a door that seemed to glimmer with gold opened before her. "The best part of it was," she later said, "I didn't even have to bang on that door to get it to open."

Numerous Confederate officers who had been captured in battle and subsequently paroled were in the river city. Knowing themselves to be a minority there, half a dozen of them, after attending a performance of *The Seven Sisters,* put their heads together and hatched a plot. Pauline, who played the sister Plutella and wore a tight-fitting man's costume part of the time, was older than most of the rest of the cast. She looked like she could use some extra cash, the conspirators agreed. So they pooled their resources and picked Capt. J. H. Blincoe as their spokesman. Blincoe approached Pauline with a proposition: If she'd break out of the play somewhere in the middle and offer a toast to Jefferson Davis, he suggested to her backstage, it would worth $300 in greenbacks "to see Louisville all shook up" over the incident.

"I'll do it tomorrow night," Pauline promised with enthusiasm. "My dead husband gave everything he had to the cause, an' I'll be proud to do my part. But I have to have the money in advance."

The Rebel with whom she was barely acquainted nodded consent and reached into his pocket. "Anything you like, little lady," he agreed, "just as long as you promise to make that toast loud enough to be heard across the county line."

After stuffing her unexpected bonanza into her shoes, Pauline hurried to the office of the Federal provost marshal, stopping strangers on the street to ask directions. When she reached it, she blurted out her story and said she was afraid she'd get shot if she didn't go through with the scheme. An officer told her to go ahead as planned and then come back to him.

She'd be considered a strong Rebel sympathizer after her performance, so he would have to smuggle her into the "secesh country" that was abundant in Kentucky. There she could look around, pick up some vital information for the Union, and take it to the nearest Federal camp. After that, she would no longer be in danger in Louisville, having done something to help the Union cause, and she might be able to return.

"I'll bring along some of my men and we'll be in Woods tomorrow night, just in case things get out of hand," he promised.

The next night, wearing the tight outfit required for her role, Pauline Cushman felt a surge of adrenaline as she slipped away from the other players long enough to grab a champagne glass. Stepping to the footlights at the center of the stage, the part-time actress, who had just celebrated her twenty-eighth birthday, raised her glass. Startled spectators sat up straight so they could see what was happening. Before a hushed house, the native of New Orleans raised her glass and cried: "Here's to Jeff Davis and the Southern Confederacy! May the South always maintain her honor and her rights!"

Her two sentences brought the night's performance to a grinding halt. Some members of the audience shouted expletives at the actress, but others cheered her at the top of their lungs. When the hubbub began to die down a bit, the theater owner stalked over to Pauline and pointed to the door. He didn't need to say a word; she had expected to be fired as a result of her performance.

Soon after passing through Union lines, Pauline found that she had become an instant heroine to both civilian and military secessionists. Passing through Kentucky and into Tennessee, she did not stop until she reached the Union-occupied state capital. Col. William Truesdail, who functioned as "chief of detective police for military governor Andrew Johnson" spent several days with Cushman. She could probably get into

The actress from New Orleans, Pauline Cushman.—Library of Congress

Rebel camps, he suggested, by saying that she was searching for her brother—who was really a Confederate soldier. Truesdail was confident that she would eventually be invited to dine with Rebel officers. His instructions were clear: Such invitations should be accepted readily, and she should keep her ears open, but should never under any circumstances ask questions about military matters. He instructed her in detail about what information she should seek, warning her not to write anything down but to "use her head as an actress and remember all of her lines."

Soon afterward, U.S. Assistant Secretary of War Charles A. Dana informed leaders in Washington that Truesdail was "deep into all kinds of plunder." He was largely responsible for inactivity of the Army of the Cumberland, said Dana, because he and his accomplices "had become rich by jobs and contracts." Though that may have been true, Truesdail nevertheless gave the female spy valuable instructions, which unfortunately, she sometimes failed to follow.

Deeply divided Tennessee held both Federal and Confederate forces, both of which wanted to see what the other would do before taking action. In this chaotic situation, it was easy for the actress from New Orleans to pass from one Rebel camp to another. Her mission was to reach the headquarters of Gen. Braxton Bragg and learn his plans, but there is no evidence that she succeeded in doing so. Here and there she picked up a bit of information that she considered to be valuable, and she seems to have passed some of it along to Federal officers. Not entirely trusting her memory when she gained access to data she consid-

Pauline brings down the house at Woods Theatre in Louisville.—THE LIFE OF PAULINE CUSHMAN

ered important, she failed to follow Truesdail's most important instruction. Apparently having hastily made rough copies of a few maps and jotting down the locations and strengths of some Rebel units, she consigned her papers to her shoes.

She had already been under suspicion as a result of constantly roaming back and forth between Shelbyville, Wartrace, Manchester, Tullahoma, and other towns. Eventually, cavalrymen under John Hunt Morgan arrested her and took her to their commander. Morgan, however, seemed more interested in her as a woman than as a Union spy, she said. Not knowing what to do with her, Morgan sent her to Forrest.

"Miss Maj. Pauline Cushman," as depicted at war's end.

Forrest was too busy planning his next move to be bothered with a woman who had been poking around a few towns held by Rebels. He sent her to Shelbyville, where she was placed in the custody of provost marshal Alexander McKinstry. After questioning her at length, he ordered her to be held under close guard until a court-martial could be convened. Once the evidence found on her person was produced, the court wasted no time in arriving at a verdict. Capt. Milton Peden, a provost marshal, brought her the news that she would be hanged within a few days.

Hours after hearing the verdict, Cushman became dreadfully ill. Although it is possible that she had indeed picked up a rapidly developing malady, it is likely that she had taken something given to her by Truesdail for use in just such an emergency. Whatever the case, she was so sick that there seemed to be no reason to hurry her execution. While she languished in her bed, soldiers in blue under the command of Gen. William S. Rosecrans struck Bragg's forces suddenly and fiercely in late June. Bragg's men left camp so hurriedly that they didn't bother to take Pauline with them.

Suddenly and unexpectedly freed by events in which she had no part, she soon went back to Nashville. Once she was safe behind Federal lines, she did not venture beyond them again. Her short career as a spy, eventful as it was, had come to an abrupt end, and she was thankful to be alive.

When she put her story into print in 1864, she confided to readers that an unexpected honor came to her when military commanders learned how close she came to be hanged while spying for the Union. Gen. James A. Garfield drew up a certificate that made her an honorary major of cavalry, she said, and it was the most precious document she ever held in her hand.

If her account is accurate, her honor was remarkably similar to that of Confederate spy Belle Boyd, who claimed that "Stonewall" Jackson made her an honorary captain (see Chapter 13).

As published in 1864 and later amplified and revised, a hasty look at Pauline Cushman's account of her adventures raises some serious doubts. One biographer has labeled parts of her story as "sheer nonsense, created one suspects, by Pauline's own not very first-rate imagination." Since she clearly exaggerated in some instances, was the entire saga that she put into print a flight of fancy by a frustrated widow who yearned to become a famous entertainer? Maybe so, maybe not.

Capsule summaries of her adventures as a spy appear in numerous standard reference works, which are carefully scrutinized by editors. Civil War historian Bell I. Wiley told audiences that "There was only one blot upon the honor and courage of Southern womanhood. That blot," he said, "was Pauline Cushman—a turnskirt who became a spy for the Union Army." According to Wiley, she may have been the only Southern woman to be condemned to death by a military tribunal.

A ringing endorsement of her story by Wiley went a long way toward convincing skeptics. Yet, it is not the most potent evidence pointing to the probability that the New Orleans native really did spy for the Union. She could have picked up the names of generals almost anywhere, of course, but even in the passion of sectional conflict, majors and provost marshals were not prominent officers known to the general public.

Pauline not only identified four obscure Federal officers; she got their names and ranks right (except for adding an extra "d" to the name of Capt. Milton Peden). Where could she have gotten such information without having actually had contact with these men? That is an even bigger riddle than whether or not a toast to Davis and the Confederacy could have propelled a rank amateur into the ranks of memorable Civil War spies.

15

Emma Sansom

Guide

A girl of only sixteen made a critical difference to the maneuvers of a hard-riding Confederate force led by Gen. Nathan B. Forrest, saving them several precious hours. Thanks largely to her service as a guide to a crossing over a waterway whose bridge was being burned, an ambitious one-of-a-kind Federal raid through three states was foiled. Afterward, the *Confederate Veteran* published her account of one of the most bizarre episodes of the war. She wrote:

> I knew of a trail about two hundred yards above the bridge on our farm where our cows used to cross in low water, and I believed he could get his men over there, and that if he would have my saddle put on a horse I would show him the way.
>
> He said: "There is no time to saddle a horse; get up here behind me." As he said this he rode close to the bank on the side of the road, and I jumped up behind him. Just as we started off, mother came up out of breath and gasped: "Emma, what do you mean?"
>
> General Forrest said: "She is going to show me a ford where I can get my men over in time to catch those Yankees before they get to Rome [Georgia]. Don't be uneasy; I will bring her back safe."
>
> We rode out into a field through which ran a branch or small ravine and along which there was a thick undergrowth that protected us for a while from being seen by the Yankees at the bridge or on the other side of the creek. When we got close to the creek, I said: "General Forrest, I think we had better get off the horse."

Acting on the advice of the farm girl, the man famous as "the Wizard of the Saddle" followed Emma Sansom through the bushes on foot. With lots of Federal rifles and one or two pieces of field artillery firing, she pointed out to him the spot where it was safe to cross Black Creek. According to her account, Forrest then asked her name and said he would like to have a lock of her hair. When the firing stopped, she started back home. "On the way," she recounted, "I met General Forrest again, and he told me he had written a note for me and left it on the bureau."

That note is the sole piece of writing by Forrest that survived the Civil War. A wealthy but barely literate slave trader in 1861, the Confederate cavalry leader was the only man in gray or blue who entered the fray as a private and became a full general before the fighting ended. His gratitude to an adolescent girl later brought her many honors. John Greenleaf Whittier wrote a fantasy about a Maryland woman of advanced years; had he known the true story of the young girl who was vital to a major military operation, his "Emma Sansom" might have become the poem of the century.

It's clearly established that Emma was born at Social Circle, Georgia, in 1847. Her father's name—and hers—is not nearly so certain. Without exception, biographers of Forrest and correspondents of the *Confederate Veteran* spelled their surname as Sansom. But in Gadsden, Alabama, residents are positive that the juvenile heroine should be remembered as Emma Samson.

Whatever her name really was, she moved with her parents into extreme northwestern Alabama when she was about five years old. Her new home was close to the Georgia state line and adjacent to Black Creek, named for its opaque waters caused by rotting vegetation. Originating on Lookout Mountain, the stream was actually much bigger than its name suggested. At many places, most notably near the Sansom farm, it was quite deep. A dirt road between Blountsville and Gadsden crossed the stream on a rough wooden bridge. It was this structure that Federal soldiers set afire on the day that Forrest's approach after a long and dogged pursuit seemed imminent.

Emma's father had died only seven years after their move to Alabama. Her brother had joined the 19th Alabama regiment and had been wearing a Confederate uniform for about two years. Though her brother was fighting for his homeland, in her wildest imagination Emma never thought that *she* would be able to do anything to help the Southern cause. But a daring plan framed far away brought the war almost to her very doorstep when Federal raiders and their pursuers swept by on their way to the iron foundry and railroad at Rome, Georgia.

One artist incorrectly thought that Emma's ride began near the cabin in which she and her mother lived.

Col. Abel D. Streight of the 51st Indiana regiment tried to execute what admirers called "the Great Plan," but there's no certainty that he devised it. When the basic outline of the proposed action became known to high-level officers, Gen. William S. "Old Rosey" Rosecrans pondered before saying that it was "fraught with great consequences." Gen. James A. Garfield reputedly pored for an hour over a map that showed Tennessee, Mississippi, Alabama, and Georgia, then gave his enthusiastic endorsement to one of the wildest schemes concocted thus far in the war.

U. S. Grant was in overall command of Federal forces throughout the region, but he and his immediate command were bogged down at Vicksburg. Some analysts assert that he approved of the raid into Georgia because he believed it would lead Confederates to move some of their units away from the strongly fortified river city. However, there is no positive evidence that he personally approved of the scheme.

The objectives of the raid were a smelter and a railroad considered vital to the Confederacy. Well to the north of Atlanta, the town of Rome seemed likely to offer little resistance to a well-armed Federal band. It wouldn't be easy to reach the target, however. It lay deep inside territory firmly held by soldiers in gray. There seemed to be no way to approach the target except by means of a lengthy and torturous route that would involve long riding through enemy territory.

By virtue of surprise, only a move so imaginative and daring that the enemy wouldn't think of it was likely to succeed. To reach his objective, Streight would have to move his men across Tennessee and through its many rivers to Eastport, Mississippi. At that point, they would have to cross Mississippi and Alabama at or close to their northern boundaries to avoid clashes with established Rebel forces farther to the south.

Because the country he expected to move across was wild and rugged, even mountainous in some spots, horses couldn't possibly make the arduous journey fast enough to stay ahead of armed pursuers. Feeling that he had no other choice, Streight decided to outfit his 2,000 men on sure-footed mules. These hardy animals could negotiate almost any terrain and readily ate things most horses wouldn't touch. Choice of the hybrid animal meant that Streight's raid would become the only memorable mule-powered operation of the war. A final aspect of the finished plan called for Gen. Grenville M. Dodge to lead a diversion to draw off Rebel forces that might otherwise make things rough for Streight and his men.

Streight, an infantry officer, was in the unusual position of leading a long-distance mounted raid. Most of his men were volunteers from infantry regiments, but he also had two companies of horsemen. Known as the Middle Tennessee Cavalry, they were natives of Alabama who had enlisted in the Union Army. Some of them knew the countryside well, and they led the way in the swift journey across their native state.

The mule riders—officially known as Streight's Independent Provisional Brigade Designed for Special Secret Service—left Nashville by way of the Cumberland River, aboard a group of river transports. From the Cumberland they turned into the Tennessee River and then headed toward Eastport, Mississippi, at the extreme northern edge of the state. They had been on the water only a day or two before C.S. Gen. Braxton Bragg received word that a large body of men in blue was on the move. He didn't have the foggiest notion where they were headed or what they hoped to accomplish, but he immediately dispatched Forrest and some of his cavalrymen to find the Yankees and stop them in their tracks.

By the time Dodge's diversionary raid fizzled, Streight had dashed through sparsely settled territory in northern Alabama to the town of Tuscumbia. Aware of growing difficulties, he left under cover of darkness. He assured his subordinates that their "lightning brigade" would move fast enough to keep far ahead of any Rebel troops and that dis-

Emma Sansom as she looked a few years after her famous ride.—THE CONFEDERATE VETERAN

abling the all-important railroad would bring glory to every man who had helped accomplish that feat.

Before they reached Day's Gap, which afforded passage through the hilly terrain, C.S. Gen. Nathan B. Forrest discovered what was happening and was riding hell-bent-for-leather to catch up with the enemy forces. He knew that his outfit was much smaller than Streight's, but hoped to outrun and outmaneuver the Federal raiders. Streight's soldiers had pushed ahead all day on April 29 and were happy to make camp at the foot of the narrow pass that led to the top of Sand Mountain. They didn't realize, however, that Forrest and his pursuing force were a mere four miles behind them that night.

Before Federal units reached the plateau on top of Sand Mountain, they realized that Confederates were hot on their heels. Streight prepared to ambush his foes by hiding two small pieces of field artillery behind bushes at a point where he was sure they could mow the Confederates down like grass. His trap didn't work as well as he'd expected, however. In a fierce fight near the top of the mountain, numerous Federals dropped when hit by Confederate balls, and Sgt. James H. Kierstead of the 3rd Indiana Infantry was captured, along with several other men responsible for the ambush of Confederates.

For the next ninety-six hours, the two forces were engaged in constant small-scale conflicts. Streight and Forrest both knew that they were engaged in a race against time. If Federal forces managed to reach the vital spot first, they could severely hamper the Confederate war effort. Provisions from the rich interior of Georgia plus munitions from the immense Augusta arsenal might be delayed in transit to Bragg and his forces.

Forrest pushed his men and their horses to the limits of endurance, determined not to let the rail line suffer damage. During hand-to-hand fighting on Hog Mountain, the Confederate cavalryman had three horses shot from under him in the course of a few hours. Each time a dead or severely wounded animal threw him to the ground, he jumped into another saddle and seemed to fight harder than ever.

Realizing that he was now too far from Tuscumbia to return to his base on the Mississippi River even if he wanted to, Streight tried every trick in the book. In addition to devising several ambushes, he burned bridges and tried to block trails by rolling boulders across them. But some of his riders had never been on the back of an animal before; and heavy rain caused very deep mud, slowing the self-styled "lightning brigade" to a crawl for a few days. By the time the Federals were moving swiftly again, Forrest was back on their heels.

Days earlier, Streight had decided largely to bypass Gadsden and to burn the only known bridge over Black Creek. His maps informed him that the Rebels would have to halt on the west bank of the creek and search up and down it for miles to find a place to cross. That should give him a lead of at least a full day, perhaps two, he calculated. Hence, he promised his weary men that once across Black Creek, they could take things a little easier on their twenty-four-mile trek to Rome—the last leg of their extremely long and circuitous journey. Eight or ten miles from Gadsden, Streight directed Capt. Milton Russell and two hundred men to race toward Rome with all possible speed in order to secure the bridge over the Oostanaula River. With that structure under his control, he could move into the town at his leisure and do a thorough job of putting the railroad out of business.

He was right in having decided that the sturdy and stubborn mule was far superior to the horse for his purposes (its omnivorous eating habits made it easy for them to feed off the land without making long stops to gather suitable forage), but their constant braying kept Rebels informed about his progress and whereabouts. Had it not been for that and the wandering Sansom cows and the girl who tended them, the Federal leader might well have achieved his goal.

Taking his men to the spot Emma identified, Forrest and his command only lost an hour or two, instead of a day or two as Streight had hoped. Ammunition for their field guns was pulled from caissons and carried across the creek by men holding the heavy shells over their heads. Using a commonly employed system of poles and ropes, it was relatively easy to get the empty caissons to the east bank of Black Creek. Guns presented more difficulty, but Forrest was able to hitch several teams of horses to the ropes that pulled each piece, and they lurched along fairly rapidly.

All the way across two states, the Rebel leader had kept careful track of the number of men Streight lost from illness, desertion, and skirmishes. Forrest had less than six hundred men in pursuit of more than twice as many Yankees, so a head-to-head confrontation around Rome would have led to quick defeat for the Rebels. In his dilemma, the commander asked one of his captains to refresh his memory about a vaguely remembered biblical adventure. His subordinate explained that at the Battle of Jericho, Joshua was badly outnumbered. To deceive his enemy, he kept his force constantly on the move, making it seem much stronger than it actually was. In the hours of darkness, Joshua sent his little army milling around carrying pitchers that hid lights inside them. When the pitchers were broken at a signal, large numbers of moving lights suddenly appeared. They created the impression that a huge host was gathering around the city of Jericho, and Joshua's enemies hastily abandoned it. Nodding satisfaction, Forrest muttered something that was taken to mean, "Fine; we'll make do with something like that."

On Sunday morning, May 3, the Rebel force that had gained precious hours as a result of Emma's service as a guide forded the Chattooga River. Still dragging the only two guns they had left, they executed a series of "Jericho maneuvers," persuading Streight that he faced a vastly superior body. He surrendered without a fight and was mortified beyond measure to discover that he had been at the head of more than twice as many men as Forrest. For having saved the Western & Atlantic Railroad, Forrest received the coveted Thanks of the Confederate Con-

The hastily scrawled note of appreciation that Forrest left for Emma. It is usually considered to read: "Hed Quartes in Saddle. May 2 1863. My highest Regards to miss Ema Sanson, for her Gallant conduct while my force was Skirmishing with the Federals across BlackCreek near Gadsden alabama. N. B. Forrest, Brig. Genl comding N. Allabama."

gress. Streight and several of his captured officers were sent to Libby Prison in Richmond, and privates in his force were scattered among several other prisons and stockades.

Nearly everyone in and around Gadsden rejoiced that Rome had not been captured by the raiders. Alabama lawmakers, keenly aware that the exploit of the Sansom girl had no close parallel, voted to show their gratitude by giving her a square mile of public land—644 acres. Though the measure passed without opposition and was signed into law, the heroine never received title to her tract. Immediately after the unconditional surrender of the last Confederate armies, Congress enacted measures under whose terms all public lands in seceded states became the property of the federal government.

A lengthy ballad was written in commemoration of Emma's service to the South, but it never achieved wide circulation. In 1904 the Gadsden chapter of the United Daughters of the Confederacy announced plans to create an equestrian statue of Emma and Forrest. Money was scarce, however, and to ordinary folk $3,500 seemed to be entirely too much money to put into a piece of granite. Consequently, the only significant tangible memorial of sorts to the girl who lived on Black Creek is Gadsden's Emma *Sampson* High School.

To Emma, none of these attempts to honor her properly made a particle of difference. Shortly before or after Lee's surrender at Appomattox, she married and moved to Texas. She and her husband spent the rest of their lives in grinding poverty. She died wearing tattered homespun, but knowing that she was the only female ever to climb aboard the warhorse of Nathan B. Forrest and ride with him. No Southern woman who survived the war years could have imagined a more rewarding memory.

16

Nancy Hart

Bushwhacker

Lt. Col. William C. Starr of the Federal 9th West Virginia regiment nodded consent when one of his men asked permission "to get a picture of the girl upstairs." Heading Companies A and F of his regiment, the officer had the hamlet under such firm control that he didn't expect any trouble from Rebels. Starr didn't like the way his men reacted to the presence of a female prisoner in the attic of his headquarters, but he figured that one picture couldn't do much harm. Neither he nor his captive knew that it would be the only photograph of Nancy Hart ever taken.

Oral tradition has it that Pvt. Marion Kerner, a regimental telegrapher, came up with the idea to take the portrait. After Starr gave his permission, Kerner went to the attic, where Hart slept on a cot, and told her the plan. At first she wanted nothing to do with it. Though she wasn't very good at reading, she did look at pictures in the illustrated newspapers that occasionally found their way west of the Allegheny Mountains. She knew what a sketch of a bushwhacker usually looked like, and she didn't want to see her face, "all uglied up," in print.

No amount of wheedling did any good, Nancy was dead set against "poking her nose in front of one of them camera things." Refusing to give up, the man who wanted her picture went to some of the women of Summersville, Virginia (now West Virginia), and borrowed a calico dress. He took his own hat, squeezed it so that it lost its military look, and stuck a plume on top of it. Offered the garments, Hart said she guessed "It won't hurt nuthin' to see if the dress fits me." When she found the garment and the hat satisfactory, she sat still for several minutes while her image was captured on an ambrotype.

Back in the attic after having been allowed to walk around for about half an hour, Hart decided that she "must be somebody special" to

Nancy Hart.—1861 AMBROTYPE

have her picture taken. The guard on duty that day was a youngster of maybe seventeen years. When his prisoner gave him her best smile and began telling him about sitting in front of a sure-enough camera earlier in the day, he showed genuine interest in her experience.

"I'd ruther have had a gun in my hand," the woman of twenty-three or twenty-four said. "That way, I'd feel like I was out o' here an' ridin' with the Rangers." She paused as though she were seventeen years old and timid before venturing, "Sure would've felt more like myself with a shootin' iron in my hand." When her guard nodded understanding, she said she guessed he'd like to see her the way she was before she was captured. "Here," she directed, "gimme yore musket, and I'll show you."

He handed his weapon to the prisoner, who was charged with being a member of the Moccasin Rangers and scheduled to go on trial as a notorious bushwhacker. She nodded appreciation, hefted the better-than-typical rifle to get a feel of its balance, and placed its butt against her shoulder. Quick as a wink, she took aim and fired. Her charge hit the guard close to his heart, and he dropped to the floor, unable to cry for help.

Nancy didn't dare risk the steps, so she climbed out of the back window of the attic and dropped nearly ten feet to the ground, her knees bent to absorb some of the shock. As soon as she was back on her feet, she raced to Starr's own horse, hopped in the saddle, and whipped the animal to top speed with a piece of brush. By the time the men of Company F realized what was happening, she was out of sight. One fellow thought she might be headed toward Charleston, fifty miles to the west. His comrades shook their heads at such a notion and told him, "She's goin' back to the Rangers for sure."

In July 1862, few sparsely inhabited sections of the divided nation were so hotly contested as western Virginia. There was already bad blood between the mountaineers and the tidewater aristocrats long before the mid-eighteenth century, when George Washington crossed the Alleghenies in search of cheap land. Methodist circuit rider Francis Asbury, who came into the region soon after Washington, was surprised by the difference between the western frontiersmen and the tobacco and cotton farmers of the east.

The passage of decades sharpened sectional differences and raised the level of Virginia's internal tension instead of lowering it. Joseph Johnson, the first elected governor of the state, was an "across the mountains man," meaning he was from the western part of the state. He gained his office in return for a promise to build a railroad from Covington all the way to the Ohio River. Though the railroad was never built along the banks of the New and Kanawha Rivers, plantation owners there immediately got the tax break for which they had bargained. Instead of paying taxes on the full value of their slaves, the levy was now capped at $300— and was abolished altogether for males and females under age twelve. Railroads and desirable state institutions sprang up in the rich eastern part of the state; the west got two asylums for the insane.

It was no wonder that the Virginia westerners saw a golden opportunity on April 17, 1861, when the state convention voted to secede from the Union. Folk living west of the mountains correctly reasoned that Washington would be on their side if they set up a new state and swore loyalty to the Union. By August, a western convention had created what they called the state of Kanawha and had named Francis H. Pierpont as its governor. But the secession of Kanawha from Virginia didn't lead to the creation of a new state for nearly two years. During part of that time, three separate state administrations were in operation—western Unionists in

The obverse of West Virginia's state seal magnifies the importance of June 20, 1863, when the region became a state.

Wheeling, eastern Unionists in Alexandria, and Confederates in Richmond—and three men claimed to be governor of Virginia.

Military events were soon as badly snarled as were political ones. With Gen. Robert E. Lee in supreme command of Virginia state troops, soldiers tried to force residents of Kanawha to rescind their declarations of statehood. Anticipating such a move, Washington sent Gen. George B. McClellan and a group of Federal volunteers to protect the interests of the Union. Fervent admirers of Lee sometimes forget that he lost badly in western Virginia, especially in the battle of Rich Mountain on July 11. His disgruntled followers began calling him "Granny" in derision. McClellan, who took his own printing press with him on the campaign, turned out such glowing reports of victories that he soon replaced Gen. Irvin McDowell as commander of the Army of the Potomac.

With soldiers in blue and gray fighting over control of Kanawha, it was all but inevitable that independent groups of rangers should spring up. Seldom under the command of a military leader on either side, these guerrillas—sometimes called partisans or bushwhackers—developed great skill in ambushing small parties of enemy soldiers. Because they were forced to live largely off the countryside in the regions where they operated, numerous bands raided farms and villages of enemy civilians when they could. When they couldn't, they plundered and foraged among friendly civilians.

Perry Conley called himself a captain but did not wear a regulation uniform and answered to no military authority. He set himself up as head of a band of pro-Confederate rangers. If he has any claim to distinction, it lies in the fact that he was willing to let a woman ride with his men. Nancy Hart, said to be a crack shot with a pistol as well as with a rifle, went along when the rangers cut a wide swath through Calhoun County late in the summer of 1861. From that time forward, she became an increasingly prominent and influential partisan—but reacted angrily any time anyone referred to her and her comrades as bushwhackers.

She didn't object to having her name appear in an occasional newspaper story, as long as it described her—like many did—as "a handsome girl with coal black eyes, who rides and shoots with the best." Because she couldn't read, her fellow rangers had to read these brief accounts to her. What she lacked in book learning she more than made up for with a keen mind and the ability to keep going when most men were ready to stop. When she wasn't busy making targets out of Yankees, she would wander into small towns and pick up military information.

Though she pretended a lack of interest in what was happening among her captors while she was in custody, she soaked up every tidbit of information she could. She learned that three men were considered sufficient for a picket post, and that there were never more than four such posts around Summersville. Though the road leading toward Sutton was the best way to get into or out of the hamlet, she discovered that Starr considered it safe and seldom had it picketed. Furthermore, she learned that most of the men who made up Starr's two companies of the 9th West Virginia regiment were sound asleep every night by 12:30 A.M.

Ten days after killing her guard and making her escape from the attic prison, Nancy Hart came back to Summersville. This time, however, she didn't come alone. A band of men from the Rebel 22nd Virginia regiment, estimated at two hundred in number, followed the female ranger into the crossroads village. As soon as they got close to Starr's headquarters, they began to whoop and yell at the top of their voices.

Lt. John W. Miller of Company F heard the commotion and understood its source, so he took to the woods and made his escape to a Federal post at Gauley Bridge. After questioning Miller at length, Lt. Col. John C. Paxton of the Federal 2nd West Virginia Cavalry put together a formal report on July 25. Addressed to Gen. Jacob D. Cox, the summary of action at Summersville said that enemy forces only fired about ten shots. They took men in blue by surprise so effectively that it was necessary for them to wound only three men. At least fifty men followed Miller to Gauley Bridge and escaped. Fortunately for the Federal forces,

Partisans, or guerrillas, owed token loyalty to one side or the other, but preyed on civilians of both sides.—HARPER'S WEEKLY

Women and children often suffered at the hands of bushwhackers.

there was no ammunition in the place except the standard twenty rounds each soldiers carried. However, most of the men were armed with exceptionally fine weapons—Enfield rifles—all of which were taken by the guerrillas.

A supplementary dispatch from Lt. Col. Augustus H. Coleman of the 11th Ohio regiment made its way up the chain of command three days later. Coleman reported that the raiding party captured Lt. Col. Starr, Capt. Samuel Davis, and Lts. Benjamin F. Stivers and James Ewing. Although he incorrectly identified the village as Summerville, his account of the damage was accurate: "They burned three houses, including the commissary storehouse; also one wagon, destroying a second wagon, capturing 8 mules and 12 horses."

Some of these partisan units owed only nominal allegiance to Union forces, and their behavior was little better than that of Confederate rangers. However, there is no solid evidence that any other band, regardless of which side it supported, was led to its objective by a woman. Aware of her unique role in the Civil War, Nancy Hart shrugged it off as inconsequential. "It just happen'd that I wuz the prisoner in Summersville an' had a fust hand look at the place," she said.

Secretly, she must have had some satisfaction in knowing that the information she gathered made possible a nearly bloodless raid in which her previous captors became her captives. All four of the commissioned officers who were taken on July 25, 1862, were sent to quarters quite different from her attic. They went to Richmond's Libby Prison, which was already crowded with captured Federal officers.

Nancy had married Joshua Douglas shortly before she was captured, and she later saw him abandon the rangers and don a gray uniform. His predated recruitment form was forged to protect him from punishment for actions during the months he rode with Nancy and Conley's male followers. Joshua was never injured in the fighting, and he survived minor bouts of illness. At the war's end, he and Nancy settled in Greenbrier County—on rugged mountain land, of course.

When the one-time female bushwhacker died soon after the turn of the twentieth century, she was buried in a remote spot. Her "tombstone" consisted of a pile of rocks gathered from the mountain knob where the grave was dug. Years later, a granddaughter searching for the gravesite discovered that the top of the crag had been leveled and a relay tower had been erected on it.

CHAPTER

17

Rose Greenhow

Banished

December 26

*In a day or two 1,200 cavalry supported by four batteries of
artillery will cross the river above to get behind Manassas and cut
off railroad and other communications with our army whilst an
attack is made in front. For God's sake heed this. It is positive. They
are obliged to move or give up. They find me a hard bargain and I
think I shall be released in a few days without condition, but to go
South. A confidential member of McClellan's staff came to see me
and tell me that my case should form an exception and I only want
to gain time. All my plans are nearly completed.*

Found in Confederate archives after the fall of Richmond, the
above document was written by an inmate of a Washington
prison, Mrs. Rose O'Neal Greenhow. She probably managed to
get it to Thomas Jordan, assistant adjutant general on the staff of C.S.
Gen. P. G. T. Beauregard. How she transmitted it to him is unknown,
but Jordan is believed to have forwarded it to the Rebel capital on
December 28, 1861.

The writer had been under guard for many weeks, so the very existence of her dispatch reveals a clever and determined Confederate spy
who was very hard to stop. Circumstantial evidence suggests that she
secured some of her military information from Gustavus V. Fox, then
assistant secretary of the navy. The writer's description of herself as "a
hard bargain" suggests that after many interrogations followed by high-
level conferences, no one knew quite what to do with her.

Confederate leaders to whom the post-Christmas dispatch was smuggled from Washington had learned to pay close attention to anything received from their most active informant in the Union capital. Hence, they acted swiftly in an effort to block a new Federal build-up in a region already infamous from the first major battle of the war.

John C. Calhoun of South Carolina was an early and close friend of Greenhow.— CHARLESTON HISTORICAL SOCIETY

Leaders on both sides acknowledged that Bull Run had been a Union debacle, partly resulting from nonmilitary events. In retrospect, Union Gen. George B. McClellan realized that the defeat of Federal volunteers there stemmed partly from the fact that "the rebels knew our plans as soon as we did." Yet, four months after Bull Run, McClellan had no idea that officials in Washington continued to talk freely with Rose Greenhow. After all, the widow Greenhow had been arrested by detective Allan Pinkerton and was being watched closely. Common sense said she no longer presented a threat to the Union cause. This time, however, common sense was wrong.

During adolescence, Rose O'Neal had been given a room in a Washington boarding house operated by her aunt. Besieged by suitors, at about age twenty-six she chose Dr. Robert Greenhow as her husband and bore four daughters. A representative of the Department of State, he traveled extensively until his accidental death in 1854. Rose, who usually accompanied him, came back to Washington as a widow at age forty; she soon became one of the capital's social queens. She spent many of her evenings at levees and dinners, the rest with one or more influential men in her comfortable quarters.

Earlier, she had cultivated the friendship of John C. Calhoun, whom she said had taught her much of what she knew about politics. President James Buchanan considered her one of the most fascinating women he had ever known and liked to spend evenings in her company. Jefferson

Physical evidence suggested that Senator Henry Wilson was an intimate of Greenhow.

Davis of Mississippi frequently dropped into her salon for a while. Perhaps through her friend Lady Napier, she met Senator Henry Wilson of Massachusetts and may have accepted him as her lover. At the outbreak of hostilities, she was careful to be seen often with her niece, who had married Stephen A. Douglas (a strong Lincoln supporter and Democratic legislator) and would soon be a widow also.

Prominent among the upper echelon of socialites in the capital and intimately acquainted with many influential persons, Greenhow easily acquired information about military plans and operations. No one knows precisely when or why she began transmitting coded messages to Confederate leaders, but, aided by Col. Thomas Jordan, she developed an efficient system of espionage within six weeks of the fall of Fort Sumter.

At least as early as July 10, Rose learned that a Federal advance was being planned. Betty Duvall had volunteered or had been recruited as a messenger; she set out for Confederate headquarters with a coded note concealed in a knot of hair. When deciphered, it warned: "McDowell has certainly been ordered to advance on the sixteenth. R.O.G."

In Richmond, Jefferson Davis was skeptical when he heard the warning from his old friend. He refused to order Johnston to withdraw from the Shenandoah Valley to join forces with Beauregard, placing Beauregard in great danger of an overwhelming defeat. Perhaps in a state of near panic, the Creole leader of Confederate forces in Virginia kept in close touch with his Washington informant. On July 16 one of his messengers, a former employee of the U.S. Department of the Interior, knocked on Rose Greenhow's door very early. She said nothing to him until after receiving and reading a note from Thomas Jordan. According to the message, she could place complete trust in the bearer, George Donellan. While Donellan waited, she framed a report and spent nearly an hour transcribing it into her private code. Part of it was later discovered to constitute a terse confirmation of earlier warnings: "Order issued for McDowell to march upon Manassas tonight."

That's how the Confederate commander got word of the Federal advance before 9 P.M. of the day on which it was launched as a supposedly top secret operation. The widow's message probably included details concerning the Federal route. Troops stationed in Alexandria and at Arlington Heights would move through Fairfax Court House to Centreville. From that one-time Confederate bastion, Union Gen. Irvin McDowell's 90-day militia would proceed in overwhelming strength to Manassas, drained by the waterway known as Bull Run. Without orders from Richmond, Beauregard adopted a battle plan and sent word to Gen. Joseph E. Johnston to come to his aid at top speed. Arrival of Johnston's troops by railroad on July 21 turned the tide on what had seemed to be a day of certain Federal victory.

At least by July 23 (perhaps earlier), another messenger from Jordan pounded on the door of his informant's Sixteenth Street residence. Again, Rose was handed a note by a man she had never seen. This time, instead of asking for her help, it read: "Our President and our General direct me to convey their thanks to you. We rely on your further information. The Confederacy is in debt to you."

Defeated at Bull Run partly because of intelligence from Greenhow, McDowell was immediately replaced. George B. McClellan, fresh from minor but well-publicized victories in what is now West Virginia, became commander of the Military Division of the Potomac just four days after the Federal loss. When Jefferson Davis met Rose Greenhow face to face months later, he reputedly pumped her hand and insisted, "But for you, there would have been no [Confederate] victory at Bull Run."

McClellan, a one-time railroad executive, had already made arrangements to use private detective Allan Pinkerton as his head of intelligence. Suspecting that someone in the capital had given away military secrets, McClellan made identifying the spy a top priority for Pinkerton and his men. Sifting through records and investigating names found in them, they followed a trail that led them to Rose Greenhow.

With one of his best men, the detective from Chicago began surveillance of the socialite. Their blundering vigil was so suspicious that both men were arrested by local police. Pinkerton complained that they were detained in a "most filthy and uncomfortable place under guard" until an assistant secretary of state came to their rescue the next morning. On August 23, a few hours after they were freed, Pinkerton placed the forty-three-year-old widow under house arrest. According to him, she became alarmed as he approached and managed to swallow what must have been another message in cipher.

The detective's official report, which was extremely long, was not filed until November. At that time, Pinkerton signed the record as Maj. E. J. Allen, an alias he frequently used. It read:

> It was a fact too notorious to need reciting here that for months before her arrest Mrs. Greenhow was actively and to a great extent openly engaged in giving aid and comfort, sympathy and information to enemies of the Government; that although she was living in the capital of the United States and [was] under its government protection her house was the rendezvous for the most violent enemies of the Government . . . that for a great number of years Mrs. Greenhow has been the instrument of the very men who now lead in the rebel councils and some of those who command their armies; who have successfully used her as a willing instrument in plotting the overthrow of the United States Government.

Reporting to Provost Marshal Gen. Andrew Porter of the Washington City Guard, Pinkerton said he and several of his operatives had spent at least two days searching Greenhow's house. They discovered what they described as "a very large amount of highly treasonable correspondence," including instructions from Jordan. Much of the material, they said, had recently been torn up; some had been thrown into a stove, but did not burn "since there was no fire therein." It greatly troubled the detective to reflect that she had "made use of whoever and whatever she could as medium to carry into effect her unholy purposes."

Angry as he was, Pinkerton was careful not to mention any names of Unionists who had frequented the Greenhow salon or engaged in any correspondence with Rose. One bundle of ten missives was found labeled "Letters from H—not to be opened, but burnt in case of death or accident." When these incriminating documents were filed with the U.S. War Department, they were listed as "Love Letters (Supposed to be) from Henry Wilson, U. S. Senator from Massachusetts." An ardent abolitionist, Wilson was a moving force in the Senate. One of his most spectacular recent triumphs had resulted in *post facto* approval to use "war powers" by the president. Wilson was so prominent that no one dared hint that letters purportedly written by him suggested that he was one of Rose Greenhow's lovers. Officials later declared that the handwriting was not that of the senator, despite the fact that Senate stationery was used.

Diarist Mary Boykin Chesnut (see Chapter 25) penned an indignant report of events that followed Greenhow's arrest. According to her, the widow was not allowed to make a single move for the eight days following her arrest without being accompanied or watched by a male guard or "sleepless sentinel." Later remanded to Old Capitol Prison, she remained there without a hearing for nearly eight months.

Threatened with a charge of treason, the spy did not flinch or cringe, despite her awareness that treason was a

Rose Greenhow's daughter accompanied her to prison.

capital offense. Even long before the Fifth Amendment was widely used by suspects, she stubbornly refused to incriminate herself. Challenged by a potentially damaging question, she calmly retorted, "That's my secret!" Her successful use of this ploy may have been aided by John A. Dix, a member of the special panel of U.S. Commissioners authorized to decide her fate. Long a prominent political leader and now a major general of U.S. Volunteers, Dix was among the men frequently seen in Rose Greenhow's company before her arrest.

She repeatedly demanded to know what law she was accused of having violated and stressed that she had been placed under detention without a warrant. After preparing a lengthy letter in which she aired her grievances, she had a copy smuggled to Richmond to be published in newspapers of the Confederate capital.

Probably helped by one of her daughters and possibly using carrier pigeons, she managed to get a number of messages to Confederates, even while guarded around the clock under house arrest. Copies of eight of these messages were found when her quarters were searched after she was imprisoned. Though experts debate about the actual value of the military information she included in her dispatches from home and

Gen. John A. Dix, an old friend of the spy, was among the commissioners who settled on banishment as proper punishment for her.
—A. H. RITHIE ENGRAVING

from prison, no one questions her skill in transmitting them. From her prison she succeeded in getting one letter to James Gordon Bennett, editor of the *New York Herald*.

No one knew what to do with Rose Greenhow, as no formal charges had been levied against her. If placed on public trial, she could cause a great many influential and important men to be embarrassed or worse. If released, she would resume her activities as a spy. An unidentified official finally suggested a resolution for the dilemma. On February 15, 1862, Rose O'Neal Greenhow was, by order of the War Department, transferred to its custody. As a political prisoner, she was later sent to Fortress Monroe. Legend says that when she stepped from Old Capital Prison on her way to her new place of detention, she delicately lifted her skirts, revealing a Confederate flag wrapped about her abdomen and thighs.

Although she had long protested such a thing, on June 2, she finally signed a document promising not to return north of the Potomac River without permission of the secretary of war after having been "set at liberty beyond the lines of the U. S. Army." After the document was signed, an officer of the 1st U.S. Volunteer Cavalry and a six-man guard escorted the beautiful widow beyond Federal lines. Arriving in Richmond as a conquering heroine, she boasted that to gain her release, she had promised not to blow up the Executive Mansion, equip a fleet, or break open the U.S. Treasury.

Confederate President Jefferson Davis almost certainly paid her a formal call while she was in Richmond. His purpose was to thank her for her part in the victory at Bull Run, he said. But aides, wondering whether he had other things in mind, soon discovered that she was headed to England and Europe on a secret mission.

Records fail to reveal precisely what she did for the Confederacy 3,000 miles away. Soon, however, she was prominent in British social circles. Often present as a guest at weekend parties, during one of them she met and talked at length with the great Thomas Carlyle. He was sufficiently impressed with her to make detailed notes about their conversation. Some evidence suggests that she may have worked with male Confederate agents whose mission was to buy as many stout ships as possible from English and French builders. Whether that was the case or not, she succeeded in securing an audience with the emperor of France. Always mindful of personal as well as Confederate interests, she persuaded a London publisher to issue her life story. It was offered to the public under the formidable title *My Imprisonment and the First Year of Abolition Rule at Washington.*

Now a celebrated author, Rose Greenhow left Greenhock, Scotland, late in August 1864 on a return voyage to the Confederacy. Her blockade runner, the *Condor,* was of the latest and fastest design—equipped with three funnels and drawing only seven feet of water. Capt. Samuel S. Ridge, commander of the vessel and son of the earl of Buckingham, was out to make a quick fortune.

No problems or delays were encountered until the *Condor* docked at Halifax, Nova Scotia. The vessel was two or three days ahead of schedule, so Ridge decided to wait for the moon to wane; darkness was a major asset in evading the warships of the blockading squadron. The delay was just long enough to enable the U.S. consul to get word to the U.S. secretary of the navy, Gideon Welles, that the *Condor* might be carrying clothing and supplies for Rebel soldiers. Welles, in turn, warned Cmdr. S. P. Lee that the vessel was likely to make port at Wilmington, North Carolina.

In the predawn hours of October 1, 1864, the warship *Niphon* spotted the *Condor* off Cape Fear and set a course to intercept. The tactic failed. However, the lookout of the *Condor* spotted a wreck in the Cape Fear River and, attempting to take action to avoid a collision, the vessel ran hard aground in the breakers. There was no cause for alarm—until the *Niphon* was seen approaching. Against Ridge's protests, Rose Greenhow had a boat lowered so she could get to shore at once. She apparently had time to get away before the Federal warship reached the stranded *Condor.*

Before her boat had even gone a dozen yards, however, heavy waves tossed Greenhow into the water. Early the next morning, the body of the female spy was found near Fort Fisher. Confederates theorized that she might have reached shore had she not been pulled under by the weight of $2,000 in gold carried in a bag slung around her neck. Rose O'Neal Greenhow was buried on October 2 with full military honors.

Greenhow in later life, as depicted by an English artist.

After a service in St. Thomas's Church, Wilmington, the cortege proceeded to Oakdale Cemetery with the coffin draped by a Confederate flag. An inquiry by the Confederate secretary of the navy concerning the whereabouts of some anxiously awaited dispatches suggests (but does not prove) that they were lost when Greenhow drowned.

Present-day analysts tend to doubt that this Washington socialite provided Confederates with military information of any great significance. Today, Greenhow is seldom perceived as having made the "invaluable contributions" credited to her during and after the Civil War. Yet caution is advisable when trying to appraise the impact of an extremely clever and audacious woman. One bizarre aspect of the arrest and imprisonment of the most celebrated early spy for the Confederacy remains intriguing even after these many years; it certainly shows the fearful regard with which the Federal government viewed Rose Greenhow. Unwilling to risk sending her to Fort Lafayette along with other political prisoners, for the first time in U.S. history, authorities banished a resident of the nation's capital from the United States.

Part IV

ANGELS OF MERCY

18

Clarissa Harlowe Barton

Feisty

Alonzo Joy tried to climb a few of the steps leading into the U.S. Capitol. He grimaced, fell, and rolled down three or four steps. Determination clearly showing on his face, the private from the Massachusetts militia crawled up half a dozen more steps. After resting, he resumed his torturous climb, eventually reaching the rotunda. Spotting an empty cot, he staggered over and fell on it, totally exhausted. When he heard a woman's voice seem to come from a spot very close to him, he wondered whether or not he was dreaming.

"You're going to be fine; I promise that you'll be walking very soon," she said.

"Are you are nurse?" the nineteen-year-old boy asked.

"No. The nurses are all males. I'm just a worker in the Patent Office. Where were you hit?"

"In my thigh, and maybe somewhere else. I don't think I'll be walking any time soon. What are you doing here?"

"I heard that some of you who were injured in Baltimore had reached the capital, so I just came over to see if I could be of any help. My name is Clara Barton, and if you think you won't pass out, I'll go get warm water and soap."

"Sure. I made it this far, didn't I? I'm Alonzo Joy, Company B, Sixth Massachusetts regiment. Go get the water; I can hang on."

Early in January, the militia unit to which Joy belonged offered its services to the national government. In response to Abraham Lincoln's call for 75,000 volunteers, on Monday, April 15, 1861, the unit was moved from Lowell to Boston. They were needed immediately, the chief executive said, to put down the insurrection in the South. With little training and even less experience, the 6th entrained for Washington on Wednesday. The cities of New York and Philadelphia were passed in routine fashion, but on Friday they and their comrades found themselves in Baltimore—in deep trouble.

In Baltimore they had to leave one railroad station and travel through the cobblestone streets of the port city to another station to finish the journey to the capital. While passing through, civilians with secessionist sympathies clashed with the uniformed young men. Many rocks were thrown, and numerous bullets were exchanged during the melee in which Joy and about forty of his comrades were wounded. At least four were killed. All of the wounded could have stayed in the Baltimore infirmary to recuperate, but the hardier of them settled for nothing less than their original destination. A few of the seriously wounded men were taken to the Washington infirmary, but most were told to choose places for themselves in the Capitol.

Finding space to place her own cot in a cubicle near the Senate chamber, Barton was all but overwhelmed by the number of wounded men who called for help. Seldom stopping except to nibble a few bites or sleep for an hour or two, she went on self-appointed duty. Much of her time and energy was devoted to Joy and two other men, George Calvin and Stephen Flanders. Still, she found time to bring wash pans and bandages to men with only superficial wounds. When Monday came, the Patent Office didn't even enter her mind until she paused to sip a cup of tea around noon.

Years afterward, the founder of the American Red Cross said that her encounter with Alonzo Joy changed the course of her life. She cared for him and a few of his friends until they were moved to Relay House on May 5. By that time, she knew that if war should really break out as expected, she would have to do all she could to help the soldiers.

Barton always insisted that she wouldn't leave the Patent Office and said simply that "it just happened." Those who knew the forty-year-old woman from Oxford, Massachusetts, were astonished when she became a self-appointed nurse to the soldiers; she made no secret of the fact that she despised men. Educated at home and enamored with outdoor sports from childhood, Barton was very early described by her elders as "uncommonly wilful [sic]." Her parents were so bewildered at her behavior that they consulted a visiting lecturer about her. Phrenologist Lorenzo N. Fowler carefully examined the bumps on Clara's head before recommending, "Give the girl some real responsibility. She has the makings of a teacher, I believe." As a result, she started teaching at age fifteen. Soon, she opened her own school in Bordentown, New Jersey, one of the first in the nation operated by a female.

Because the education was free, pupils flocked to her from the start. Within weeks, the school outgrew its facilities; after two years, its six hundred students required a new, larger building. Once it was completed, town fathers decided it wasn't proper for a female to be in charge. When informed that a male principal had been named, the thirty-three-year-old, who now called herself Clara, resigned in a huff. She informed the parents of some of her pupils that she planned to go to Washington and find a paying job. An acquaintance had told her that the Government Patent Office allowed eighty cents for sewing a book, and she was fast with a needle.

Clara Barton, first high-level female employee of the U.S. government.—JOHN SARTAIN ENGRAVING

Once she reached the capital, the woman who said she didn't like men simply because they were male meekly presented herself to a section foreman in the Patent Office. He ignored her proffered letter of recommendation from Congressman Alexander De Witt of her home district. Handing her one of his own documents, he gestured toward pen and ink and gruffly ordered her to copy a few lines. After she handed her work back to him, he examined her strong and clear copperplate handwriting and told her to report to the chief clerk on Monday morning.

Some senior employees, who didn't try to conceal their resentment at having a woman working among them, taunted her mercilessly. Clara gritted her teeth and pretended not to hear what they said. She performed her work so well that her efforts came to the attention of the commissioner of patents. To the consternation of many employees, Charles Mason selected her as his confidential clerk at the generous salary of $1,400 a year. Hence, Clara Barton may have been the first woman to hold a government white-collar position.

By the time her first patients had shown signs of beginning to heal, Edward Coburn of Lowell was brought in on a litter. Ill at ease in secessionist-filled Baltimore, he had insisted on leaving the infirmary there to rejoin his regiment. Before he reached Washington, Coburn was delirious. Under Clara's care, he regained consciousness and was able to drink a little broth. On April 26, he sat up for the first time and requested solid food. Finally, for the first time in a week, after dressing his wounds and slowly feeding him, his nurse gave priority to her own weary mind and body.

With about 3,000 men now quartered in the Capitol, it was time for them to acknowledge new authority. Drawn up into companies in the square that includes the Capitol, they were sworn into Federal service. This ceremony made them no longer simply members of state militia units but 90-day soldiers answering the president's call.

Barton slept through the late afternoon and the entire night that followed, then went to her room for a bath and a change of clothes. Believing her interlude as a nurse was over, she was ready to go back to the Patent Office. No one in the capital knew, however, that leaders in Richmond, Virginia, were ready to offer their city as the new Confederate capital, and it was only about one hundred miles from the Patent Office.

Because Richmond would soon be the center of Rebel planning, President Lincoln and his advisors decided that the city must be taken imme-

After most of the wounded left, the rotunda of the Capitol was used as a temporary barracks for volunteers.—HARPER'S WEEKLY

diately. In New York, Horace Greeley's influential *New York Tribune* was daily trumpeting the challenge "ON TO RICHMOND!" A quick victory in Virginia would mean that the struggle would soon be over and little blood would have been shed. Gen. Winfield Scott and other military advisors cautioned the president not to act hastily. He knew, however, that if his 90-day men were to fight at all, they would have to do so very soon. He dispatched them toward Richmond under the leadership of Gen. Irvin McDowell.

The men fought their first big battle in a region near Manassas Junction. A stream called Bull Run ran through the battlefield and gave the battle its name in the North; in the South, however, it was generally referred to as Manassas. By whatever name, the battle of July 21, 1861, yielded a casualty list that was staggering in comparison with earlier clashes. Clearly, a single battle would not put down the insurrection; the contesting regions would send more armies to do battle on other fields.

"Bull Run changed my life forever," Barton later told audiences eager to hear her story. "When the news came, I knew I couldn't watch the wounded from a distance. Through the influence of Senator Henry Wilson of my own state, I was permitted to remain on the rolls at the Patent Office. That meant I had to hire a substitute, so I found Edward Shaw and paid him from my salary. I immediately found an empty hall, engaged it, and began filling it with sheets, towels, soap, jellies, preserved fruit, and other necessities."

Many necessities were in short supply and no governmental agency was striving to supply them. Barton used the *Worcester (Massachusetts) Spy* to publicize an appeal for food, clothing, and bandages. Scores of packages were sent in response to the single appeal in this newspaper with only a small circulation. They arrived too late, however, and were too little for the flood of casualties faced after Bull Run, which Clara described as a "shattered army streaming back into the capital." Even if she could have met all the demands for supplies, she would not have been satisfied operating from the sidelines. She would have to bathe fevered foreheads herself and pack the wounds of injured soldiers with her own two hands.

Institutional resistance by male officials was all but overpowering. She badgered every leader who would see her, but for months received little except rejection at the federal level. Governor John A. Andrew of Massachusetts took up her cause and wrote to the surgeon general, Alfred Hitchcock, on her behalf. But Hitchcock crisply informed the governor that he didn't think Barton should go into the field "to act as a nurse" for men commanded by Gen. Ambrose E. Burnside of her native state.

When the assistant quartermaster general in charge of transportation learned that she had huge stores of supplies, however, he developed sudden interest. Maj. D. H. Rucker issued a pass that permitted her to drive a mule-drawn wagon to the front. One by one, other department heads grudgingly took similar action. August 12, 1862, was a red-letter day for Clara Barton: An aide to Gen. John Pope gave unqualified approval to her request to go to Culpeper Court House, Virginia. There she found that every available building near Cedar Mountain had been turned into field hospitals, crammed with some of the 1,445 Federals wounded in the battle on August 9. In a tiny church, one of the first places she stopped, she found a man whose right arm had been taken off at the shoulder. Private Parker, a member of a Massachusetts unit, lamented that the battle should be remembered as Slaughter Mountain. "We had about 8,000 men here, and they say our casualty list tops 2,000," he told her bitterly. She bandaged his massive wound as best she could, then gave him a clean shirt and a loaf of bread before moving on to his stricken comrades.

Proceeding to Alexandria in company with nearly six hundred men who had been badly wounded at Cedar Mountain, she later saw Washington go into a fresh panic over carnage at Second Bull Run. This time,

At Bull Run, fierce fighting at close range led to many casualties.—VIRGINIA MILITARY INSTITUTE MUSEUM

she was given a freight car for her trip to the battlefield. On arriving at Fairfax Station, she talked a provost into assigning dozens of prisoners to her under a work detail. Since they had no stretchers, some of the prisoners carried wounded men in their arms. Others were put to work digging graves. During her first evening at the new site, Barton stumbled upon one of her old pupils, Charles Hamilton. Though his right arm was mangled, he awkwardly tried to embrace her with his left.

Before she had even finished with men wounded at Second Bull Run, casualties from Chantilly began flowing into Fairfax Station in what seemed to be a never-ending stream. If Chantilly represented a stream, Antietam could only be called a tidal wave. Having learned that "a big battle [was] shaping up," she drove an army wagon to a sight close to Sharpsburg, Maryland. There she slept on September 16, 1862, on the edge of the battlefield. She was the only woman known for sure to have been among the 75,000 men of the Army of the Potomac.

Not until long afterward did anyone even make an approximate tally of the more than 25,000 casualties incurred between daylight and dark on September 17. About the same number of men from each side fell, and Barton gave stricken Confederates the same care she extended to Federals. Finding a wounded man lying in a field, she bent to offer him a drink of water. Suddenly, the object of her compassion jerked. According to her own account, "The poor fellow sprang from my hands and fell back quivering in the agonies of death. A bullet had passed between my body and the right arm which supported him, cutting through my sleeve and passing through his chest from shoulder to shoulder."

Official resistance to her volunteer work, already beginning to melt, was completely dissipated in the aftermath of Antietam. When the Army of the Potomac moved slowly into Virginia, she went with the IX Corps at the head of four wagons and an ambulance. By mid-December, she was at Fredericksburg again. Hurrying in response to an appeal from the surgeon of the 21st Massachusetts regiment, a shell took off part of her dress as she scurried across a pontoon bridge. Without even attempting to mend it, she proceeded to an improvised hospital for her work as a nurse. That night, perhaps for the first time, she used her untrained voice to encourage the wounded by singing "Rally Round the Flag, Boys."

Her mind, she said afterward when questioned about Fredericksburg, was not "big enough to deal with 12,000 casualties." Her most vivid memory of the place was a waist-high pile of amputated arms and legs near one of the city's elegant dwellings. Used as a hospital, the mansion's floor was so thick with blood that she had to stop periodically and wring it from her skirt.

In 1864 she went far to the south and worked for a time at Hilton Head, South Carolina. There she learned that the U.S. Navy was trying to besiege Charleston, where the conflict was certain to cause many casualties. She was on Morris Island, close to Charleston, when black soldiers from Massachusetts tried to take Battery Wagner from its Rebel defenders.

Back in Washington for the second inauguration of President Lincoln, whom she never met in person, for the first time she gained an official title from Gen. Benjamin F. Butler. Wounded men had long known her as "Angel of the Battlefield"; officers now saluted when they encountered the new superintendent of nurses, Army of the James.

With the U.S. Sanitary Commission and the huge staff of the surgeon general working hard, Clara Barton continued doing practically everything she had been doing before as a volunteer. Despite her splendid title, she needed a new goal in life. She realized that with the conflict winding down, tens of thousands of relatives and friends knew nothing about the fate of their loved ones. She had found her new goal: It was time, she decided, to turn from hauling supplies and tending the wounded to "collecting and imparting information respecting the lost."

Three attempts to see Lincoln to get his backing for her new crusade proved fruitless. For a month, however, she carried with her everywhere a letter from Gen. William Hoffman, commissary general of prisoners. Himself a prisoner of war in 1861, the New York native took a bold step in February 1865 when he ordered officers at Camp Parole in Annapolis, Maryland, to give Barton every possible assistance. She was granted permission to post notices and ask questions of parolees from the South. She was warned that under no circumstances was she to try to get information "on which to base a claim [by a Union veteran] for pay or allowances." As publicly announced, her goal seemed deceptively simple. She said she wished "to be the means of informing the friends of prisoners who have been in the hands of the enemy of their fate." To do so, she'd have to find the names of men who had died and try to locate their graves.

At the time, she had no idea what she was starting. Of the estimated 300,000 graves of Union soldiers, only about 165,000 bore any identifying information. At least 40,000 men seemed to have vanished without a trace and were believed dead. In Georgia, officials at Andersonville prison alone had put their dead into about 10,000 unmarked graves.

Probably through the influence of Senator Henry Wilson, Lincoln signed a terse directive only a few days—but possibly only a few hours—before he made his fateful trip to Ford's Theatre:

To the friends of missing persons:

Miss Clara Barton has kindly offered to search for the missing prisoners of War. Please address her at Annapolis, Maryland, giving name, regiment, and company of any missing prisoner.

Brief as it was, the undated memorandum was enough to get started for the woman whom some officers called "Hell-cat in Calico." During the days the assassinated president's body lay in state, she wrote more than one hundred letters concerning soldiers whose records were not complete.

Clara Barton, president of the American Red Cross.

Soon she had a new and official title: general correspondent for the friends of paroled prisoners. From her Annapolis headquarters she issued in early May a preliminary list of men missing from some units. To her dismay, the list was so long that no private printer in Washington had a sufficient number of capital letters to set it in type.

When President Andrew Johnson learned of the dilemma, he acted with the promptness Barton had sought but did not get from Lincoln. John Defrees, superintendent of the Government Printing Office, received a June 3 notice: "Let this printing be done as speedily as possible, consistent with the public interest." Though it didn't have its modern name in 1865, the Patent Office clerk who was still on leave from her job had launched the beginning of the MIA movement.

At Andersonville Prison in Georgia, Dorence Atwater was her unpaid chief assistant for many weeks. Together they compiled incredibly long lists of missing men. Eventually, many of their graves were identified and marked. When Barton ended this phase of her work, she claimed to have identified about 16,000 men whose relatives had received no information from the War Department. Some present-day analysts say that she actually found and transmitted evidence of at least 22,000 MIAs.

Without seeking fame, it was bestowed on her by the general public. She became one of the most highly paid lecturers of the period and used some of her earnings to visit Geneva, Switzerland. There she became acquainted with leaders of an organization called the Red Cross.

Much of its work was based on the 1864 Treaty of Geneva for the Relief of Sick and Wounded Soldiers. Twelve nations had accepted this document, but the United States had not been among them.

After years of hard work at home, in 1882 Clara Barton persuaded President Chester Arthur to put his influence behind a movement to get Congress to ratify the Geneva Treaty. Once that was accomplished, the American Red Cross came into existence, and the "angel of the Civil War battlefield" became its first president. In that capacity, she succeeded in extending the scope of the organization's work to include "any great national calamity," such as hurricanes, tornadoes, forest fires, earthquakes, epidemics, and floods. Known internationally as the American Amendment, her modification of the original goal was accepted by the international Red Cross movement.

Though she was notable as "the most decorated woman in American history," she remained a maverick to the end. In her leadership role, it was inevitable that she come under criticism from some quarters. Fuming that she didn't have to suffer such indignities, she resigned from the American Red Cross. She promptly founded a rival society, the National First Aid of America.

Had she been less feisty and more willing to take orders, Barton might have stayed on the government payroll until she retired and faded into obscurity. Because she ignored conventional standards and did what no sensible person believed any woman should or could do, Clara Barton's Civil War accomplishments will be recounted for generations to come.

19
Phoebe Pember
Observant Matron

"Will you let me have your hair cut? You can't get well with all that dirty hair hanging about your eyes and ears."

"No, I can't git my hair cut, 'cause as how I promised my mammy that I would let it grow till the war be over. Oh, it's unlucky to cut it!"

"Then I can't write a letter for you," matron Phoebe Pember responded, according to her account written later. "Do what I wish you to do, and then I will oblige you."

Attenuated and jaundiced, the homesick Confederate from Georgia, called Gouber by many of his comrades, yielded. Once his hair had been cut, Pember sat by his bed as he talked and wrote for him a letter that began "My Dear Mammy."

Gouber was one of more than 78,000 men who passed through Chimborazo, the largest military installation to escape listing in the index of the *Official Records*. Omission from its approximately 126,000 pages about the Civil War is even more striking because 168 volumes of records about Chimborazo and Head Matron Phoebe Yates Pember eventually found their way into the National Archives.

Phoebe Yates, daughter of wealthy Jewish parents, had moved to Savannah, Georgia, at about age seventeen. There she married merchant Thomas Pember of Boston, who died of tuberculosis a few weeks after Fort Sumter. The widow of the Savannah merchant is said to have had a premonition that the port city of Richmond would soon be the subject of attack by soldiers in blue. Two years before Sherman's 1864 March to the Sea, she left the Georgia coast and headed north. Travel was restricted, and no one knows how she managed to get there, but she arrived in the Confederate capital just before the close of the year.

Authorities in the Confederate capital were initially suspicious of the Jewish woman who had no good reason for being there. Probably suspecting she was a spy, they questioned her at great length for several days. In the course of these sessions it was learned that she had more than casual knowledge of medicine and had experience as a nurse. Confederate Surgeon General Samuel Moore was happy to learn that a native of his hometown of Charleston had just reached town. Furthermore, he was eager to find a woman to head much of the work at the city's hospital. When Moore learned that Pember was a close friend of the wife of Confederate Secretary of War George W. Randolph, he offered her a post as head matron at Chimborazo.

"We have erected here a truly great hospital," an officer told Mrs. Pember in almost the same breath with which he informed her that she was no longer under suspicion. "One of the divisions of the hospital has no head matron; the woman who was there died of bilious fever only last week. Will you take her place?"

"I am loyal to the Confederate States of America," said the woman who had been born in Charleston. "If you need me, and if you think I can do the job, I will give it my best."

Escorted to the sprawling facility, she was dismayed to find that it was not as splendid as she had expected. Row after row of long frame buildings stretched from the edge of a ravine "nearly as far as the eye could see." A hasty inspection showed the hospital to be great only in size. Many of the attendants wandered about aimlessly, letting sick and wounded men fend for themselves much of the time. Rotting filth plus the odor from gangrenous wounds produced a stench so distinctive and powerful that residents of Richmond dubbed the fumes simply "Chimborazo."

Scores of buildings dotted the side of a ravine when Pember took charge of housekeeping at the immense Chimborazo Hospital.

Confederate leaders decided that much of the institution's problems stemmed from the use of male nurses. Many of these nurses were soldiers recovering from wounds or illness themselves, and were not yet strong enough to return to their units. They were, however, considered suitable for nursing duty. These men, plus many of the ragtag patients under their care, were usually so disheveled that society ladies of the capital derided them as "hospital rats." Phoebe made a mental note to be sure to remember that name—not knowing that she would herself later stir up quite a commotion about these rodents.

Partly in order to get rid of "the Chimborazo odor," she discovered, the Confederate Congress had taken a bold step. In September 1862, shortly before Pember reached the capital, lawmakers set aside a substantial appropriation. Under the terms of their action, this money was to be used to hire female nurses to care for most or all of the thousands of men who were found in the hospital's wards.

Pember was expected to oversee "the entire domestic economy of fifteen buildings." She was instructed to take charge of the administration of medicines, see that food was properly cooked, and supervise subordinates in such a fashion that "beds and bedding will be clean and orderly." As if that was not enough to keep a woman busy, formal legislation instructed these female nurses to "attend to all such other duties as may be necessary."

Inquiry revealed that at least 17,000 critically wounded men came to the immense installation. Others who spent time there were suffering from a variety of maladies that had nothing to do with combat. Many were simply worn out from constant marching and fighting. Much more than a hospital in the modern sense, the Richmond institution was a major site for what today would be called "rest and recuperation" for battle-weary soldiers. In official papers, it was listed not as a general hospital but as an army post.

For reasons she never explained and perhaps didn't fully understand herself, the new head matron responsible for one of the hospital's five divisions began carefully observing her surroundings and the people in it. She immediately began making lengthy notes about what she saw and heard. On her first day, Pember learned that Chimborazo Hospital got its name from a South American site that was vaguely similar to the tract of land on which the hospital was built. She was elated to learn that the hill on which the institution sat had three good springs, which could furnish more pure water than could be used. When she noticed a cavernous ravine and asked about it, she was told that it separated the hospital from the city very well.

Head Matron Phoebe Yates Pember was some-times painfully observant of persons and events around her.

According to Pember's records, Chimborazo included seventy-five wards, each three hundred square feet in size and designed to accommodate forty to sixty men. Borrowing from military terminology, the wards were grouped into five divisions and each was named for a seceded state. As head matron of a division, she was responsible for six to nine hundred men.

Pember joyfully began her official duties for the Confederacy on December 1, 1862. Surgeons soon noticed what they described as "a remarkable change in the atmosphere." More than 8,000 beds and the rooms in which they sat were now clean and tidy, meals were being delivered to patients on time, and formerly despondent men began to smile as a result of having had a bedside visit from the chief matron.

Surgical fever, inflammation of bones, and blood poisoning were probably reduced as a result of the bold move toward cleanliness. These and other "hospital killers" were by no means conquered entirely, however. Many nights found the dead-houses of two or more wards literally packed with corpses. An estimated 77,800 men were sent to Chimborazo, and about 16,000 of them died there. Most were buried in Richmond's Oakwood Cemetery, but some bodies were shipped to other points throughout the South.

Under Pember and her matrons, use of adjunct physical facilities also flourished. At Tree Hill Farm, loaned to Chimborazo by Franklin Stearns, the hospital's herd of cows grew to about two hundred head. At times, the place also held five hundred goats. A canal boat bearing the name of the institution began to make regular runs to cities such as Lynchburg and Lexington to barter cotton yarn and hospital-made shoes for fresh vegetables, fruits, poultry, and eggs.

One problem proved insoluble, however. Officially listed as an adjunct of the Quartermaster's Corps, Chimborazo depended on that organization for many basic supplies. Mounting shortages among Confederate armies made it difficult for matrons to secure enough wood to fire even one of the stoves in each ward, regardless of how cold it might be outside. Food was supposed to be provided by the Commissary Department, but salt and flour were often in short supply—to say nothing of coffee and meat. Sometimes it was possible to get a few days' supply of meat by slaughtering the goats at Tree Hill Farm.

The price of rations, about 35 cents per person per day in 1861, soared to $2.50 in 1865. On any given day when any supplies stipulated by the regulations were not needed, Phoebe Pember had the cash equivalent deposited in the hospital fund. No other money was ever received by Chimborazo; yet, by the end of 1863 books of the institution showed that a balance of $316,712 was available—all of it squirreled away, bit by bit, from the rations allowance.

April 2, 1865, saw the institution caring for only 1,453 patients. Those who were even marginally ambulatory had left in a hurry because they feared Federal takeover of Richmond. When the evening check was made on the day bluecoats moved into the Confederate capital, only 644 beds were occupied. Walking through her nearly empty wards, Pember mused that:

> Every man who could crawl had tried to escape a Northern prison. Beds in which paralyzed, rheumatic, and helpless patients had lain for months were empty. The miracles of the New Testament had been re-enacted. The lame, the halt, and the blind had been cured. Those who were compelled to remain were almost wild at being left in what would be the enemy's lines the next day; for in many instances they had been exchanged prisoners only a short time before. I gave all the comfort I could, and with some difficulty their supper also, for my detailed nurses had gone with General Lee's army, and my black cooks had deserted me.

She probably didn't know it at the time, but the observant matron was the last Confederate holding an official position to leave conquered Richmond.

She wrote page after page about what she saw and heard during the hours in which the death knell of the Confederacy was sounded

One page of the hospital's report for May 1864.

by explosions and fires that decimated the once-proud city. "Our Confederacy is gone with a crash," she told her journal.

The arrival of the Federal troops was not nearly as fearful as many folk had believed it would be, she noted. Many citizens of the capital had boasted earlier that he had never seen one of the newfangled "greenbacks" that Abraham Lincoln had ordered into use in lieu of currency that could be redeemed in gold or silver. "People who had boxes of Confederate money and were wealthy the day previously," Pember noted, "looked around in vain for wherewithal to buy a loaf of bread. Strange exchanges were made on the street of tea and coffee, flour and bacon."

Representatives of the U.S. Sanitary Commission reached Richmond soon after it was occupied by Union soldiers. They opened shops and handed out "order to draw rations," noted the hospital matron, "but to effect this, after receiving tickets, required so many appeals to different officials, that decent people gave up the effort."

At this point in her notations about life that swirled around her, the matron-turned-writer inserted one of her many flashes of wry humor. The difficulty of finding one's way through the bureaucratic maze aside, she noted, "The must corn-meal and strong cod-fish were not appreciated by fastidious stomachs [of Richmond's remaining citizens]—few gently nurtured [persons] could relish such unfamiliar food."

Pathos was more prevalent than humor in her record of what happened when Federal soldiers took over Richmond. She wrote:

> Bravely dressed Federal officers met their former old classmates from colleges and military institutions and inquired after the relatives to whose houses they had ever been welcome in days of yore, expressing a desire to "call and see them" while the vacant chairs, rendered vacant by Federal bullets, stood by the hearth of the widow and bereaved mother. They could not be made to understand that their presence was painful.

Women of the South, she emphasized, still fought a battle for the dead; they "fought it resentfully, calmly, but silently! Clad in their mourning garments, overcome but hardly subdued, they sat within their desolate homes."

Nearly two decades after she witnessed the fall of Richmond and its aftermath, the former head matron succeeded where many diarists failed. She managed to publish her memoirs under the title *A Southern Woman's Story*. No other account of hospital life in the Confederacy or the political intrigues of the Rebel capital is as filled with explicit details. Numerous complicated surgical procedures were described by her in layman's terms. She told how shattered portions of a femur had been removed, shortening the victim's leg barely an inch. Several vivid accounts deal with the treatment of compound fractures of the skull.

One report of what she labeled "a surgical procedure" would never have been penned by a male physician. Wounded in the instep of his left foot, a Virginian identified only as Patterson developed "a great lump of proud flesh, which formed in the center of the wound like an island." Surgeons were afraid to remove this mass, fearing that it was connected with nerves in his foot.

Making her rounds one morning, Pember found Patterson almost delirious with joy. He showed her that "the little island was gone, and a deep hollow left, but the wound [was] washed clean and looking healthy." Patterson, she said, dozed off the night before and slept so soundly that he was not awakened by the work of "some skillful rat surgeon," who ate the putrid flesh and left the wound clean.

Thinking of that rodent and the many others she saw in Chimborazo, the high-born Charleston native offered the "curious gourmets" among her readership a recipe unlike any other ever put on paper by a cultured and educated woman. Even if she had committed no other experiences to print, this unique recipe, formulated by ravenously hungry men, would have told us more than volumes could about everyday life in the world's biggest hospital at the midpoint of the nineteenth century.

> The rat must be skinned, cleaned, his head cut off and his body laid upon a square board, the legs stretched to their fullest extent and secured upon it with small tacks, then baste with bacon fat and roast before a good fire quickly like canvas-back ducks.

20

Katharine Prescott Wormeley

70,000 Army Shirts

*To think or speak of the things we see would be fatal. No one must
come here who cannot put away all feeling. Do all you can, and be
a machine—that's the way to act; the only way. . . . Such a scene as
we entered and lived in for two days I trust never to see again.*

Katharine Wormeley, Civil War Nurse

Born in England to a rear admiral in the British Navy, Katharine
Prescott Wormeley was an unlikely candidate to serve as a nurse
during Virginia's Peninsular Campaign in the summer of 1862.
But she and many like her traded in their pampered lifestyles to care for
wounded soldiers in the early months of the Civil War.

Few of these women kept any record of their experiences; Wormeley
was an exception. At every opportunity, she paused to write family and
friends, who saved her correspondence. Following is one of the few records
available about the contributions of the Civil War nurse—an important
personality of the era that received little documentation or attention.

Her unforgettable experiences during four months aboard a hospital
transport were published in 1888 with the title *The Other Side of War;*
it was an intimate depiction of a nurse's life. In one of her early letters,
she wrote: "Men in every condition of horror, shattered and shrieking
were brought in on stretchers borne by 'contrabands,' who dumped
them anywhere, banged the stretchers against pillars and posts and
walked over the men without compassion."

Her service following the Battle of Fair Oaks was perhaps her most
trying assignment. She wrote:

> Conceive of the Medical Director sending down over
> four thousand five hundred wounded men without—
> yes, almost literally without—anything for them: with-
> out surgeons; no one to take charge of them; nothing

but empty boats to receive them. . . . You can't conceive what it is to stem the torrent of this disorder and utter want of organization. . . . Imagine a great river or Sound steamer filled on every deck—every berth and every square inch covered with wounded men; even the stairs and the gangways and guards filled with those who are less badly wounded; and then imagine another fifty well men . . . rushing to and fro over them, every touch bringing agony to the poor fellows, while stretcher after stretcher came along hoping to find an empty place. . . . I do not suffer under the sights; but oh! the sounds, the screams of men. It is when I think of it afterwards that it is so dreadful.

Women of the early 1860s were generally not exposed to such a scene. But Katharine felt called to do her part. In spite of her British birthplace, she considered herself an American. Her father was born in Virginia as a grandson of Attorney General John Randolph. Her mother, a native of Massachusetts, was the niece of Cmdr. Edward Preble, who founded the U.S. Navy. Her parents undoubtedly nourished her sense of obligation to public service.

The transition from aristocratic young woman to seasoned nurse began in the spring of 1861. Katharine lived with her mother in Newport, Rhode Island, at a time when patriotic citizens felt the call to aid the Union. Many people there were removed from the war, but wanted to do something to support the cause.

Women in particular were eager to assist, so they formed societies and sewing circles to make articles for the soldiers. All too often, however, the groups would either send totally useless items or have them delivered to the wrong location. As this trend rippled across the country, it became clear that a central organization for the effort was needed.

At an informal gathering in New York in April 1861, the Women's Central Relief Association organized to coordinate the work. Similar groups were formed that spring and summer in Ohio, Connecticut, Massachusetts, and Rhode Island. The head of the Woman's Union Aid Society of Newport, Rhode Island, was none other than thirty-one-year-old Katharine Wormeley. Women first met in her home and accumulated supplies and clothes. Patrons, churches, and the nearby U.S. Naval Academy funded their efforts.

To assist the women in organizing, several gentlemen made an excursion to Washington to see what other roles citizens could play.

One of these men was the Rev. Dr. Henry W. Bellows, a Unitarian minister from New York. He suggested meeting with government officials to find out what the medical corps was already doing, what jobs they could not do, and what help they desired.

At first, the powers that be were less than enthusiastic. Some doctors were neutral, some dubious, and others flatly opposed. The president himself reportedly called the idea "a fifth wheel to the coach." It was the surgeon general who was finally convinced. On June 9, 1861, President Lincoln and his secretary of war established the United States Sanitary Commission—often regarded as the predecessor of the American Red

Like the unidentified nurse shown here, Wormeley initially thought she could care for the wounded in "street attire."— "In the Hospital," 1861 watercolor, William Ludwell Sheppard

Cross. Fortunately, a man of great skill was readily available to serve as general secretary. In Wormeley's opinion, "The organizing genius of Frederick Law Olmstead made the Sanitary Commission what it practically became—a great machine running side by side with the Medical Bureau wherever the armies went." She was awed when she realized that under Olmstead's direction and "during its existence, it received $4,924,480.99 in money, and the value of $15 million in supplies."

From inspecting drainage sites and hospitals to providing for the needs of cooks and nurses, the commission's charge was to ensure the health and safety of Union soldiers. Perhaps the most useful role the Sanitary Commission played was bringing order to the civilian relief effort. Branches of the commission were set up in several large cities, where they received supplies from smaller collection centers. Contributed items were sorted, labeled, and shipped in an organized fashion. Weekly reports of on-hand items were generated so supplies could be sent to the proper locations.

The twenty-one-member all-male commission oversaw the inspections of 870 regiments in the first two years of the war. Dr. Henry G. Clark, along with sixty volunteers, led inspections of all general hospitals in the

Logo of the U.S. Sanitary Commission.—LIBRARY OF CONGRESS

country. Many records of the commission now rest in the Astor Library in New York

While the Sanitary Commission was being established, Katharine Wormeley's local society was busily at work. On one occasion, the society received a notice from Washington that stressed an immediate need for bed sacks. The ladies went to work procuring materials. Every available sewing machine in Newport was put to work. Within twenty-four hours, the society had shipped seventy-five bed sacks and did the same the next day.

But the production of common flannel shirts set Katharine's work apart from others. Here, her great skill as an organizer and administrator flourished. She saw a problem and was not content until she had solved it. Newark, New Jersey, had an annual influx of wealthy summer residents who supported the work of the society by "sponsoring" underprivileged women in town by supplying the money needed for their wages as employees of the Woman's Union Aid Society. Many of these underprivileged women had sons, brothers, and fathers serving in the war, and they needed employment to support themselves and their families. Wormeley trained them to make flannel shirts and hospital clothing. The women produced these essential items in great quantities.

Unfortunately, at the end of the summer when their benefactors departed, these workers were left jobless. Katharine grappled with a solution. She contacted the sympathetic Col. D. H. Vinton, who was in charge of the U.S. Army office of clothing and equipment. Using her persuasive personality, she convinced him to give her a contract for army shirts. She wrote:

> During the winter of 1861–62, we made over seventy thousand. The Department paid me fourteen cents a shirt, and furnished the flannel and the buttons. I paid the women eleven cents a shirt (they could easily make four a day, without a machine), and the remaining three cents just covered the cost of linen-thread, transportation to and from New York, office and workroom expenses. The ladies of Newport helped me cut the shirts.

Katharine was particularly proud that not one of her shirts was returned as flawed. Close to $6,000 was earned by members of one hundred families who would have been otherwise unemployed.

But Katharine was not finished yet. Just as her shirt contract was running out, another challenge for her to engage surfaced. The Sanitary Commission had recently formed the Hospital Transport Service to shuttle supplies and care for the wounded in a swampy area near the Potomac. Steamboats large enough to hold a thousand men were chartered and refurbished as floating hospitals. These vessels received the sick and wounded straight from the battlefields and transported them to safe destinations.

One of Olmstead's first volunteer appointees was Mrs. William Preston Griffin, an acquaintance of Katharine Wormeley. Griffin left on the first run of the first commissioned ship, the *Daniel Webster*. On hearing about the new program, Katharine quickly wrote a letter volunteering her services; she boarded the *Daniel Webster* when it returned.

Other ships in service were the *Elm City,* the *S.R. Spaulding,* the *Knickerbocker,* the *Vanderbilt,* the *Elizabeth,* the *Wissahicken,* the *Louisiana,* and the *State of Maine.* The *Wilson Small* also provided living quarters for Olmstead and his associates and served as the headquarters for the Hospital Transport Service. Once, near Yorktown, Katharine had been assigned to the *Wilson Small.*

The female volunteers were mostly from wealthy families and unaccustomed to physical labor—much less caring for the seriously wounded. They soon experienced a completely different way of life on the boats. To their credit, they endured the circumstances and worked steadfastly. One of the first changes Katharine noted was a change in the dress code:

> I have done my first work—making the beds. How you would laugh to see me without a hoop mounted on the second tier of births, making the beds on the third tier. . . . We shuffle about without hoops. Mrs. Griffin says it is de rigueur that they shall not be worn in hospital service. I like it very well aboard ship: it is becoming to Miss Whetten, who is symmetry itself; but it must be owned that some of us look rather medieval.

Her duties ranged from bathing and feeding the incoming patients to cooking to organizing and replenishing supply closets and pantries. Newly arrived patients were always thirsty; many had been stranded in

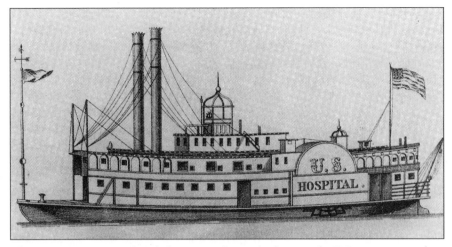

The USS D. A. January, *a truly luxurious ship under lease to the U.S. government that was converted for hospital use early in 1862.*—LIBRARY OF CONGRESS

the fields for days without food or water. Beef tea, milk punch, lemonade, and a gruel-like soup called panada were the usual fare. Often, there were several hundred soldiers to serve on a ship that carried only a handful of staff members. On one occasion, eight hundred lemons were squeezed in one day.

The staff of the ship was on call constantly when new arrivals came in. Sleep was a luxury, and traditional furniture was not to be found. "Our dinner table [was] the top of an old stove, with slices of bread for plates, fingers for knives and forks, and carpet-bags for chairs—all this because everything available is being used for our poor fellows," Wormeley observed. One evening she was roused from sleep to receive a clean mattress because the previous one had been occupied by a typhoid patient.

One of the most important tasks of a nurse was to write letters for the soldiers, many of whom were dying. Pen in hand, Wormeley listened patiently and jotted down a few of her own thoughts in the intervals:

> I went . . . to attend . . . to a Southern colonel, a splendid-looking man, who died, saying with raised hand: "Write to my wife and tell her I die penitent for the part I have taken in this war." One of our men stopped me saying: "He's a rebel; give that to me." I said, "But a wounded man is our brother!" and they both touched their caps.

Death was a daily occurrence and often presented new tasks for the nurses. The wife of deceased soldier Simeon A. Newman had written numerous letters requesting that his sash be returned. No one could honor her request because his knapsack was lost. While searching for supplies, Katharine found the missing knapsack on board the *Wilson Small*. This presented her the unpleasant task of sending it to his grieving widow. Mortality was so high that one of the nurses on the ship developed the practice of pinning name tags on the patients so that notifying the families in the event of death would be more efficient.

Bathing the sick soldiers was one of the more difficult tasks, even under the best of circumstances, and almost impossible when supplies were inadequate. Wormeley wrote of this aspect aboard a hospital transport:

> I started each row with two tin basins and two bits of soap, my arm being the towel-horse. Now, you are not to suppose that each man had a basinful of clean water all to himself. However, I thought three to a basin was enough, or four, if they didn't wash too hard. But an old corporal taught me better. "Stop, marm!" said he, as I was turning back with the dirty water to get fresh; "that water will do for several of us yet. Bless you! I make my coffee of worse than that."

Nurses rarely had an opportunity to bathe or to change into clean clothes themselves; Wormeley, being from Newport, one of the most elegant cities in the nation, admitted:

> This matter of dirt and stains is becoming very serious. My dresses are in such a state that I loathe them, and myself in them. From chin to belt they are yellow with lemon-juice, sticky with sugar, greasy with beef-tea, and pasted with milk-porridge. Farther down, I dare not inquire into them. Somebody said the other day that he wished to kiss the hem of my garment. I thought of the condition of that article and shuddered.

The only readily available solution for filthy clothing was to borrow old shirts from a doctor who was returning to New York.

A nurse's work was greatly complicated by the many doctors' lack of medical training and knowledge of sterilization techniques. Many "doctors" were merely apprentices. Harvard University did not acquire microscopes or stethoscopes until after the war. The surgeon general of Federal forces was quoted as saying that the Civil War took place "at the end of the medical Middle Ages." It became taken for granted that one patient in four would die—and many of the most seriously wounded men never even reached a hospital.

In the field, doctors went for days without washing their hands or their instruments. A soldier was much more likely to die of disease than injury. Researchers estimate that three out of five Union solders and two out of three Rebel soldiers died of disease. Intestinal illness accounted for close to half of the deaths from disease, with pneumonia and tuberculosis taking a heavy toll. Typhoid fever was a major culprit—accounting for nearly one-fourth of deaths from disease. Doctors and nurses were far from immune; out of the small staff on Katharine's ship, one doctor died and another became so ill that he was sent home.

In the middle of the most tumultuous period in America's history, nurses aboard a hospital transport kept going, despite the filth and suffering, because they felt that they were helping their nation. They were in close proximity to crucial battles, military leaders, and historic sites. Barely two weeks into her volunteer position, Katharine boarded a ship crossing the Chesapeake Bay. When she spotted a fire in the distance she wondered what it could be and learned that the vital Gosport Naval Yard at Norfolk had been torched. She later heard a noise so deafening that she couldn't imagine its source, but was soon told that it was produced by an explosion that destroyed the CSS *Virginia*—previously the USS *Merrimac*.

On a trip to Yorktown, Katharine collected some relics to send to a friend. Her coworkers were particularly envious of one item—an iron pulley from a gun that Gen. George B. McClellan had called "impertinent this morning." Katharine also saw the former headquarters of the Marquis de Lafayette, who played a crucial role in the American Revolution. On this same excursion, the staff visited the hospital at Lord Cornwallis's headquarters and met Dorothea Dix (see Chapter 21), who was in charge of nurses serving in the Army Medical Bureau.

Katharine and the other nurses were close to battles, such as Williamsburg, Fair Oaks, and Malvern Hill (also known as Seven Pines). They even helped occasionally in the field hospitals. One of her letters speaks of a close look at the president. Katharine wrote:

> For the last two hours I have been watching President Lincoln and General McClellan as they sat together, in earnest conversation, on the deck of a steamer close to

us. I am thankful, I am happy, that the President has come—has sprung across that dreadful, intervening Washington, and come to see and hear and judge for his own wise and noble self. The President stood on deck with a glass, with which, after a time, he inspected our boat, waving his handkerchief to us. We watched the earnest conversation which went on, and which lasted till 6 P.M.; then they rose and walked side by side ashore—the President, in a shiny black coat and stove-pipe hat, a whole head and shoulders taller

Young Frederick Law Olmstead dressed for a tour of inspection.—MUSEUM OF THE CITY OF NEW YORK

than the General. Mr. Lincoln mounted a horse and together they rode off, the dragoons wheeling round to follow, their sabres gleaming in the sunlight. The cannon are firing salutes—a sound of strange peacefulness to us, after the angry irregular boomings and the sharp scream of the shells to which we are accustomed.

The Union fell short of its goals in the Peninsular Campaign, leaving Washington in a vulnerable position. Some historians call it the high point of the war for the Confederacy. Katharine Wormeley was in the midst of the retreat and saw firsthand the famous USS *Monitor* on the James River as the campaign came to a close.

When her duties with the Hospital Transport Service ended, she was appointed by the U.S. surgeon general as superintendent of nursing for a general hospital. In the publishing world, she gained quite a bit of fame as a translator for the works of Honoré de Balzac and as the author of two books, *The Other Side of War* (her letters), published by the Massachusetts Loyal Legion of the United States in 1888, and *Civil War Nurse,* published by Ticknor in 1889.

Her experiences as a Civil War nurse made a lifelong impression on her. The gratitude of the men stayed with her throughout her years. One amputee, turning to her with tears streaming down his face as he strained to pull something into his bunk, pressed some wrinkled pink paper (its contents unspecified) into her hand and said, "I heard you tell that man you gave him the last pin out of your dress: don't give us everything; please take these." Gratitude was the positive part of her service, but as the title of her book *The Other Side of War* suggests, she saw something quite different in it:

> Any one who looks over such a deck as that, and sees the suffering, despondent attitudes of the men, and their worn frames and faces, knows what war is, better than the sight of wounds can teach it. It is a piteous sight to see; no one knows what war is until they see this black side of it. We may all sentimentalize over its possibilities as we see the regiments go off, or when we hear of a battle; but it is as far from the reality as to read of pain is far from feeling it.

21

Dorothea Dix

Indomitable

S weeping into a reception room, a woman described by the clerk as "old enough to be my grandmother, but lookin' like she had royal blood" flashed a *carte de visite*. She had personal business with the surgeon general, she told him, and it was most urgent. Minutes later Dorothea Lynde Dix was ushered into the private office of Robert C. Wood.

Few men, much less women, could have gained such quick access to a high-level military officer. Most women would have waited three or four days without even getting a glimpse of the man they wanted to see. Wood's visitor of April 20, 1861, was not "of royal blood," but she was as imperious as any American female at the midpoint of the nineteenth century could be. The acting surgeon general had not yet met this woman from the Northeast in person, but he was nonetheless keenly aware of her influence in the capital. It was generally known that Secretary of State William H. Seward regarded her as an intimate and highly influential friend. She had proposed using proceeds from the sale of public lands to build institutions for the insane, and it had passed both houses of Congress—only to be vetoed by President Franklin Pierce.

"What brings you back to the capital?" he inquired. "According to the city's newspapers, you should be in Tennessee, making plans to establish a new institution."

"I left there some time ago, assured that my time had not been wasted," Dix replied. "My heart is still with the nation's poor wretches who are treated worse than animals, but my head has told me that I am likely to be needed here.

"I was at the New Jersey State Lunatic Hospital when Governor Andrew sent a regiment here," Dix continued. "Three hours after I heard that these men had been fired upon in Baltimore, I left Trenton

193

Confidential secretaries John Hay, standing, and John G. Nicolay were thrilled by Dix's offer, which was not immediately accepted. —Harper's Weekly

with only a few essential items in my valise. I am here to organize an Army Nursing Corps that will be made up of mature and experienced women who will serve without pay."

Taken by surprise, Wood only nodded his comprehension. He then explained what she already knew—that the U.S. Army used only male nurses. Pulling out a sheaf of papers, he thumbed through them and found a recent report that labeled hospital facilities for soldiers as adequate.

Even in the far west at Leavenworth, Kansas, the post hospital could accommodate twenty men, he told her. With twenty-seven surgeons and sixty-two assistant surgeons on the rolls, plus men from every regiment designated as nurses, the Army's top medical officer hesitated to encourage Dix. He told her that her offer, which he judged to have been inspired by the president's call for 75,000 volunteers, was certainly appreciated. But these men would be going home in ninety days at the outside, probably much sooner. That made it highly improbable that any females would be needed for hospital duties.

Dorothea Dix realized that she was getting nowhere with Wood, so she expressed appreciation for his time and said she'd call again soon. When word of her unexpected arrival reached the Executive Mansion, both of the president's confidential secretaries recorded their reaction to the news. In his journal, John G. Nicolay noted that Miss Dix was said to have offered herself "and an army of nurses to the government gratuitously." His immediate subordinate, John Hay, considered her gesture to be "munificent and generous." Still, there is no reason to believe that her visit to Wood was reported to the president himself.

Instead of returning to New Jersey (as most sensible persons would have done after receiving such a rebuff), Dix found lodgings and dug in her heels. Having dealt with governors, legislatures, foreign military commanders, and heads of state for twenty years, she certainly did not regard Wood's verdict as final. Regardless of what he might think, if 75,000 volunteers plus the 15,000 or so professional soldiers of the U.S. Army should clash with Rebels, male nurses wouldn't be able to wipe up all the spilled blood.

The woman rebuffed as an organizer of a corps of female nurses turned her rented home at 500 Twelfth Street into what she called "a receiving station for hospital supplies." She sent notices to Massachusetts newspapers and soon began receiving shirts, havelocks (designed to protect fighting men from unaccustomed exposure to the sun), sheets, and canned foods.

Soon after a conference with U.S. Secretary of War Simon Cameron, Wood called on Dix at her temporary home; unfortunately, she was out. He immediately wrote a memorandum in which he told her, "A very large quantity of medical supplies [had] been ordered from New York." She could help, he suggested, by "instituting preliminary measures" to secure quantities of bandages and lint. On the following day he asked if she could secure five hundred hospital shirts. These garments should be made "long, from common cotton material," he pointed out.

Only a few days after the patriotic women of Boston learned of the Federal need, they sent Dix the hospital shirts she required. Other women spent their spare time unraveling fabric to produce lint, which was "a surgical necessity" when deep wounds had to be packed. Bag after bag of it arrived, along with donations of jelly, milk, eggs, and even chickens from residents of the Washington area. Anything considered likely to prevent scurvy would be received with special gratitude, she informed the public. Soon her home was overflowing; the would-be nurse, who had ample means from her inheritance, rented another house on nearby H Street.

While these preparations to care for wounded men were

Dorothea L. Dix, superintendent of women nurses.—LIBRARY OF CONGRESS

being made, Dix's request to develop an all-female nursing corps was under more serious consideration by Cameron. On April 23 he notified her that the War Department would accept her services. Less than three weeks later, she received a document that certified her as the holder of a newly created post. For the first time in the nation's history, its army would be cared for by women, all of whom would be headed by the Superintendent of Women Nurses.

Before assuming her new role, Dix arranged for the Union Hotel in Georgetown and other properties to be turned into infirmaries. At that moment, she had no idea how they might be used. Each regiment of about a thousand men was supposed to have its own hospital, made up of three special tents and served by a surgeon and two assistants. Drummers, most of whom were small boys, were expected to get men off the field if they were wounded in battle.

Convinced that they'd be needed, regardless of what military leaders believed, Dix sent out calls for women. She specified a number of conditions, however, making it clear that only those who met her criteria would be accepted. The requirements that she laid down included details such as:

> No women under thirty need apply to serve in the government hospitals. All nurses are required to be plain looking women. Their dresses must be brown or black, with no bows, no curls, no jewelry, and no hoop-skirts.

All applicants had to be interviewed by and approved by Dix. She seldom modified her strict standards. She was so taken by one woman, however, that she accepted her despite her cycling costume, which Dix considered "abominable." For her own "hospital costume," She selected "a grey cottonish cross-grained skirt and a Zouave jacket" that allowed her arms to move freely.

Dorothea Dix's early childhood had fostered a great disdain for the Catholic Church. At about age sixteen she was employed as a private teacher for the children of Rhode Island Unitarian Rev. Dr. William Ellery Channing. She became a staunch member of his congregation and traveled to the West Indies with the Channing family. More than a decade later, she was advised to go to England for therapy for her persistent lung trouble. It would have been impossible for her to receive the eighteen months of therapy, had Channing not contacted friends who lived near Liverpool and persuaded them to take Dix into their home as a guest. Her regard for Channing and his views was so great that she did not try to hide her scorn for the Roman Catholic Church and all its adherents. Rigidly opposed to using members of Catholic orders as nurses, she turned away many nuns who were superbly qualified.

She also erected barriers, however, that many Protestant women could not surmount. Working on her organization for only a short time, she spelled out the qualities for which she was looking in a letter to a New York associate, saying:

> No young ladies should be sent at all, but some who can give their services and time and meet part of their expenses or the whole, who will be ready for duty at any hour of day or night—those who are sober, earnest, self-sacrificing, and self-sustained; who can bear the presence of suffering and never lose self control; who can be calm, gentle, quiet, active, and steadfast in duty.

Dix berated the prevalent practice by which commanders permitted many soldiers' wives (or "daughters of the regiment") to stay with troops and act as nurses to the soldiers. She was positive that such women couldn't possibly function in the aftermath of a battle, so she wanted nothing to do with them.

Writing to another friend on May 26, she revealed some of her concerns about having proper nurses available:

> I have written to the secretary of War for a pass to Fortress Monroe where a hospital must be organized. There is soon to be active service, I fear, and our brave men must be provided for if wounded. It would be better to be there during the battle, if there is one, since then we could do the most good. These are strange times and this war truly seems now not unreal.

She and thousands of others found out how very real the struggle was when Federal volunteers with little training and no combat experience met Rebels on the field of Bull Run.

Though she had seen some of the action in the Crimean War, Dix was not prepared for the aftermath of the first significant battle of the Civil War. Wounded and desperately sick men streamed back from Bull Run in such large numbers that the government installations and the infirmaries established by Dix were not big enough to take care of more than just a small fraction of them. She hurried from place to

U.S. Secretary of War Edwin M. Stanton relegated handling of the corps of women nurses to his assistant surgeon general, who subsequently relegated control of it from Dorothea Dix.

place, arranging for the Fairfax Theological Seminary, a Methodist church, and a female seminary to be converted into hospitals and be marked by yellow bunting. Having learned that the Forces commanded by Union Gen. Irvin McDowell had not taken enough ambulances with them, she purchased one from her own funds and dispatched it toward Centreville, Virginia.

In nearby Georgetown, she commandeered the unfinished Union Hotel, even though she knew that it could take care of only about two hundred men if their beds were crowded close together. One of her Georgetown nurses, a Massachusetts woman who was suitably plain, became quite ill and was frequently visited by Dix. Louisa May Alcott (see Chapter 27) said of Dix in her own *Letters and Journals:* "Daily our Florence Nightingale climbed the steep stairs stealing a moment from her busy life, to watch over the stranger of whom she was as thoughtfully tender as any mother."

Anticipating that more hospitals would be needed everywhere that a likelihood of battle existed, Dix traveled far westward in response to a telegram from Gen. John C. Fremont. When she reached St. Louis, she was astonished to find that many residents openly supported the Confederate cause and wanted nothing to do with her work, which was designed to comfort sick and wounded soldiers in blue. Angrily reacting to the mood of the divided city, she sent emergency appeals for funds back to long-established friends in the East, and from Massachusetts alone she received about $500,000.

Regardless of where they were stationed, many military surgeons treated her coldly; others were positively rude. They didn't have to put their feelings into words to make it clear that if they had to put up with female nurses, they preferred to pick their own. Many of the complaints channeled back to Washington had a recurrent theme: Surgeons repeatedly said that nurses chosen by the superintendent of the corps were old enough to think they could ignore military regulations, so long as they pleased Dorothea Dix.

To complicate matters, representatives of the U.S. Sanitary Commission and other relief organizations often clashed with Dix and her aides. Noted reformer George Templeton Strong, an organizer and leader of the Sanitary Commission, received many complaints from St. Louis and once wrote in his diary that "General Fremont seems to have set up a local Sanitary Commission of his own to act under the direction of Miss Dix." An anonymous military analyst reported to Washington that in his opinion, the superintendent of women nurses wanted nothing less than "total control of every phase of her operation."

Dix functioned primarily as an hospital organizer, fund raiser, and supply depot manager. Though never a hands-on, person-to-person nurse in the fashion of Mother Bickerdycke (see Chapter 22) and hundreds of lesser-known volunteers, dozens if not scores of new hospitals, both small and large, sprang up under her direction and were partly or fully staffed by women whom she recruited. Tens of thousands of sick and wounded men got some of the medicine, food, and bandages she distributed in massive quantities. Most of them had no idea that a woman older than sixty years played a dynamic role in the way they were treated when they were incapable of reporting for duty.

One major change in her method of operation became necessary early on. Once the women who met all of her qualifications had enrolled, many fell short of financial independence, and they often came knocking at her door. Male nurses, most of whom were soldiers on special assignment, were paid $20.50 per month plus rations, clothing, and housing. Dix realized that her nurses simply had to be provided trans-

From this miniature of Dix, the U.S. Postal Service designed a commemorative stamp.

portation, food, and a place to sleep. Once this concession had been made, it was only a short step to adopt a cash pay scale of forty cents per day. With this system of compensation by the government in place, the size of Dix's corps soared into the range of 50,000 women.

Numerous women of the period found that success could be dangerous and costly. Dix's organization had become so large and efficient that more and more surgeons registered complaints about its personnel and methods. Keenly aware that her nurses didn't dare question her directives, some of them labeled Dix "a dictator in a petticoat."

To move him out of the cabinet, Lincoln named Cameron as U.S. Minister to Russia in January 1862. Edwin M. Stanton, who succeeded him, was an admirer of Dix, but had his days and nights more than full trying to help direct the course of the war. A new assistant surgeon general, E. D. Townsend, soon became the Washington official with whom Dix dealt. On October 29, 1863, he issued General Orders No. 351. Addressing the matter of "the employment of women nurses in the United States General Hospitals," the lengthy directive was divided into four major parts.

A hasty glance at the document might have suggested that its chief purpose was to record a list of prevailing practices. Any surgeon or hospital administrator who carefully read every word would have recognized, however, that it was carefully drawn up to relegate Dix to a more subordinate role. After December 31, no woman except a few career hospital matrons would be "borne upon the Muster and Pay Rolls" without authorization by a War Department official. On January 1, all female nurses would become directly responsible to the senior medical officer of the hospital in which they worked.

Dix, however, swallowed her pride and concentrated more heavily on matters not covered by the Washington order, which radically altered her status. In the month before Townsend's directive was circulated, Dix had been on the battlefield at Antietam. Holding the head of a badly wounded man in her lap in order to give him water, she saw him jerk and die instantly when a ball hit him directly in the head. She put the man's head down and took her water to the nearest prone sufferer, without bothering to see whether his uniform was blue or gray. Any woman who could do that would have continued to do the best she could, regardless of limitations placed on her work.

Dix tendered her resignation four months after Robert E. Lee surrendered at Appomattox, stipulating that she'd like for it to become effective on September 10. Until then, she devoted most of her time to mustering out her volunteers by the score. Offered both financial compensation and the highly coveted Thanks of Congress award, she let it be known that she wanted neither honor and quietly returned to the Trenton hospital she had founded earlier. There she devoted nearly two years to raising $8,000 to erect a monument to 6,000 men buried near Fortress Monroe. She then resumed her work for what she always called "lunacy reform."

Late in January 1867, she was surprised to receive a large box accompanied by a letter. Opening the letter, which was dated December 3, 1866, she was overcome by emotion. It read:

> In token and acknowledgment of the inestimable services rendered by Miss Dorothea L. Dix for the care, succor, and relief of the sick and wounded soldiers of the United States on the battlefield, in camps, and hospitals during the recent war, and of her benevolent and diligent labors and devoted efforts to whatever might contribute to their comfort and welfare, it is ordered that a stand of arms of the United States colors [a national flag, complete with all accouterments] be presented to Miss Dix.
>
> *Edwin M. Stanton*
> *Secretary of War*

Telling her friends of the unexpected gift from Washington, she said of the flag, "No possession will be so prized while I am alive to love and serve my country."

In retrospect Dorothea Dix's Civil War work was eclipsed by her pioneer crusade for the humane care of the insane. Hence, numerous reference works deal primarily with her long and successful labors on behalf of the mentally ill and give only cursory mention to the establishment and organization of many hospitals and her huge corps of female nurses. Years later, Congress took belated action by providing $10,000 with which to erect "a lasting memorial" to the Civil War's only superintendent of women nurses.

22

Mary Ann Ball Bickerdyke

Human Cyclone

"**C**ome here, young fellow!" the stout woman commanded. "Whadda you want?" was the flippant reply. Not deigning to reply herself, the woman, twice the age of the fledgling lieutenant, demanded: "Bend over."

When he obeyed, Mary Ann Ball Bickerdyke yanked at the neckband of his shirt. Observers in the hospital ward, laughing without restraint, quickly noticed the letters NWSC inside the officer's shirt.

"I thought so," observed the woman, who looked as though she had just stepped off a farm. "Shuck it, this instant!"

When the lieutenant hesitated, his powerfully built inquisitor grabbed him around the waist and wrestled him to the floor. Calmly sitting on him, she casually pulled the offending garment loose, then gestured for him to turn so she could remove it.

With onlookers crowded about them in a tight circle, she examined the waistband of his underpants, shook her head, then turned her attention to his feet. After yanking off his crocheted slippers, she climbed off her target. Extending her right hand to help him rise, she brought the encounter to a close with the comment:

"Young fellow, some of your clothes came from the North Western Sanitary Commission in Chicago. These things ain't for the likes of you; they're for men too sick to get off the flat of their backs."

Thousands of men stationed at Cairo, Illinois, remembered this incident on August 7, 1861, as "the day a cyclone hit the Federal base at the bottom tip of Illinois." The two-legged "cyclone" in a skirt came there from the town of Galesburg, Illinois, near the town of Galena, where Ulysses S. Grant had been living.

Oral tradition supports that humiliation of an officer by a civilian woman took place immediately after Bickerdyke reached Cairo. She

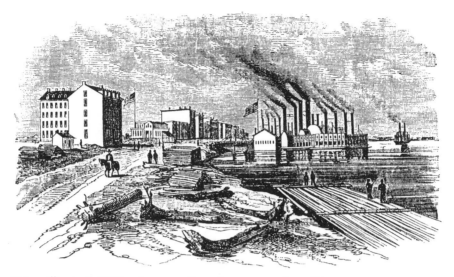

Cairo, Illinois, in 1861.—Pictorial Field Book of the Civil War

came by means of the Illinois Central Railroad in response to a letter from Dr. Benjamin Woodward received by the pastor of the Brick Congregational Church in Galesburg. When Woodward's letter was read from the pulpit, women of Galesburg got busy and didn't stop until they had raised $500. Once the cash was in hand, no one seemed to know what to do with it. According to Woodward's letter, sick Illinois volunteers in the Federal camp were short of just about everything they needed. At a quilting party, inspiration emerged.

"Let Mary Ann buy supplies and take 'em to the base," a friend suggested. "She doesn't have a man about the house to need her, and we can take turns looking after her boys."

A newcomer to Galesburg, Mary Ann Bickerdyke had moved there from Ohio just five years earlier. When her husband of a dozen years dropped dead one day, she decided she might as well continue to make Galesburg her home. Skilled in finding herbs and using them as home remedies, the Quaker woman was soon listed in the city directory as a botanic physician. Plying this vocation, she managed to make a living of sorts for herself and provide for her two sons. Since it was the sick who needed help down where the Ohio flows into the Mississippi, she was a logical choice as the unofficial agent for the women of Galesburg. Many of them were aware that back in Ohio she had spent four years at Oberlin College. What's more, she had trained as a nurse at Cincinnati.

When she stepped off the train, pulling hard on a canvas bag stuffed with $100 worth of supplies for the sick, she asked directions to the hospital. "Which one?" was the response. The organization of volunteer units, she soon learned, was on a regimental basis. With six regiments camped in and around Cairo, there were six hospitals in the sprawling river town, along with half a dozen sets of doctors and nurses. Convalescent soldiers not yet strong enough to drill filled all of the facilities.

When Bickerdyke finally located Dr. Woodward and the men over whom he had charge, she might have gotten sick to her stomach had she had the time. Instead, she swung into action. She instantly discovered that the half dozen sheets stuffed into the bottom of her bag were the only bed linens in the big tent that served as a sick bay. So she gave one sheet to each of the men whom Woodward pointed out as having the worst cases of ague.

Within days of her arrival, the whole place had been scrubbed. Two or three at a time, sick men had shed their grimy underclothing and watched the woman they had begun to call "Mother" take their garments to the tub and wash them clean. Woodward was, if possible, more astonished than the sick men. He jotted in his diary a memorandum that described the volunteer nurse from Galesburg as being "a large, heavy woman of forty-five years, strong as a man; muscles of iron; nerves of steel; sensitive, but self-reliant; kind and tender; seeking all for others, nothing for herself."

"My women got up another $400," she confided to the sufferers from ague. "Soon as I get this place halfway cleaned up, I'll go get so many sheets that a few of you can have a pair."

During most of her second month in the camp, she spent her afternoons inspecting the other five hospital tents and making a start at cleaning them. Each seemed to be dirtier than the last; frustrated and exasperated, she stomped into the headquarters of Gen. Benjamin Prentiss and announced: "We've got five hospitals too many here. Don't need but one, but it has to be big. And a revival tent won't do."

Not sure whether to laugh at his fist-shaking visitor or to signal aides to escort her out, Prentiss pondered her demand. "Maybe you're right," he admitted. "Things couldn't be much worse than they are. There's a half-finished hotel close to the center of town that has never been used. I'll see what I can do."

Long before the hotel had been transformed into a camp hospital, Bickerdyke realized that no matter how hard they worked, the women of Galesburg couldn't keep up with her needs. They had spent the additional $400 they had collected and more for sturdy zinc chamber pots, quilts and blankets, and ticking with which to make pillow sacks and mattresses. That's when she turned to the strong Chicago chapter of the fledgling U.S. Sanitary Commission, which had its headquarters in New York. She was never officially connected with the Sanitary Commission, yet she begged, wheedled, and demanded so constantly that a stream of supplies was soon flowing to Cairo from Chicago: bandages, under-clothing, hand-crocheted slippers, sheets, even a few towels, iodine, jel-lies and preserves, flour, salt, sauerkraut, pickles, and an occasional can of Gail Borden's evaporated milk.

Walking past the guardhouse one afternoon, Bickerdyke noticed that nearly every man in the place seemed to be hale and hearty. "Ought not to waste all that good energy," she grumbled to herself. Within days, convalescents who had been serving as nurses were replaced by sturdy men from the guardhouse who served the balance of their time in what was beginning to look like a real hospital. When one of Woodward's aides demanded to know on whose authority she acted, she snapped: "By the authority of the Lord God Almighty; have you anything that outranks that?"

Firmly established at Cairo and accustomed to getting her way even when officers—especially those in the medical corps—disagreed with her, Mother Bickerdyke made the river city her headquarters for the duration. But just like the men who headed brigades and armies, she often went into the field with troops for weeks or months at a time.

Mother Bickerdyke rejoiced during the Christmas season of 1861 when Gen. U. S. Grant, whom she had known in Galesburg, was placed in command of the District of Cairo, Department of Missouri. Though she had tried hard "to treat officers as equal to enlisted men," that approach had not always worked. Her frequent brushes with men in authority, in which she never backed down and seldom lost, had earned the nickname of "Cyclone in Calico."

With Grant in command, the cyclone was sure that Cairo would soon be lifting itself out of its eternal mud and slime. Even men down with the bloody flux ought to feel better if they could breathe a little clean air, she insisted. Grant soon issued to the forty-four-year-old widow a document that she always kept on her person and prized for the rest of her life—an unrestricted pass to go anywhere she wished within Union-held territory.

When camp scuttlebutt informed her that Grant was about to attack Forts Henry and Donelson in Tennessee, she began making plans to go along, but said nothing to anyone. The Sanitary Commis-

Mary Ann Ball Bickerdyke during her years with soldiers.—A. H. Ritchie engraving

sion, she had learned, had outfitted one of the finest Mississippi river passenger steamers as a floating hospital. All personnel aboard were male, as was standard procedure. But when the USS *City of Memphis* reached Fort Donelson a few hours after Grant had scored the first big Union victory of the war, one woman was aboard.

Bickerdyke never revealed whether she had talked her way past sentries, had bribed her way past them with home-packed jellies and preserves, or had flourished the pass signed by Grant. But once she came out of hiding, the only woman aboard the vessel took charge of it and filled every cot with a wounded man in order to go back up the river to Cairo. By early dark she was bone weary, but too worried to sleep. Maybe, just maybe, one or two fine young fellows who had been hit by Rebel bullets and overlooked by stretcher bearers still lay somewhere in the area of fiercest fighting. Lighting a piece of fat pine and using it as a torch, she had combed only a small part of the battlefield when she was placed under arrest and escorted to the tent of Union Col. John A. Logan, still brandishing her torch.

As soon as she saw the ex-Congressman from Illinois, who had forsaken the Democratic party to fight for the Union, she recognized him and exclaimed: "Black Jack, what on earth do you want with me at this time of night?"

Logan looked her over, chuckled, and said, "You look harmless—but I thought you might be robbing the dead, with that light of yours bobbin' up and down out there."

She explained her mission; he nodded understanding and said he was proud to know that a woman from Illinois was with the troops. Soon the two were fast friends; when Logan became a brigadier general on March 21, she wrote letters to Galesburg in which she told friends,

"Now that there are two good generals in charge of our boys; we're going to win this thing before long."

Directed by the woman who had taken charge of the steamer, the *City of Memphis* took a full load of wounded to Cairo—then went back for more. When every cot in the fine Cairo hospital was filled, she sent the ship to Mound City, Illinois, and then to St. Louis. After at least four (perhaps five) trips up the river, all survivors among the wounded from the first major Union victory of the war—Mother Bickerdyke's beloved boys—were in hospital cots somewhere.

Barely two months later, she was in the thick of things again. After steaming down the Mississippi River and turning into its tributaries, she reached Savannah, Tennessee. Located nearly ten miles below Pittsburg Landing, this was the site where many wounded Federals were being brought from the fighting near Shiloh Church. Casualties were so great that everyone trying to care for the wounded was working day and night.

Governor Lewis Harvey of Wisconsin arrived soon after the battle, bringing along ten tons of supplies for the men of his state. When every wounded soldier from Wisconsin had received care, he still had nearly half of his supplies left. Impetuously, the governor turned them over to Bickerdyke, confiding to aides that he'd seen representatives of the official agencies at work and was sure that Mother Bickerdyke could run rings around all of them.

Unable to personally stand guard over her mountain of supplies, the cyclone in calico soon discovered that someone was stealing wine from

"Midnight on the Battlefield," an artist's conception of Bickerdyke at work.

it. She found the culprit to be a physician. She went straight to Gen. Grant and within a few hours watched with satisfaction as the thief was put under arrest. A few hours later, she presided over the opening of the first of many U.S. Army laundries. Until she took action, it was customary to burn or bury clothing and bed linens that had been used by badly wounded men. She managed to find and purchase two hand-powered washing machines with mangles. Soon she put runaway slaves, known as contrabands, to work with these devices. Her contrabands were also sent on battlefields to salvage anything usable that had been left behind by combatants. By means of these two devices, Bickerdyke was credited by the U.S. War Department with having "cleansed and redistributed supplies worth a small fortune."

Wherever action was fierce in the Western Theater, Mother Bickerdyke was there. She washed, fed, and cared for men who took part in nineteen major battles, of which Vicksburg was one of the most crucial. Men in blue found her at Resaca, Kingston, Atlanta, Chattanooga, and Lookout Mountain. In addition, Marietta, Georgia, had no hospital when she arrived, so she promptly established a large one.

Once, an officer under Gen. William T. Sherman noticed that Bickerdyke was the only woman in the Federal camps, so he went to his commander and asked why an exception was made in her case. Sherman reputedly answered in three words: "She outranks me." Yet he shook his head in response to her plea to accompany his armies on the March to the Sea. "It will take weeks," he told her. "Go home and rest a little, then meet me on the coast."

Instead of following Sherman's suggestion, Bickerdyke toured much of the Midwest in a whirlwind of fund-raising activity. To a Milwaukee audience she gave a rare, impassioned public speech:

> Suppose, gentlemen, you had got to turn loose tonight of one thousand dollars or your right leg; would it take you long to make up your minds? Which would you give up first, two thousand dollars or your right arm? Five thousand dollars, or both of your eyes? Right now, I've got eighteen hundred boys in my hospital at Chattanooga. Half of them have given an arm, a leg or both. Beyond the hospital, there's a big graveyard. It holds the bodies of thousands who gave their lives to save you and your country from ruin. Open up your pocketbooks tonight, and empty them for the sake of the legs and arms and eyes of my precious boys!

Few if any observers of the Grand Review of May 1865 noticed that it included one female.—E. B. Treat engraving

Concurrently with her fund-raising, she conducted what became nationally notable as "a cow and hen expedition." Her goal was to get enough animals and fowls to provide her "precious boys" with fresh milk and eggs. Though she didn't quite reach her goal, her experience in working with community leaders prepared her for a significant postwar career.

In 1866 the cyclone from Cairo managed to be certified as a pension attorney. In this capacity she helped hundreds of nurses and veterans to get pensions. Yet she never asked to receive one herself. After a year at the Chicago Home for the Friendless, she launched and led a movement to persuade destitute veterans to migrate to Kansas and get free land. At least three hundred men and their families went to the West through her influence. Later she worked for New York's Board of City Missions before going to California as an employee for the U.S. Mint.

Twenty years after having secured pensions for many others, she reluctantly accepted from Congress a pension of $25 per month for herself.

At war's end she traveled to Philadelphia, where a telegram from Logan was waiting for her. Headed for Washington with his army, he was in desperate need of rations and knew he could depend on her to do something about it. Heavy fighting in the Eastern Theater, she soon discovered, had exhausted U.S. Army supplies. Even the storerooms of the Sanitary Commission in Washington were all but bare. So the widow, who was then nearly forty-five but looked much older, sent a telegram of appeal to New York. That single telegram produced a loaded freight train, five cars long, that had right-of-way over other traffic to reach Alexandria, Virginia, before Logan's hungry men got there.

By the time they arrived, plans had been finalized for the mightiest celebration ever staged in the United States. For weeks, a Grand Review of the Union Armies had been planned for May 23–24, 1865. On the first day of the biggest military exhibition held in North America up to that time, Pennsylvania Avenue vibrated to the tread of 80,000 men. Led by Gen. George G. Meade, veterans of the Army of the Potomac took hours to pass in front of President Andrew Johnson and a host of dignitaries.

May 24 saw Sherman's 65,000 tattered followers go by the presidential reviewing stand. Two horses with riders were near the head of the immense column. One of them was Logan's Slasher, bedecked with red, white, and blue ribbons. The other animal was Mary Ann Bickerdyke's faithful Old Whitey, who was adorned with a mass of forget-me-nots.

When Gen. William Tecumseh Sherman reached the Treasury Building, he looked back at a sight he described as "simply magnificent." As described by him:

The column was compact, and the glittering muskets looked like a solid mass of steel, moving with the regularity of a pendulum. The steadiness and firmness of the tread, the careful dress of the guiders, the uniform intervals between the companies, all eyes directed to the front, and the tattered and bullet-riddled flags, all attracted universal notice.

When he penned that description, it is improbable that Sherman knew his ranks included one person who had never signed any sort of enlistment paper, had never participated in a drill, and had never drawn a paycheck. Thanks to Logan, the widow who had left her home and her sons for the sake of sick and wounded strangers, still wearing the cheapest kind of calico, passed in review with 145,000 veterans in blue uniforms.

Part V
Movers and Shakers

23

Harriet Beecher Stowe

Novelist

Had Lyman Beecher's daughter, Harriet, remained in Connecticut (where she was born in 1811), she might have died a struggling writer. Her only claim to fame would have been the fact that she was the sister of the famous Rev. Henry Ward Beecher. But in 1832 her father decided to go to what had once been "western Connecticut" and took her to Cincinnati, where he founded the Lane Theological Seminary. For the career of the woman who began dabbling with poetry and other forms of writing very early on, the place could not have been better. The self-proclaimed "capital of the West," Cincinnati had most of the cultural advantages of big eastern cities.

Three years after the Beechers arrived, *Western Magazine* offered a $50 prize for the best story submitted. Harriet easily walked away with the honors. She became active in the city's Semi-Colon Club, whose members encouraged her to put even her wildest fantasies on paper. She responded by penning a series of fictional letters, which she wanted readers to believe were genuine.

According to her own account, when Harriet finished the first of these letters, she took great pains with the manuscript, saying:

> I smoked it to make it look yellow, tore it to make it look old, directed it and scratched out the direction [address], postmarked it with red ink, sealed it and broke the seal—all this to give credibility to the fact of its being a real letter.

Many folk of the time were suspicious of fiction in general and novels in particular. This prevailing attitude probably accounts for all her work to make the bogus letter appear genuine. Yet, when she married

At age forty, Harriet Beecher Stowe looked as though she might have been a student in her father's seminary.

Calvin Stowe, a professor in her father's seminary, Harriet's burning ambition was not discouraged by her mate. In effect, he told her, "Go to it, and see what you can do with a pen!"

Calvin was no ordinary professor. His absorbing interest in the improvement of education persuaded the state of Ohio to send him abroad to study European methods of teaching. In his private life, he was a proper subject for what later came to be called gothic novels. Constantly in contact with the supernatural, he told Harriet that he once woke up to find an ash-colored skeleton in bed with him. Calvin spent a considerable time in the company of a very large invisible Indian woman and a small Indian man, who played the bass viol. His especially vivid juvenile vision had centered around a spirit named Harvey, who regularly squeezed between boards in order to enter Calvin's bedroom. Once, he saw tiny fairies who danced with such abandon that he never forgot them. When he confided these secrets to his new wife, Harriet mumbled, "You must be of Goblin origin!"

An early collection of Harriet's short pieces, *The Mayflower*, didn't earn enough to pay the grocery bills for a month. Undiscouraged, however, she kept plugging away and eventually became one of the most widely published writers of her day, seeing at least thirty-one of her books roll off the press. Her novels ranged from *Pearl of Orr's Island* to *Agnes of Sorrento* and *My Wife and I*. She wrote widely for a juvenile audience: *Betty's Bright Idea*, *Little Pussy Willow*, *First Geography for Children*, and *Queer Little People*; "Domestic science" was treated in *The American Woman's Home*, *The Chimney Corner*, and *House and Home Papers*. Largely because she expected them (correctly) to be profitable, she turned out nonfiction volumes such as *Men of Our Times*, *Our Famous Women*, and *Bible Heroines*. While producing a constant stream of books, she wrote magazine articles on subjects ranging from travel to Charleston, South Carolina, dogs and cats, and spiritualism.

Imaginary letter writers and characters conjured up by Harriet seemed tame, almost prosaic, in comparison with her husband's spirits. Had she married any other man, he might have scoffed at the notion of wasting time on fiction, and her life would have been quite different.

Like Calvin, she was intensely interested in educational reform. Like her father, she took a hands-off attitude toward the burning question of the day—abolition of slavery. But during her Cincinnati years, in which she bore seven children, Harriet could not ignore the tensions created by those who wanted to abolish it.

Theodore Weld, one of her father's students, was so incensed at Beecher's middle-of-the-road views that he withdrew from school. Taking other students with him, he formed the nucleus of what later became Oberlin College and wrote a passionate volume called *African Slavery as It Is.*

As the largest city situated squarely between free and slave sections, Cincinnati was in constant turmoil. One of Weld's converts, James G. Fee of Kentucky, liberated his slaves and went home to preach abolition. He was run out of the state and disowned by his father. Another Kentuckian, Van Zandt, did not get off so lightly. When he freed his slaves and moved to an Ohio farm, he used it as a station on the Underground Railroad. Authorities seized him, Harriet remembered in later life, "attached his property and threatened him with utter ruin." He escaped disaster only because he was represented in the courts by "a rising young Cincinnati lawyer, Salmon P. Chase," later U.S. Secretary of the Treasury.

Another of Weld's converts, identified only as Birney, came to Cincinnati to help edit an antislavery newspaper. When a mob destroyed his press, Harriet was so furious that she confided to Calvin, "I can easily see how such proceedings may make converts to abolitionism. I wish [Birney] would man [his building] with armed men, and see what can be done. If I were a man I would go, and take good care of at least one window."

Clergyman and educator Lyman Beecher took his daughter to Cincinnati, the largest city between the Cotton Belt and the abolition-minded Northeast.— Dictionary of American Portraits

The house in which Uncle Tom's Cabin was written.—
NATIONAL CYCLOPEDIA OF AMERICAN BIOGRAPHY

In spite of strong emotional reactions against mob violence and awareness of the plight of slaves living just south of the Ohio River, Harriet was not an emotionally charged abolitionist. Rather, she was a dedicated writer in search of a subject. She found that subject, after accompanying Calvin to his new faculty position at Bowdoin College in Maine, by turning back to her Cincinnati years.

During a very cold winter, she began experimenting with a story in which slavery took a central theme and that was embellished from her memories of the Bible and the novels of Daniel Defoe and Sir Walter Scott. With sectional strife becoming more strident, she thought antislavery advocates would probably buy a book depicting the horrors of slave life below the Ohio River. The first draft of her first chapter described the death of a central character whom she called Uncle Tom.

If she ever approached publishers with her brainstorm, none showed any interest. After all, her firsthand knowledge was extremely skant. She had never lived in the South. Her knowledge of the region's culture and residents was limited to what she'd read, plus a few anecdotes brought to Cincinnati by runaway slaves. (The city was their first stop on the underground railroad to freedom.) Furthermore, very few refugees reached the campus of Bowdoin College. Perhaps that was just as well; instead of depending on interviews, she turned her imagination loose. Even if her novel had never been published, it probably would have given her considerable personal satisfaction to write it.

When he got wind of a potential novel about the brutality of slaveholders and the horrors of life as a slave, editor Gamaliel Bailey of the antislavery *National Era* magazine of Washington expressed interest. His offer wasn't much, but if she cared to publish her story in serial form, he said, it would bring her a byline and a tiny but regular remittance. Previous contacts with Bailey led Harriet to be confident that her serial would be run in full. When the first chapter was dispatched in

April 1851, she launched a full-length account about which famous novelist George Sand soon commented: "The life and death of a little child and of a negro slave!—that is the whole book!"

Eventually brought to completion in the *National Era*, Harriet's story earned little initial attention. Many of the intellectuals of her time were more concerned with questions about admission of new states to the union and the rights of existing states in their dealing with the national government. Who really cared to delve into the darker side of life in the Cotton Belt?

But March 1852 saw publishers taking a great risk. Serialization of Harriet's novel would end in April. If it was ever to become a book, this was the best time to give it a try. The John P. Jewitt Company of Boston carefully hedged its bets by splitting the venture with Cleveland investors. *Uncle Tom's Cabin, or, Life Among the Lowly,* was so long that it was divided into two volumes. The anti-slavery publishers who saw it into print fervently hoped that they would break even on the venture.

Harriet hoped to get enough money from the publication of *Uncle Tom's Cabin* to afford a new silk dress. As late as July 9, 1851, she was working hard to call attention to her novel. In a letter to noted abolitionist Frederick Douglass, she expressed hope that he had seen the early chapters. March 20, 1852, saw publication in book form before the April issue of the *National Era* brought the serialization to a close.

The tangible feeling and size of hard cover around a full-length book (perhaps coupled with shifts in public sentiment and other factors) helped work a publishing miracle. The so-so serialized story was trans-

Uncle Tom as depicted on many theater posters. The play was on stage somewhere continuously beginning in 1852 until at least 1931.—Historic Landmarks of Black America

"TOPSY"

·UNCLE·TOM'S·CABIN·

Topsy, as portrayed on posters advertising one of scores of "Tom companies," which gave unlicensed dramatic renditions of the novel.

formed into a best-selling novel. Within five years after the two-volume book came off the press, it was in 500,000 American homes. Jumping across the Atlantic Ocean, the highly imaginative book was soon offered by eighteen different British publishers. Few buyers paid much attention to the subtitle that expressed Harriet's major purpose: to depict life among the Southern lowly.

Any teacher of a college course in literature could have torn the book to shreds. It had no well-structured plot, and it was entirely too long. Much of the "lowly life" it claimed to depict was about as close to reality as tales about the man in the moon. But *Uncle Tom* was dripping with pathos. Dramatic incidents, however unbelievable, abounded. Characters were depicted with such vividness that their names became everyday labels: Uncle Tom, Simon Legree, Topsy, and many more.

Most of all, Harriet's book had a message. Readers who plowed through both volumes were seldom neutral about slavery, the plantation system, or the rights of oppressed Americans. More than any other single factor, this novel helped transform the long-simmering North-South feud into a great moral battle.

No one has ever succeeded in compiling an accurate account of the impact of the book and the stage plays based on it. Before it was even a year old, it had been translated into at least two dozen languages. When U.S. sales reached one million copies, admirers insisted that the author had established a record that "no other female will match for decades to come."

Throughout the western world, celebrities praised the book and its writer; a letter from opera singer Jenny Lind was especially treasured by the author. Yet even that trophy was soon relegated to second place.

England's Lord Shaftesbury sent her twenty-three morocco-bound volumes that held the signatures of 562,448 women who sent through Harriet "an affectionate and Christian address to the women of America." Transformed into an instant celebrity by *Uncle Tom,* Stowe wrote stories, articles, and books on practically any subject she thought would generate revenue. Even the death of her husband seemed a fit subject for two articles in the *Atlantic Monthly,* which she suggested to the editor "at my usual rates."

Her runaway best-selling novel turned Harriet into a reformer. Once the book was in hundreds of thousands of American homes, she could no longer be moderate in regard to slavery. Hence, she was vociferous in scolding Abraham Lincoln on two separate scores. He had never been known to read a novel, she correctly said, and his first inaugural address seemed tame and insipid by comparison to the fervor of most abolitionists.

Possibly, but not positively, at the urging of his wife, on May 26, 1862, Abraham Lincoln ordered for the library of the Executive Mansion one of Harriet Beecher Stowe's novels—*Agnes of Sorrento,* which sold for $1.25. On June 16 he borrowed from the fledgling Library of Congress a piece of her writing with a much longer title: *A Key to Uncle Tom's Cabin; Presenting the Original Facts and Documents upon which the Story is Founded. Together with Corroborative Statements Verifying the Work,* which was published simultaneously in Boston and Cleveland in 1853.

The president by then was interested in the most famous novel of the period. His *Collected Works,* which does not include papers burned by his son, makes no mention of Stowe, but oral tradition too strong and too old to ignore says that upon meeting Harriet the man from Springfield greeted her with a wonder-filled comment: "So this is the little woman who started this big war!"

Widely circulated stories according to which Lincoln addressed Stowe as "the little woman who started this big war" cannot be documented. Yet her novel was a conspicuous factor in helping fan the flames of the sectional rivalry and hatred that cost the lives of 623,000 fighting men. When it was over, the author whose own outlook was transformed by her own handiwork rejoiced—not that the Union had been preserved, but that slavery had been abolished.

24
Mary Todd Lincoln

Haunted

A decade after an assassin's derringer took her husband's life, Mary Todd Lincoln received news of yet another tragedy in a series that punctuated the last twenty years of her life. Her sister, Elizabeth Todd Edwards, wrote that Mary's four-year-old granddaughter had just died. Abraham Lincoln's widow summed up her own years since leaving Springfield, Illinois, by writing of "sweet, affectionate little Florence," whom she loved dearly:

> The information saddened me greatly & rendered me quite ill. I have drank so deeply of the cup of sorrow, in my desolate bereavements, that I am always prepared to sympathize with all those who suffer, but when it comes so close to us, & when I remember that precocious, happy child, with its loving parents—what can I say? In grief, words are a poor consolation—silence & agonizing tears, are all that is left the sufferer.

Mary Todd was envied in her girlhood; her friends said she had everything. Her prosperous and influential father saw to it that his daughter, born and reared in Lexington, Kentucky, wanted for nothing that money could buy. His ample income couldn't fend off grief, however, when at age seven, Mary lost her mother. Her father's second marriage, to Elizabeth Humphreys, brought Mary half-brothers and half-sisters in rapid succession. Mary later contended that her stepmother devoted all of her time and attention to her own children. Whether or not that was the case, the girl began spending more and more time next door, at the home of Henry Clay; by the time she passed puberty, she had come to despise her stepmother.

Mary attended Madame Victorie Mentelle's boarding school, where she received an education not normally available to women of that period. Years later, a French dignitary who visited the Executive Mansion in Washington expressed astonishment that the president's wife understood his conversation so well. She gave a demure smile and explained—in the visitor's language—that at her finishing school girls were not permitted to speak except in French when they were on the grounds of the institution.

Linguistic skills, however, did nothing to ease the tensions between Mary and her stepmother. Hence, a family conference ended with a decision that the twenty-one-year-old

Until he became president-elect of the United States, Mary's husband did not wear a beard.

Mary should pay a protracted visit to her sister in Springfield, Illinois. Married to Ninian W. Edwards, son of the territorial governor of Illinois, Elizabeth Todd Edwards took Mary into the highest social circles of the new state capital. She soon met attorney Abraham Lincoln, an aspiring politician, and they developed a mutual affection that led to what was then known as "an understanding," but they did not set a nuptial date.

Incomplete and confusing records suggest that the man soon to become famous as the "rail splitter" cooled things off a bit and by late 1840 had backed away from marriage. Recent research indicates that he was interested in other young women. Apparently, he also didn't like the weight Mary had put on since leaving Kentucky. He once quipped, "It looks like a woman puts on an extra pound for every ten miles she travels into the West."

Disconsolate for months, Mary seems to have initiated the reconciliation that took place in 1842. Tradition has it that from girlhood she had wanted to marry a future president of the United States, and Abe Lincoln seemed to her to be a great prospect for the role. Whether that legend is accurate or not, Abe and Mary were married in the Edwards parlor on November 4, 1842. Many years later William H. Herndon tried to assemble all the evidence he could find about the life of his longtime law partner. If even a tenth of what he wrote is accurate, the newlyweds had only a brief period of bliss. As soon as she became Mrs. Lincoln, Herndon asserted, the woman from Lexington "began ruling the roost."

Herndon's findings are given considerably more credence today than in earlier decades. Whether his verdict was accurate or not, an impartial observer of Mr. and Mrs. Lincoln could not possibly have escaped noticing that they were totally unlike each other in many respects. Mary had received a splendid education; her husband had spent only a few weeks at a time in what he called "blab schools," so was almost entirely self-educated.

Abe spoke in a high-pitched nasal whine and never learned to spell. Mary had the voice of culture and frowned whenever a word was not pronounced or written correctly. Because Mary simply could not tolerate her husband's uncouth relatives, Abe's parents did not attend their wedding and never saw their grandchildren. She was an accomplished ballroom dancer, but her husband's extremely long legs and complete lack of experience made him unwilling to learn even the simplest steps. Abe's boyhood was spent in poverty and hard manual labor; Mary was accustomed to affluence and didn't have the foggiest notion of how to manage a kitchen, let alone an entire household. Given the situation, the newlyweds decided to pay $4 a week for the privilege of taking their meals at the Globe Tavern. It was there that their first child, named for his grandfather Robert Todd, was born in August 1843.

Zealous work took the new father away from home much of the time, but his income increased enough for them to buy their first and only home in exchange for a small piece of real estate and about $1,200 in cash. Their second son, Edward Baker, was born at home in the spring of 1846. When Abe went to the U.S. House of Representatives in 1847, his wife was elated beyond words. Her joy was short-lived, however; he served only one term and did not hold another elected office for more than a decade.

Both of them had physical ailments that gave them considerable trouble. Abe suffered from long periods of despondence. It is speculated that this was caused by having been kicked in the head by a mule as an adolescent and lying unconscious for hours afterward. Mary's spirits usually stayed fairly high, but she frequently suffered from headaches so severe that nothing could reduce their severity or duration.

The first lady with her husband and her two surviving sons.—19TH-CENTURY LITHOGRAPH

On February 1, 1850, Mary was hit very hard by the first in a series of tragedies and crises that marked the rest of her life—the death of their four-year-old son Eddie. Mary never fully recovered from this loss, despite the birth of their third son Willie—baptized as William Wallace in honor of one of Mary's brothers-in-law—just eight months later. When their fourth son, Thomas, was born in 1853, his father said his big head made him look like a tadpole, so the boy instantly and permanently became known as Tad.

Willie and Tad didn't quite know how to react when they learned that their father had become the first Republican president of the United States, but Mary's head soared into the clouds and didn't come down for weeks. Upon arriving in Washington she set about making the seedy and run-down Executive Mansion fit for levees, balls, and receptions. Congress appropriated $20,000 for the project, but Mary didn't stop spending until after "the insurrection in the Cotton Belt" was under way and her bills had reached $26,700. That's when her husband indulged in a rare display of open anger and rebuked her soundly. He's believed to have told her, "It would stink in the nostrils of the American people to know that flub dubs for this damned old house" cost a small fortune at a time when "soldiers can't have blankets" because there was no money to purchase them.

If that stinging reprimand wasn't enough to give her tremors for days, the first contingent of Federal troops sent into Virginia caused the Executive Mansion to be swathed in black crepe. Young Col. Elmer Ellsworth, a protégé of Lincoln, was killed on May 24, and his body was brought to the Executive Mansion. Lincoln had loved Ellsworth like a son, and Mary couldn't go about her daily activities without repeatedly seeing the catafalque on which the young officer's body lay.

Furthermore, she soon became the target of bitter accusations that rocked the capital. Since she was born and reared in now-divided Kentucky, had spent her early years pampered by slaves, and had numerous male relatives who were in the ranks of Rebel soldiers, she was accused of being a traitor to the Union. Things got worse when the husband of one of her half-sisters was killed in action. Out of respect for her brother-in-law, Ben Hardin Helm, she ordered the black crepe out again, despite her knowledge that the gesture would surely create a storm of protest. Legend has it that Lincoln was called before a Congressional committee whose members demanded that he account for his wife's conduct and swear to her loyalty. That incident never took place, but members of what today would be called "the power circle inside the beltway" did everything they could to make life more miserable than ever for Mary Todd Lincoln.

Her chief source of comfort seems to have been her mulatto housekeeper. Little is known about the early life of Elizabeth Keckley, but her middle years were filled with action. She was the only person in the nation who knew from firsthand observation what life was like in the households of both Jefferson and Varina Davis and Abraham and Mary Todd Lincoln. She had worked in both, but if she ever confided to Mrs. Lincoln what she knew of the Davis family life, she never admitted it. The book she wrote and published in the postwar years says nothing of it.

According to Keckley, before the end of 1861 her Kentucky-reared mistress was in the habit of saying to her over and over, "I am pursued by evil forces; since the nomination of my husband, my life has been nothing but a series of disasters." When she first voiced these feelings, she did not know that Willie, who had been conceived about the time his brother Eddie died, would soon come down with what doctors diagnosed as "bilious fever." Mary sat by the boy's bedside, holding his hand for hours during periods of delirium. Occasionally, his father came into the bedroom, tried to express encouragement, then choked up and fled in tears.

Like every member of the household, Willie drank water from the taps of the mansion. Piped directly from the Potomac River, it probably caused the eleven-year-old to contract his sickness (which was most likely typhoid fever). Even if attending medical personnel had arrived at a correct diagnosis, they would have been all but helpless to combat the illness. Most typhoid victims and their relatives were told simply to fight it out, and hope for the best. Willie seems to have been a fighter, for he lingered longer than some grown men who came down with the same malady. From the beginning of his struggle, however, his mother held little hope for his recovery. When he died on February 20, 1861, he was buried in nearby Georgetown. Willie's bones lay there until his father was killed by John Wilkes Booth; then the small coffin was put aboard the Lincoln funeral train and taken to Springfield with the body of the first assassinated president.

Elizabeth Keckley, who worked in the Jefferson Davis home before becoming seamstress and confidante to Mary Todd Lincoln.—BEHIND THE SCENES

Mary never pretended to get over Willie's death and refused to enter his room again. Desperate to "make contact with my son," she consulted spiritualists and with the guidance of Keckley arranged for seances to be held in the Executive Mansion. Her husband, who was almost totally absorbed with directing his armies, is believed to have attended only one of these sessions.

Thomas, who was now seven years old and full of life, offered some consolation of a sort. Tad was not at all like his other brothers, however. When Tad cut his baby teeth, it was obvious that they were badly aligned, and his permanent teeth proved no better. His first attempts at speech revealed that he had a lisp, but this was the least serious of his impediments.

In Washington, Tad had the run of the Executive Mansion and delighted in tormenting visitors. Wearing a juvenile version of a Federal officer's uniform, he darted in and out of his father's office, regardless of what business was being conducted. By today's standards, he probably would have been labeled hyperactive, possibly developmentally delayed. He certainly gave his mother more headaches than pleasure.

In the aftermath of the Union victory at Gettysburg, the first lady hurried back to the Executive Mansion from the Soldiers' Home by carriage. Her horses bolted or her carriage failed, and she was thrown from it, hitting her head on a large stone. Though rushed to a military hospital and given the best available treatment, her fall led to infection, and her skull had to be opened by a surgeon. Although her injury was not fatal, it may have caused her headaches to become progressively worse and her outbursts of temper to become more frequent and prolonged. Probably from surveying what he knew of this period, Herndon labeled the wife of his former law partner as "the female wildcat of the age."

With Tad showing no signs of outgrowing his handicaps and two of his brothers in the grave, Mary Todd Lincoln's hopes were pinned on her first-born son, Robert Todd. When the Illinois draft quota was not met, public pressure was exerted on the first lady. Why was her son attending Harvard when the sons of ordinary folk were being forced into blue uniforms even if they badly wanted to stay out of the Civil War?

Tormented by the very notion of possibly receiving word that Robert had been seriously wounded or killed in battle, his mother used all of her wiles and every word her sharp tongue commanded on Abraham. Weary of fighting both his wife and mounting public indignation, the chief executive arranged for his son to become an aide to Gen. U. S. Grant. This put him into a captain's uniform, but guaranteed that he'd remain at a headquarters post and would never be exposed to Rebel minié balls or canister shot.

Mary paid a joyful visit to her soldier son at City Point, Virginia, and for the first time in many months returned home in a positive mood. But her euphoria vanished forever just two months after visiting her handsome boy.

With her husband she went to Ford's Theatre on Good Friday to see a performance of *Our American Cousin*. Had she not alienated the wife of U. S. Grant (Julia Dent Grant despised being in the company of the first lady), the couple might have accompanied them to the theater and Gen. Grant might have provided some protection to President Lincoln. But Julia persuaded her husband to leave Washington immediately and go to their New Jersey home, leaving Lincoln virtually unprotected that evening, when he was assassinated by John Wilkes Booth.

Mary Todd Lincoln was physically and emotionally unable to attend her husband's funeral. Tad knew what had happened, but was not capable of fully understanding it. Trying to console his mother at age twelve, he solemnly promised her that he'd begin to dress himself in the mornings without aid. But even as she began to recover from her latest and greatest loss at the hands of the "demonic forces that pursued her," she assessed her financial condition and received still another shock. Abe left what was then considered to be a substantial estate of at least $70,000. But her share of this sum (one-third) amounted to an annual income of only about $1,700—a fraction of what she needed to maintain her standard of living.

Possibly—but not positively—at Keckley's suggestion, she shipped trunks full of her clothing and accessories to New York and offered them for sale anonymously. The merchant, however, who had promised to shield her identity, soon made it public. Even so, when things belonging to the former first lady went on sale, there were few buyers. Although a great deal of newspaper publicity was stirred up by "the Old Clothes Scandal," the sale did not generate enough cash to help her pay debts accumulated from what some analysts call her compulsive spending.

With a financial crisis pending and his mother now finding little consolation except in the company of her "dear little Taddie," who was far from being a normal adolescent, her son Robert decided it was time to act decisively. He may have had his mother's interests at heart, but he also probably had his eye on the share of his father's estate that she controlled. It is likely that he also knew his mother habitually squirreled away substantial sums of cash, even when pressed by creditors. Probably impelled by a complex set of motives, Mary's oldest son had his mother committed to an asylum for the insane and took over the management of her affairs. Although she remained in the asylum only a few months before

Mary Todd Lincoln during her years as first lady.— LIBRARY OF CONGRESS

the diagnosis was overturned, her relationship with Robert was permanently and irreparably damaged.

With Tad in tow, she spent a protracted period in France—as much an exile as former Rebel officials who fled from their birthplaces when the Confederacy collapsed. She returned to the United States after the protracted absence to find that the public had virtually forgotten that she had once been mistress of the Executive Mansion.

Ignored by the press and the public and inconsolable after the early death of "dear Taddie," she died in virtual isolation and in what seemed to be a state of near poverty. One discovery, however, constitutes the final irony in the life of one of the most tragedy-haunted women of the nineteenth century. In her old age, the woman who had accumulated huge debts for clothing and jewelry for which she had little or no need had become a miser. She had ample money, but had lost all desire to spend it. When her quarters were emptied and their contents examined, Robert was astonished to find that she had hidden more than $50,000 in cash.

25

Mary Boykin Chesnut

Analyst

In the hospital the better born, that is, those born in the purple, the gentry, those who are accustomed to a life of luxury, are the better patients. They endure in silence. They are hardier, stronger, tougher, less liable to break down than the sons of the soil.

—*Mrs. Louisa S. McCord in* A Diary from Dixie

Mrs. Mary Boykin Chesnut, author of *A Diary from Dixie*, the most celebrated and widely read woman's analysis of life in 1861–65, preserved these words. Her diary has appeared in at least three versions, and numerous books have been written about it. But because she twice made extensive revisions of her wartime notes, there's no certainty that her friend's comment hadn't been altered at some point. A few analysts think Chesnut's voluminous writings should be called memoirs rather than a diary, since much of her work in revision was done long after the conversations, events, and observations that constitute her book. Whether or not she quoted McCord verbatim is beside the point. As clearly as any fifty-word section in the 400,000 or so words she wrote, the second- or thirdhand comment she attributed to her friend reveals a basic aspect of Chesnut's own life and thoughts.

Until her world came crashing down on her during the Civil War, Mary knew nothing but prestige and affluence. Her father, Stephen D. Miller, had been governor of South Carolina, a U.S. Congressman, and a U.S. senator. She married one of the wealthiest men in the state and saw him leave the Senate to fight for secession and states' rights before becoming a Confederate brigadier general.

Poor whites of the time would have said of the woman, "She's every bit plantation born 'n bred." Because she knew little except high society until 1861, logic suggests that she would lavish unadulterated praise on the high and mighty and their lifestyle. In this instance, logic is badly askew. She did look down her nose at "sandhill tackeys," or poor whites,

Mary Boykin Chesnut, author of A Diary from Dixie, *managed to step aside from her culture and her era and look closely at both.*
—THE VALENTINE MUSEUM

and she extolled friends and acquaintances who had "everything of the best—silver, glass, china, table linen and damask, etc." But at the same time, she castigated her peers for what she considered the inability to work hard and long at winning the war against the Yankees. "South Carolinians," she wrote, "have pluck enough, but they only work by fits and starts; there is no continuous effort; they can't be counted on for steady work. They will stop to play or enjoy life in some shape."

A comment like that might have caused her to be ostracized had the Civil War not obliterated plantation life as she knew it. What's more, she was a caustic and analytical critic of slavery, despite the fact that she reveled in having slaves wait on her for more than forty years.

Her work is much more than mind-boggling in its sheer quantity. No man of the period came close to matching her skill as a commentator on the society that disintegrated before her eyes. Louis Untermyer once observed, "Few private papers and fewer public documents give a greater sense of the havoc wrought by the Civil War than the diary of Mary Boykin Chesnut." In many respects, her observations and notes are to Civil War reporting what *Gone with the Wind* is to fictional accounts of the period.

During her late adolescence and young womanhood, Mary wrote both prose and poetry and kept a journal. With sectional warfare looming, she radically altered her writing style. Her wartime diary, which started soon after Federal forces occupied Fort Sumter at Charleston in late December 1860, includes little banter and no jokes. It deals with the unremitting struggle made endurable for her by the social circles in which she moved in Birmingham, Alabama; Charleston and Columbia, South Carolina; and Richmond, Virginia.

Young Mary Miller grew up in Camden, South Carolina, the site of a significant battle during the American Revolution. Like Mary Todd of Lexington, Kentucky, she studied at an exclusive boarding school. Both institutions required girls to use French rather English during school hours. Madame Talvande's location on Legare Street in Charleston was enough to tell any knowledgeable person that all her students came from the state's most prosperous and influential families.

When only thirteen years old and still a schoolgirl, Mary met twenty-one-year-old James Chesnut Jr. of Mulberry Plantation. A graduate of Princeton, the heir to an immense fortune was reading law under James L. Petigru in his Charleston office. Petrigu was known and despised in much of the South because he was a vocal and articulate critic of John C. Calhoun, who had widely proposed that a state could nullify Federal legislation at will. Although he was universally known to be a strong Unionist, Petigru spent the war years in Charleston, where the Civil War started.

Chesnut married Mary Miller four years after they became acquainted. Initially ecstatic over her role as mistress of three or four plantations, the seventeen-year-old woman soon began to resent being assigned a subordinate role in a male-dominated society. Though James Chesnut would have found it difficult to spend all of his prewar wealth, he kept a close eye on his wife's spending and frequently took her to task for what he considered extravagance. She wrote years later that her husband once "locked the door and put the key in his pocket" when he stalked out of her room after a quarrel.

The diary that Mary started in the aftermath of South Carolina's secession proved extremely therapeutic. Luckily for modern readers, she said precisely what she thought in her diary. Because it was locked in a safe place, there was no danger that James or anyone else might read it and take offense.

Already planning to become an officer in the state militia, James asked her opinion about a matter in March 1861. She did not record the question or her reply, but to her diary confided:

> Mr. Chesnut thinks himself an open, frank, confiding person and required an answer to his proposition. Truth requires me to say that I know no more of what Mr. C. thinks or feels on any subject now than I did twenty years before. Sometimes I feel that we understand each

other a little—ever so little—then up goes the iron wall between us. He never gives me the impression of an insincere person, or even a cold one—only reticent; like an Indian, his pride is to hide all feeling.

But her husband's stoic and reticent behavior was far down the list of Mary's grievances. Near the top of the list was a matter that everyone knew about, but no one discussed—the nocturnal visits of plantation owners to the cabins of their female slaves. Her frequently expressed preference for city life may have stemmed at least in part from this master-slave relationship on plantations. Charleston, Columbia, Atlanta, Montgomery, New Orleans, Richmond, and many smaller cities had auction houses at which slaves were bought and sold. But none of them included a long row of cabins like the plantations, where a white man could go unobserved and unquestioned.

Once the sectional struggle reached critical mass and war became inevitable, Mary got into in the thick of things and stayed there. Her husband became a colonel in the South Carolina militia in 1860 and was elected to the Provisional Congress of the Confederate States of America. Hence, she was in Montgomery when Jefferson Davis—whose youthful wife was among Mary's most intimate friends—reluctantly agreed to become chief executive of the new nation. He'd have much preferred to be a field general of Rebel forces, Mary observed.

Col. James Chesnut Jr. played a leading role in the negotiations that preceded the battle of Fort Sumter.

Fort Sumter, which had no garrison prior to its occupation by Maj. Robert Anderson's small Federal force, became the chief focal point of a bitter contest over ownership. Because it sat on her soil, the self-declared Independent Republic of South Carolina claimed the installation. But Federal money had built it and the artificial island on which it stood, so Lincoln and his immediate aides stood firm; it would never be handed over peaceably, they warned.

A stalemate developed in April 1861. Lincoln wanted to send enough food and other supplies to Anderson so that his men could hold the fort for weeks or months. Secessionists, most of whom didn't yet call themselves Confederates, were adamantly opposed to any action that would bar them from taking possession of the fort. U.S. Secretary of State William H. Seward fed a stream of promises to secessionists that Washington would soon come to terms about the transfer of ownership. When it became apparent that Lincoln had never authorized a deal and had no intention of making one, Southern tempers flared.

Mary and her husband were in Charleston when negotiations broke down. They had hoped that their close friend Louis T. Wigfall would persuade Federals to hand over the fort. A native of Virginia who had practiced law in South Carolina and had been sent to the U.S. Senate by Texans, Wigfall tried his level best. He even made an unauthorized visit to Fort Sumter, where he unsuccessfully begged Anderson—whose men were at the point of starvation—to give up the struggle. Col. Chesnut, who was officially authorized to act, demanded the immediate evacuation of the fort, but could not persuade Anderson to make the move. When the last desperate effort to preserve peace failed, men on both sides knew that an artillery duel would begin within hours.

From her husband, Mary learned that the Yankees had until 4 A.M. on April 12 to yield the fort. She went to bed, but could not sleep. She counted the chimes that rang from St. Michael's Church, knowing that the deadline had arrived, hoping against hope that it had passed without bloodshed. Soon she heard the unmistakable boom of a heavy cannon. She jumped out of bed and prayed as she had never prayed before. By daylight, telegraph messages had informed much of the nation that the long-awaited military struggle had begun.

On the following night, Mary Chesnut was on the roof of a Charleston mansion located close to the waterfront. She and other civilians watched with breathless excitement as forces that included her husband sent balls and shells screaming toward their target, lying more than a mile from the city. Describing herself as "weak and weary," Mary accidentally sat down on a chimney top and her clothing caught fire. She might have become a civilian casualty, had not other ladies quickly doused the flames. By morning, it was widely known that not a man on either side had been killed, so Mary described the night's action as a "sound and fury, signifying nothing."

Later, she welcomed the news that President Davis had selected her husband to become one of his confidential aides. Before he resigned from the U.S. Senate, Mary had reveled in Washington society. She was positive

Cannon fire directed at Fort Sumter by Col. Chesnut and his fellow secessionists caused April nights "to put July 4 celebrations to shame."

that the Confederate capital would offer the same pleasures that abounded in the nation's capital, only a hundred miles away. One brief comment after another in her diary reveals that she enjoyed Richmond more than any other place she lived.

Richmond was close to Manassas, where Rebel and Federal forces fought their first significant battle, so Mary felt almost as close to the battle as the throngs of civilians who took picnic lunches to watch the action. Many leaders on both sides had been confident that one genuine battle would bring an end to what President Lincoln called an insurrection. Many of her observations concerning later battles are surprisingly accurate; however, this one was not. Mary recorded her astonishment that soldiers in gray did not pursue their fleeing enemies into Washington, take the city, and put an end to the whole sorry business. Gen. P. G. T. Beauregard and his victorious troops didn't have the strength or the necessary supplies to push fifty or so miles from the battlefield into the national capital.

Mary Chesnut's revealing insights into military struggles make fascinating reading. Yet her commentary concerning leaders and the two separate societies into which Americans had been formed are even more significant. Passage after passage reveals that she was an ardent feminist in an era when that label was rarely used. To her diary she confided:

> Dogmatic man rarely speaks at home but to find fault. At his every word the infatuated fool of a woman recoils as if she had received a slap in the face; and for dear life she begins to excuse herself of what is no fault of hers.

Very soon after she and James reached Richmond, she wrote of him:

> After dinner he sat smoking, the solitary chair of the apartment tilted against the door as he smoked, and my poor dresses were fumigated. I remonstrated feebly. "War times," said he; "nobody is fussy now. When I go back to Manassas tomorrow, you will be awfully sorry you snubbed me about those trumpery things up there." So he smoked the pipe of peace, for I knew that his remarks were painfully true. As soon as he was once more under the enemy's guns, I would repent in sackcloth and ashes.

Mary never quite understood the role that Southern women voluntarily assumed to try to help win the war. Pondering their actions without emulating them, she wrote:

> I do not know when I have seen a woman without knitting in her hand. Socks for soldiers is the cry. One poor man said he had dozen of socks but only one shirt. He preferred more shirts and fewer stockings. We make a quaint appearance with this twinkling of needles and the everlasting socks dangling below.

Mary Boykin Chesnut devoted many paragraphs to Abraham Lincoln, whom she characterized as being "of the cleverest Yankee type." He had barely taken his oath of office before this female analyst wrote, "I must read Lincoln's inaugural. Oh, 'comes he in peace, or comes he in war?' Lincoln's aim is to seduce the border states."

Echoing some of the jibes of Northern cartoonists, whose sketches she never saw, early in the war Mary called the president, "Awfully ugly, even grotesque in appearance, the kind who are always at the corner stores, sitting on boxes, whittling sticks, and telling stories as funny as they are vulgar." Later she revised her judgment and confessed to her diary that some Southerners had stopped laughing at the man from Illinois as a rough clown. "You never hear now of Lincoln's nasty fun," she observed, "only of his wisdom. Doesn't take much soap and water to wash the hands that sway the rod of empire."

Though she was often in the company of President Jefferson Davis and his wife, the woman from South Carolina once found herself repelled by the Confederate chief executive during a dinner party. Back

Senator James Chesnut Jr.—
NATIONAL CYCLOPEDIA OF
AMERICAN BIOGRAPHY

home, she described his activities of the evening in two words: "coarse talking."

As U. S. Grant chalked up one victory after another, the outspoken female Rebel wrote of him in a fashion that almost sounds as though the words came from Lincoln. "He don't care a snap if men fall like the leaves fall; he fights to win, that chap does," Mary observed. "He is not distracted by a thousand side issues; he does not see them. He is narrow and sure—sees only in a straight line." Musing about the man who had conquered supposedly impregnable Vicksburg, she said to herself, "He has the disagreeable habit of not retreating before invincible veterans."

Her analysis of politicians and their actions was almost always critical. Surveying the Montgomery scene before the provisional Confederate constitution was adopted, she mused, "Everybody who comes here wants an office." This prevailing mood, she observed, had dire consequences: "The many who are disappointed [office seekers] raise a cry of corruption against the few who are successful."

Having met nearly all of the early Confederate leaders, she dismissed the entire lot with a single sentence: "Every man wants to be the head of affairs himself." Strife among these men started early, and it soon became ugly. She could be happy in Richmond, she wrote in her diary, except for the fact that "this cabinet of ours are in such bitter quarrels among themselves—everybody abusing everybody."

As might be expected, she had nothing but scorn for Harriet Beecher Stowe and *Uncle Tom's Cabin.* She knew the famous writer had little or no firsthand knowledge of her subject. Hence, she said of Stowe's novel that "People can't love things dirty, ugly, and repulsive, just because they ought to do so—but they can be good to them at a distance; that's easy."

Until the defeated South lost its slaves, they were integral to Mary Chesnut's world. Yet she succeeded in seeing "the peculiar institution" of slavery with a detachment that was rare in her time and place. Part of her unique analytical capacity in this respect may have stemmed from her loathing of her father-in-law. In the aftermath of Bull Run, she observed of him, "Old Mr. Chesnut sees his fine estates slipping away. These are his Gods, for he worships his own property."

She must have learned soon after her marriage that her father-in-law could readily find his way to the slave cabins on a moonless night. Revolted, but unable to change the structure of the society into which she was born, the diarist wrote:

> God forgive us, but ours is a monstrous system. Like the patriarchs of old, our men live all in one house with their wives and their concubines; and the mulattoes one sees in every family partly resemble the white children and every lady tells you who is the father of all the mulatto children in everybody's household but hers.

There's no certainty that Mary Boykin Chesnut was ever fully satisfied with the revisions to her diary. She had hoped to extract material from it for novels, but even had she succeeded in writing them, with the emphasis she included in her personal notes, she would have found it impossible to get them published in the postwar South. Having spent her last years in near destitution, she willed her memories of the war to a friend, who brought out the first version of *A Diary from Dixie* in 1905. Today, nearly a century later, it's going stronger than ever before.

CHAPTER

26
Julia Ward Howe
Poet

I went to bed as usual and slept soundly. I awoke in the gray of the
morning twilight, and as I lay waiting for the dawn, the long lines
of the desired poem ["Battle Hymn of the Republic"] began to
twine themselves in my mind. Having thought out all the stanzas, I
said to myself, "I must get up and write these verses down, lest I fall
asleep again and forget them." So with a sudden effort I sprang out
of bed and found in the dimness an old stump of a pen which I
remembered to have used the day before. I scrawled the verses
almost without looking at the paper. I had learned to do this when,
on previous occasions, attacks of versification had visited me in the
night and I feared to have recourse to a light lest I should wake the
baby, who slept near me. I was always obliged to decipher my
scrawl before another night should intervene, as it was only legible
while the matter was fresh in my mind. At this time, having com-
pleted my writing, I returned to bed and fell asleep, saying to
myself, "I like this better than most things I have written."

—*Julia Ward Howe*, Reminiscences, *1899*

T his account of the origin of the Civil War's most famous song was penned nearly forty years after the actual event, but the author's mind was still very keen. No novice at writing—especially poetry—the Boston woman who was spending a few days at Willard's Hotel in Washington had crammed her mind with vivid imagery, plus words from the Old Testament. Were she alive today, she'd probably say that her subconscious mind, accustomed to putting words together in verse, wrote the poem without conscious participation.

Wealthy from inheriting a New York banking fortune, the woman who grew up as Julia Ward probably paid for the publication of her first book of poems, *Passion Flowers*. When it appeared in 1854, it created little or no interest. *Leonora, or the World's Own*, her play produced in

New York in 1857, evoked criticism whenever men and women spoke of it. Genteel folk who saw it or heard about it wanted to know why on earth a refined female chose to write about "a fallen woman." A second volume of poems, *Words for the Hour,* was so low in controversy that it was all but ignored, even in her hometown of Boston. Even *A Trip to Cuba* didn't excite the literary world of the Northeast when it appeared in 1860, but it probably added to Julia's ability to put words together rapidly and skillfully.

But things changed in February 1862. On rereading and reflecting on her predawn scrawling, the author scrapped her sixth and final stanza, judging it to be anticlimactic. But except for altering those four lines, which may have been scrawled so hastily in the predawn hours that she couldn't be sure of what she had written, she made no other change in her

Cover page of an early edition of Howe's poem that became a song.

Abolition-ist Samuel Gridley Howe went to Washington in order to supervise dis-tribution of supplies to Massa-chusetts soldiers.

poem before dispatching it to a publisher. Editors at the *Atlantic Monthly*, concurred that the image-filled lines were worthy of being presented to readers. They scheduled them for publi-cation on the front cover of their February 1862 issue. They also instructed their bookkeeper to send payment to the author in the sum of $4.

Whatever else she may or may not have been, the poet was a true Yankee blue-blood. She was descended from colonial pioneer Roger Williams and was related to the famous "Swamp Fox" of the American Revolution, Gen. Francis Mar-ion. Her father, Samuel, spent most of his career with the banking firm of Prime, Ward, and King and was its head for many years.

A stream of governesses came to their Broadway mansion, and Julia eventually left it for a whirl at the finest finishing schools of the period. Like all women of her generation, she was excluded from study at a col-lege, but she more than made up for this by learning Latin and Greek on her own. She was related to the Astors by marriage, so it was easy for her to get the head of the Astor Library to be one of her tutors. As an adolescent, she often confounded her elders by pulling from her vast store of memorized lines a particularly apt saying by philosopher Immanuel Kant. By age seventeen she had largely ceased to quote other persons and had turned to putting her own ideas and rhymes on paper.

Since she could have had any eligible male in New York, Connecti-cut, or Rhode Island as her husband, some of her friends wondered aloud why on earth she chose a man who was doing nothing but oper-ating a school for blind children. Some of these fashionable young women probably didn't know that Samuel Gridley Howe practically worshiped England's immortal poet, Lord Byron. Howe purchased Byron's helmet (his most prized possession) at an auction and left home to help the Greeks fight the Turks. Made a Knight of St. George Cross during his six years as a warrior and surgeon, he gave up military life to head Boston's Perkins Institution for the Blind. One of his early pupils, Laura Bridgman, was the first blind and deaf child to learn to commu-nicate with others.

Their mutual love of poetry may have influenced twenty-four-year-old Julia Ward to marry the forty-two-year-old former soldier of fortune. Although they seem never to have considered a divorce, their interests soon began to diverge. To make matters worse, Howe often revealed to friends his jealousy of his wife's ample fortune and her prowess with the pen.

By 1860 Samuel was regionally prominent as an educator and reformer; Julia was beginning to achieve limited, local recognition as a poet. During the following spring, long-simmering North/South tensions boiled over and led to a state of armed confrontation. A few far-sighted Northerners, among them Samuel, looked ahead and didn't like what they saw. To them it was clear that illness, hunger, and lack of suitable clothing might be more dangerous to Union volunteers than Rebel bullets. Pooling their ideas and their resources, they established the United States Sanitary Commission.

John A. Andrew, governor of Massachusetts, was among the first state executives to send troops to Washington. While the Federal disaster at Bull Run was still very fresh in everyone's mind, Andrew decided that his fighting men badly needed essentials that were not readily available through government channels. As a result, he planned a fall trip to Washington and notified Dr. Howe that he had been selected to supervise the distribution of supplies to the fighting men of Massachusetts.

Governor and Mrs. Andrew, Dr. and Mrs. Howe, and the Rev. James F. Clarke traveled to the capital in November 1861. As they approached the center of the Federal government, Julia was all but overcome by a strange sense of discouragement. Describing it afterward, she said:

> I thought of the women of my acquaintance whose sons or husbands were fighting our great battle, the women themselves serving in the hospitals, or busying themselves with the work of the Sanitary Commission. My husband was [sixty years old and hence] beyond the age of military service, my oldest son but a stripling; my youngest was a child of two. I could not leave my nursery to follow the march of our armies; neither had I the practical deftness which the preparing and packing of sanitary stores demanded. Something seemed to say to me, "You would be glad to serve, but you cannot help anyone; you have nothing to give, and there is nothing for you to do."

Some of Julia's self-doubt vanished when she came into Washington and saw "mounted men and orderlies galloping to and fro" while companies and regiments drilled in the crowded streets. The visible military might of the Union, she decided, helped create an almost tangible atmosphere of optimism. Suddenly brimming with confidence in the Union, the fighting men of Massachusetts, her husband, and her own ability to put words together even if she couldn't roll bandages, Julia had a gala time of it.

She went for long drives in the countryside, cheerfully packed and helped consume a picnic lunch, and long afterward said she remembered noticing her heart beating rapidly when she and Samuel entered the Executive Mansion. Abraham Lincoln, seated on a sofa beneath a Gilbert Stuart painting of George Washington, showed the strain he was experiencing with the news of one delay or defeat after another. Julia studied the chief executive's deep blue eyes and made a mental note that every other feature of his face could only be called "quite plain." When he greeted his visitors, she was surprised by his high-pitched Western twang and observed that the sleeves of his coat and the legs of his trousers were much too short.

On November 18, Julia and other visitors from Massachusetts were invited to see a review of troops scheduled to be held across the Potomac River. A day that had begun with expectation soon turned sour when Rebel skirmishers appeared and broke up the review. Bugle notes that notified soldiers in blue to retreat seemed "to stick in the mind" of the poet when their coachman wheeled about and raced back to the capital.

Longstanding tradition, for which she herself never vouched, asserts that she and her companions sang snatches of military songs as they rode back across the river. They allegedly sang a few lines of the popular song that begins "John Brown's body lies a-moldering in the ground / His soul is marching on." It is clear that Samuel Howe would have been especially sensitive to these words. A longtime fervent abolitionist in a city that held many friends of the South, he was forced to flee briefly to Canada in the aftermath of John Brown's raid at Harpers Ferry and the anti-abolitionist sentiment that it spawned across the country.

This brings us to the fitful night in her Willard's Hotel room in the aftermath of this nearly disastrous conflict, when Julia experienced her memorable "attack of versification during the night." The result was the "Battle Hymn of the Republic," a poem that appeared in the *Atlantic Monthly* four months later.

Undocumented tradition that credits the clergyman from Boston with having encouraged her to "write some new words for the melody of

'John Brown' is suspect, to say the least. But consciously or unconsciously, Julia Ward Howe had selected her words—or they had forced themselves into her semiconscious brain—in such fashion that they truly did fit the rhythm of "John Brown's Body."

Julia regarded the work that "came to her" while in Willard's Hotel as a poem, but editors who first put it into print called it the "Battle Hymn of the Republic." Consisting of only fifteen lines and a short refrain with each stanza, it was not immediately popular. Men in blue

Julia Ward Howe waited for many years to publish her Reminiscences, *in which she told how her poem "came to her."*

already had a number of rousing songs, such as George F. Root's "The Battle Cry of Freedom" and his "Tramp, Tramp, Tramp." A unique combination of words and melody made "We Are Coming, Father Abraham" especially popular, despite general knowledge that Lincoln's call for 300,000 volunteers (on which James Gibbons based the song) was an abysmal failure. Favorites such as these, along with sentimental "Lorena" and strident "Marching Along," gave stiff competition to any and all brand-new songs.

Charles Cardwell McCabe, chaplain of the 122nd Ohio regiment, is generally credited with helping catapult Julia's poem-that-became-a-song. Noted for his splendid baritone voice, he may have taught the "Battle Hymn" to men of his regiment and may have led them in singing it. Whether he actually did that or not, it is fully documented that he was captured at Winchester, Virginia, and sent to Richmond's Libby Prison. Because inmates could do little else to make their days go by more swiftly, they often sang. McCabe is believed to have taught the song to fellow prisoners and to have led them in a rousing rendition of it when they received grapevine news about Gen. George G. Meade's great victory at Gettysburg, Pennsylvania.

As word of the Libby Prison incident spread, Julia Ward Howe's words, widely associated with the defeat of the Army of Northern Virginia, soon became familiar throughout the Northern armies. Henry Steele Commager has pointed out that "there was little organized entertainment in the Civil War." This factor, he suggests, encouraged soldiers to amuse themselves by engaging in communal singing around campfires and on the march. "Civil War soldiers," Commager emphasized, "were not mechanized; soldiers marched afoot, and as they marched they sang."

More and more, they sang the words that were scribbled at Willard's Hotel in the dim predawn light. Ralph Waldo Emerson soon noted in his *Journal* that he honored the author of the "Battle Hymn" despite her New York background. "I could well wish she were a native of New England," he mused. "We have no such poetess in New England." Decades later, Commager reminded his readers that her poem was "the one great song to come out of the Civil War—the one that transcends that particular conflict and embraces every great moral crusade."

Few (if any) Confederates sang the "Battle Hymn" during the years 1861 to 1865. They favored Dan Emmett's "Dixie," "The Bonnie Blue Flag," "Lorena," and "Maryland, My Maryland." If they had been familiar with the words of the Boston poet, they would have scoffed or sneered at them because of their Northern origin. With the passing of generations, things have changed greatly, however.

First smuggled into hymnals issued by long-established religious denominations and then boldly thrust into them with an article added to its title, today "The Battle Hymn of the Republic" is sung throughout the United States and much of the rest of the world. How Julia would rejoice if she could know that her words are now used as readily and as enthusiastically in the South and the West as in her native Northeast.

27

Louisa May Alcott

Nurse and Author

"We're glad to have you; what shall I call you?" the head nurse asked. "At home, they all call me Louy," was the reply.

"No proper name for a nurse; I think I shall call you Alcott," the head nurse continued. "Now that we know one another," she said, although she had not given her own name to the newcomer, "I'll give you a quick look."

"Our wards are ready for twenty men each," continued the woman known only to Alcott as Nurse. "Everything here is brand-new."

"The building isn't exactly what I expected," ventured Alcott.

"No wonder. It has just been converted from the Union Hotel. In Washington, didn't they say you'd be working in the Union Hotel Hospital?"

"No, Nurse. They did not. It wouldn't have made any difference, though. I came to serve wherever I am most needed."

"You're likely to be needed here soon. You'll see only a handful of men this morning, but I hear that there may be some fighting at Fredericksburg, Virginia. General Ambrose Burnside and his men are on the way to capture the Rebel capital. Rumor has it that they will face some resistance on the way. If they do," gesturing toward beds that were mostly empty, "some of these will soon be filled. I hope you will not object to serving alongside male nurses."

"Not a bit," responded the not-so-young woman who had come from Massachusetts. "I've been seeing pictures in *Leslie's Illustrated Weekly*. I found a splendid sketch of a hospital at Hilton Head, South Carolina, in it; I framed it and hung it in my room. I don't think it shows a single female nurse."

"Things are changing fast, Alcott. There's a shortage of males for hospital duty. Otherwise, you wouldn't be here."

"Yes, I know. Have I seen everything I need to see? We've only been walking and talking for ten minutes. When I was in Washington for my interview, they took me through Carver Hospital."

"This is not Carver. This is the Union Hotel. They say that Washington has at least fifty hospitals, and that some of them are full. Until we have more patients, you will be assigned to the laundry."

On that day in December 1862, neither woman had any idea of what lay immediately before them. Even as they made their way through the small new hospital, soldiers in blue were close to the Rappahannock River, singing "John's Brown's Body" with gusto as they marched. Their commander, who had held his post for barely six weeks, had been forthright about his plans. First, the town of Fredericksburg would be "shelled to the bare ground" by batteries of cannon. Once the place was occupied, the army would move on Richmond by forced marches. With that city in the hands of Federal troops, Rebels would quickly capitulate, and the men making up the Army of the Potomac could go home.

Helping wash and fold blood-stained linens that had just arrived from Washington facilities, Alcott was plagued with doubts. Maybe she had acted too hastily. She could have found work in a laundry room in Boston or maybe even in Concord. "But that wouldn't have helped the cause," she told herself.

Soon after moving with her family to Concord, Louisa May Alcott had found herself among neighbors whom she regarded as distinguished men of letters—Ralph Waldo Emerson, Nathaniel Hawthorne, and Henry David Thoreau. Frequent visitors to the home of Bronson Alcott, all of them were outspoken foes of slavery, as was Louisa's father. They probably were responsible for bringing to the Massachusetts town in 1859 a fiery abolitionist who thrilled his overflow audience in Concord's biggest auditorium.

John Brown, Louisa remembered as she filled shelves with sheets and towels now clean but still stained, had warned that blood would be

Federal hospital, Hilton Head, South Carolina.—W. T. CRANE IN THE SOLDIER IN OUR CIVIL WAR

shed very soon. He said nothing about his personal plans to form a new nation made up of freed slaves, but railed against "complacency in sheltered New England." Already calling herself an abolitionist, Louisa had walked home with her head held high after listening to a man who "really knew what was going on in the Kansas Territory."

A few months later she learned that Brown and a few followers had attacked the U.S. arsenal at Harpers Ferry, Virginia. When she read that he had gone to the scaffold with the proud claim that his death would count more than his life, she turned to her diary. "Glad I have lived to see the Antislavery movement and this last heroic act in it," she wrote. Though she had never seen him, she despised "that horrid Lieutenant-colonel Robert E. Lee," who had led the body of men who had captured Brown and had broken the back of his movement. "Wish I could do my part to make John Brown's words come true," she had mused when she saw a sketch of the execution.

Things looked different from the perspective of the laundry room of a nearly empty hospital in Georgetown, but one of the major players in the Southern insurrection seemed likely to suffer the same fate as John Brown. At the head of the Rebel body he called the Army of Northern Virginia, Lee would be facing Burnside. Louisa felt a twinge of guilt at realizing that she would be glad to see him in a coffin so that the war would end.

Despite the unforgettable hour she had spent listening to Brown, the man who went to the scaffold in the name of abolition had no direct influence upon her sudden decision to leave New England for a while. At age thirty, her life seemed to be going nowhere. All of her female friends and acquaintances were now wives and mothers. For years, she had dreamed of earning her living as a writer, but despite publishing a few things, she was forced to take whatever menial job she could find. Work as a nurse couldn't possibly be harder than some of the things she had been doing back home to support her ne'er-do-well father, she reasoned. If she could bring a few wounded men back to health, she would have done her part in the war to end slavery.

Louisa had been caught up in the "war fever" that swept Concord after secessionists fired on Fort Sumter. "When Concord gets stirred up it is a sight to behold," she noted in her diary. "All the young men & boys drill with all their might. The women & girls sew & prepare for nurses."

Had Bronson Alcott's health not seemed as fragile as his finances, Louisa might have gone to Washington in May or June 1861. Having taught for several years with little enthusiasm and no advancement, she had gone to Boston and taken rented rooms, where she hoped to write.

Noted abolitionist Theodore Parker had encouraged her to take this step, but even his influence didn't enable Louisa to earn enough to help her destitute father. "I shall open a kindergarten and find success!" she told Parker early in 1862.

That venture failed after only a few months; during a period of morbid self-doubt, she read in a newspaper that women were now being accepted for service as military nurses. Suddenly deciding to do what she could to aid the cause of abolition, she spent her first forty-eight hours at the Union Hotel Hospital wondering if she had done the right thing.

Back on the war front, Burnside was confidence personified as he perfected his plans to take Fredericksburg and overwhelm his armed foes. With at least 130,000 men against no more than 80,000 foes, the anticipated struggle should be a pushover for Federal forces. Even the fact that pontoons—needed to bridge the river—didn't arrive on schedule failed to trouble the Federal commander. He had such overwhelming numerical superiority that he felt he could take his time.

Lee, who had expected a battle about the middle of November, used the extra month given to him by his foe to prepare a defensive position on the outskirts of Fredericksburg. More than six miles long and nearly two miles from the river, the Confederate front was greatly strengthened by placement of nearly three hundred guns. A stout stone wall that ran along an elevated position called Marye's Heights would shield its defenders when the vast body of Federal troops crossed the Rappahannock River and converged on their foes.

Only two days after Louisa May Alcott began her work as a nurse, the Army of the Potomac was unleashed on Confederate positions behind Fredericksburg. Charge after charge, launched with spirit and fervor, wilted under the withering fire of Rebel cannon, muskets, and rifles. Unwilling to give up or to change his battle plan, Burnside ordered new bodies of troops to continue in the path of comrades who had been mowed down. He stopped what strategists later labeled as "senseless slaughter" only when darkness fell. Two days later, he drew back across the river, having already dispatched thousands of dying and wounded men toward Washington's hospitals.

Henry Villard, a newspaper correspondent who witnessed the Fredericksburg debacle, was the first to reach the capital. Senator Henry Wilson met him at Willard's Hotel and learned the dreadful truth. Determined that the president must know what had happened, Wilson took his new acquaintance to the Executive Mansion. Lincoln listened with rapt attention, but when Villard had finished his account he was told simply, "Let us hope that it is not as bad as you believe."

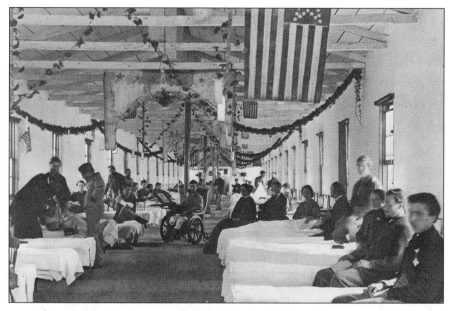

A ward in Washington's Carver Hospital; note the arrangement of stars on the flag.—
U.S. SIGNAL CORPS

Before the newspaper correspondent returned to his hotel, casualties from Fredericksburg began streaming into the capital. Lightly wounded men were the first to arrive; many of them had already been assigned beds when men who had lost arms or legs began crowding into every hospital of the city. Close on their heels were men who had taken direct hits of Rebel canister and minié balls in the abdominal and chest areas. Before the last of Washington's hospitals was filled beyond capacity, many soldiers considered to be in critical or terminal condition were directed to the adjunct Union Hotel Hospital. Extra beds were hastily pulled out, and wards were rearranged to hold twice as many groaning and unconscious men as had been planned for.

Anticipating being unable to cope with the odors she was sure to encounter, Louisa found a bottle of lavender water with which to sprinkle herself frequently. Instructed to go to ward one, and wash them, she was momentarily perplexed at finding on the door of the ward a single word: BALLROOM. Before opening the door, she resorted to her lavender water, for "a regiment of the vilest odors that ever assailed the human nose" warned her of what was to come. Inside, some men were stretched on beds, and others were sprawled on the floor. Describing the first patients for whom she was responsible, she later wrote:

Round the great stove was gathered the dreariest group I ever saw—ragged, gaunt and pale, mud to the knees, with bloody bandages untouched since having been put on days earlier. Many were bundled up in blankets, their coats being lost. All were wearing that disheartened look which proclaimed defeat, more plainly than any telegram about the Burnside blunder [at Fredericksburg].

Handed a basin of water, a bar of brown soap, and a sponge, she went to work. Remembering that living nightmare, she said that she drowned her scruples in the basin of water "and made a dab at the first dirty specimen I saw." One by one, she sponged the heads, shoulders, and feet of her patients, correctly assuming that male nurses would finish the job she had started.

Men diagnosed as suffering with pneumonia were put into one corner, "with diphtheria close by and typhoids next in line." Having finished her first scrub session, a memory suddenly popped into her head and made her laugh aloud, startling some of her patients. Tramping along trails leading into and out of woods that surrounded Concord she had always thought she'd like to be a deer or a horse "because it is such a joy to run." Now, she found herself running (and working) at top speed and seeming to get nowhere.

On the following evening she was suddenly promoted and put in charge of Ward One. The woman who had held that position found the deluge of human flotsam and jetsam too much for her, and she walked off the job without so much as saying that she wouldn't be back. Louisa described her typical day during this period by writing:

Up at six, dress by gaslight, run through my ward and throw up the windows though the men shiver and grumble; but the air is bad enough to breed a pestilence, and as no notice is taken of frequent appeals for better ventilation I must do what I can. Poke up the fire, add blankets, coax and command but continue to open doors and windows as though my life depended upon it. Mine does, but doubtless many another, for a more perfect pestilence box than this house I never saw—cold, damp, full of vile odors from wounds, kitchens, washrooms, and stables. No competent head, male or female, to right things, and a jumble of good, bad, and indifferent nurses, surgeons, and attendants to complicate the chaos still more. After this unwelcome progress through my stifling ward I go to breakfast and find the inevitable fried beef, salt butter, husky bread and washy coffee.

For years, the woman whose favorite literature was sentimental poetry had forced herself to write poems and stories under difficult circumstances. Now those years of discipline enabled her to pen frequent long letters about her experiences. Almost daily, despite weariness and periodic inclinations to vomit, she sent her loved ones paragraph after long paragraph about her encounters with the wounded men.

Any seasoned veteran of work in a military hospital could have told her she should have increased her work load gradually. Not aware of danger or knowing how to avert it, she kept at her chores and her letter-writing for fourteen hours every "good day" and much longer on bad ones. Inevitably, her health began to fail after only three weeks of giving everything she had to the war effort.

When her cough became so deep and pronounced that it could be heard from one end of her ward to the other, she consulted the surgeon in charge of the Union Hotel Hospital. He examined her briefly, grunted that she had fever, and jotted down a memorandum. Trying desperately to decipher it, Louisa Alcott couldn't be sure whether she had typhoid fever or pneumonia.

Soon, she became delirious and was confined to her bed. Immense doses of calomel, administered to "put her back into her ward in a few days," made her worse. Although U.S. Army surgeons would conclude within months that the "mercurous chloride," the chief ingredient of the purgative, was too poisonous to be used, their verdict came too late to help Louisa. Too weak to stand on her feet unaided, she notified her father of her condition. Bronson Alcott rushed to her side and brought her home to recuperate.

Her recovery, which was never complete, was much slower than anyone had anticipated. After nearly three months in bed, she felt strong enough to go to the dinner table for one meal a day. By that time, many of her teeth were coming loose, and one had dropped from its socket. Not until long afterward did she learn that mercury in the calomel forced on her at the hospital caused her to lose all her teeth.

On many days, her only diversion was the reading and rereading of the letters she had sent to Concord from the Union Hotel Hospital. Sometimes she came across a passage that caused her to smile and occasionally laugh; many times, she wept over rekindled memories of men whose faces she knew well, but whose names she did not remember. Her

Louisa May Alcott, successful and prosperous author.

account of days and nights in the Georgetown hospital constantly caused her to reflect on her journey and her brief experience there.

Washington never disappeared from her mind. "Though I'd often been told that it was a spacious place, its visible magnitude quite took my breath away," she said. During her single evening in the capital, she was afforded the time to "stare hard at the famous East Room of the

White House" from outside, which she would have liked to see, even through a crack in the door. Ladies who formed the queens of society in the capital, she said, wore "three-storey bonnets and walked like ducks." When the mail brought her payment for her hospital services in the sum of $10, she handed the money to her father without a word.

By the time she felt strong enough to resume some of her prewar activities, a few of her letters had been seen by people outside the family. One of them, James Redpath of Boston, persuaded her that she didn't need to sit down and write a book as she had earlier dreamed of doing. "You already have a book in these vivid and detailed letters," he told her. Edited to appear in third-person voice, her *Hospital Sketches* filled a little book of 102 pages. It attracted little attention at the time, but is today regarded as a classic description of what a cultured woman was expected to do when she offered her services as a nurse.

Robert Brothers, an executive of a Boston publishing firm, had known that the woman from Concord yearned to write a novel. After scanning her book of *Hospital Sketches,* he encouraged her to try her hand at something much longer—perhaps a story designed for young girls. By the summer of 1868, the one-time volunteer nurse had completed her manuscript about the four girls of the March family of New England. Published as *Little Women,* the experiences of Meg, Jo, Beth, and Amy was an immediate and a lasting success.

Brief as her wartime service turned out to be, Louisa May Alcott confessed that for every ounce of courage it took to volunteer, she needed "ten times as much to stay in Ward Number One for a single hour after casualties began pouring into it." Had she lacked the courage and zeal that took her to the nation's capital and the Union Hotel Hospital, she may never have had the experiences and motivation that propelled her into the ranks of great writers of the Western world.

CHAPTER

28

Barbara Frietchie

Flag Waver

E mma Dorothy Eliza Nevitta Southworth, a noted novelist, knew
how hard it was for a writer to find a very compelling topic.
That's why she was delighted to come across material that she
thought was perfectly suited to the pen of John Greenleaf Whittier. Writing from Georgetown, Virginia, in August 1863, she informed him of an
incident that took place nearly a year earlier and enclosed newspaper
accounts of it. The famous woman usually referred to as E.D.E.N. told
the poet:

> When Lee's army occupied Frederick, the sole Union
> flag displayed in the city was held from an attic window
> by Mrs. Barbara Frietchie, a widow lady, aged ninety-
> seven years.

E.D.E.N. said she received her information from a friend who lived in
Frederick and from stories in Washington newspapers. In her letter to
Whittier, she told him that Union flags in Frederick were lowered on the
approach of the Army of Northern Virginia under the command of
Gen. Thomas "Stonewall" Jackson. Frietchie, however, had refused to
follow the example of her neighbors. Instead, she ascended to the garret
of her home and threw open a window. She then vigorously waved the
Stars and Stripes over the heads of marching Rebels. An officer who
saw what she was doing barked two orders in quick succession: "Halt!"
and "Fire!" The resulting volley damaged Frietchie's flag, E.D.E.N.
wrote, but the aged widow was not intimidated. Leaning from her garret, she cried to Confederates below, "Fire at this old head, then, boys;
it is not more venerable than your flag!" When the incident came to
Jackson's attention, he ordered his men to leave the old woman alone.

Whittier must have experienced a rush of adrenaline on reading this dramatic story. Singlehandedly, a woman nearly a century old had defied invading Rebel troops under the command of the mighty Stonewall Jackson! Barbara Frietchie's exploit would be a hot topic of conversation long after she was dead. Jackson was too much of a Southern gentleman to retaliate, but he must have seethed inwardly.

Inspired in a way that he had experienced only a few times in his long life, the Quaker poet who was also an ardent abolitionist informed

Dame Barbara Frietchie.—Pictorial Field Book of the Civil War

his Washington friend that he had written the incident in verse. "It will appear in the next number of the *Atlantic*" he told her. "And you can judge whether it is good for any thing." He probably had no idea that his version of the brief drama in Frederick would be listed more than a century later as one of his four most widely known poems. As published in the *Atlantic Monthly* of October 1863, Whittier's ballad read:

BARBARA FRIETCHIE

Up rose old Barbara Frietchie then,
Bowed with her fourscore years and then;
Bravest of all in Frederick town,
She took up the flag the men hauled down;
In her attic window the staff she set,
To show that one heart was loyal yet.
Up the street came the rebel tread,
Stonewall Jackson riding ahead.
Under his slouched hat left and right
He glanced: the old flag met his sight.
"Halt!" The dust-brown ranks stood fast.
"Fire!" out blazed the rifle-blast.
It shivered the window, pane and sash;
It rent the banner with scam and gash.
Quick, as it fell from the broken staff,
Dame Barbara snatched the silken scarf;

> She leaned far out on the window-sill,
> And shook it forth with a royal will.
> "Shoot, if you must this old gray head,
> But spare your country's flag," she said.
> A shade of sadness, a blush of shame,
> Over the face of the leader came;
> The nobler nature within him stirred
> To life at that woman's deed and word:
> "Who touches a hair of yon gray head
> Dies like a dog! March on!" he said.
> All day long through Frederick street
> Sounded the tread of marching feet.
> All day long that free flag tost
> Over the heads of the rebel host.

Frederick storekeeper Henry M. Nixdorff wrote and published a brief account of the life of the woman immortalized by Whittier. According to Nixdorff, she was the faithful wife of a glove maker. Having come to Frederick from elsewhere, she soon became well known throughout the village and was locally renowned for her ardent patriotism.

"I shall never forget her appearance as she came into my store during the earlier part of the war [when nearly every week saw a Confederate victory]," Nixdorff wrote. "With the greatest earnestness, she said: 'Do not for a moment despair; stand firm.'" According to him, whenever bad news about Union forces was received, Barbara would urge: "Do not be cast down! It will all come right! I am sure it is God's will that the Union shall continue."

No emblem was more hated and coveted during wartime than the enemy's flag. A soldier who captured a flag in battle became an instant hero, and his trophy was usually shipped to his home state for exhibition on special occasions. More than a year before the drama took place in Frederick, a Rebel flag triggered events that led to what Northerners called "our first martyrdom."

Col. Elmer Ellsworth of the famous Fire Zouaves, or 11th New York regiment of volunteers, led soldiers to Alexandria, Virginia, on May 24, 1861. Invading troops caught sight of a Rebel flag flying above the Marshall House tavern. Their dauntless commander, a protégé of Abraham Lincoln, stormed into the tavern, rushed up the stairs, and hauled down the offending emblem. He was shot and killed on his way back down the stairway by James T. Jackson, owner of the tavern. Almost instantly, Pvt. Francis E. Brownell returned a fatal shot and killed Jack-

A gable window of this house was identified as the place from which a Union flag was waved at Rebels.—National Cyclopedia of American Biography

son. In the aftermath of the tragedy, about which the entire North soon learned in detail, the Executive Mansion in Washington was draped in black. No doubt about it, a flag could make the blood of a man or a woman boil with anger.

Despite difficulties of transportation and communication, the poem "Barbara Frietchie" soon reached Rebel readers. Without exception, they moaned and screamed with indignation that Jackson, or for that matter any other Confederate commander, would never have told his men to fire in the general direction of a woman. Throughout the Confederacy, Whittier's ballad and the story on which it was based was dismissed as Northern propaganda. Rebels initially denied that there had been a flag-waving incident of any sort in Frederick. Whittier, deeply offended, hotly retorted that he based his poem on solid evidence from an impeccable source, that he had received a clear account, and that he wanted to make Barbara Frietchie memorable as "a hater of the Slavery Rebellion." At the end of the Civil War, former C.S. Gen. Jubal Early sent Whittier a courteous letter, which never received a reply. Early later wrote:

I called his attention to the overwhelming proof that he had been imposed upon by the parties who gave him the incident, and asked him for a note acknowledging his mistake. But he did not deign a reply to my letter. No doubt "the great American poet" who used his genius so generously in misrepresenting and slandering the South rejoiced at having put down "the Rebel Jackson."

Despite having ignored Early's letter, as late as 1886 Whittier went on record as "still constrained to believe that the poem had foundation in fact." Two years later, he notified the editor of *Century* magazine that he had "received letters from several responsible persons who wholly or partially confirmed" the story he put into verse. By then it had been reprinted countless times, unchanged except for Anglicizing the heroine's name as Fritchie.

Caroline H. Dall seems to have made an early start on a book whose purpose was to defend Frietchie's claim to fame, but it was not published until much later. When she issued a volume about the life of her famous husband, Stonewall Jackson's wife took pains to repudiate the story that was by then almost universally known. Mrs. B. A. Keane of Roxbury, Massachusetts, tried to launch an organized move to have the Whittier poem banished from public schools. Describing herself as "not a Southern woman, only a good American," she said she didn't want her children to grow up with sectional prejudice spawned by this verse.

Long before 1888, many other people had given their own accounts of the controversy. Barbara's nephew Valerius Ebert, who allegedly had strong secessionist views, claimed his aunt had been bedridden and couldn't possibly have climbed into her garret. Even had she been carried up the steps, her nephew alleged, "she would have been unable to wave a flag." What's more, he added, her mind had started to wander long before and could not have thought clearly enough to defy the Confederate invaders.

His analysis of the physical and mental condition of the heroine is strongly challenged by a well-documented chain of events. Units of Gen. George B. McClellan's Army of the Potomac reached Frederick on September 13, less than a day after Jackson pulled out and headed toward Antietam Creek. Union Gen. Jesse L. Reno's aides claimed that shortly before or after noon, Reno heard a version of the Frietchie tale. He reputedly exclaimed, "The spirit of '76!" Intrigued by the story, the Federal commander went to West Patrick Street in Frederick and quickly located the Frietchie residence on the bank of Carroll Creek.

An artist's concept of Barbara Frietchie in action.—SAMUEL SARTAIN ENGRAVING

When he knocked on the door, Dame Barbara came to the door, giving him a warm smile because of his blue uniform. Records indicate that he shook hands with the aged resident and accepted from her a glass of homemade currant wine. He then asked Frietchie if she would sell him her flag. She told him that she had two flags, one of which was made of silk and was kept in her Bible. She wouldn't part with it under any circumstances, but she would be honored to present him with a large bunting flag that usually flew from a dormer window. If anything was said about the recent flag-waving incident, the conversation was not recorded. Clearly, however, either Reno's immediate subordinates or Barbara's nephew lied about the woman's physical and mental condition on September 12, 1862.

To further complicate the already tangled story, Jackson's aides consulted their records. They unanimously agreed that Stonewall couldn't possibly have come near the Frietchie home as he passed through Frederick. While encamped for four days, the noted Confederate leader had recuperated from injuries sustained by a fall from a spirited horse. He had not entered Frederick until 5:15 A.M. on Saturday, when he finally climbed on his favorite horse and rode through the Maryland town to visit a friend and clergyman. His route took him, said Col. Kyd Douglass, "along Mill Alley, about three hundred yards from the Frietchie residence." When he failed to find his friend at home, Jackson turned due west toward Antietam and hence did not reenter Frederick.

Anyone known or believed to have been in Frederick at the time of the famous flag-waving incident was questioned. Frederick's mayor, Jacob Englebrecht, a man with strong Union feelings, lived close to Barbara on the other side of the street. He shook his head when asked what had taken place and allegedly said that he saw Lee as he rode along his street, but never saw Jackson. His aged neighbor, said the mayor, did not appear at her window on the morning in question.

Dr. Oliver Wendell Holmes hurried to Maryland in the aftermath of Antietam. The famous writer came in search of his son, having received news that he had been wounded during the bloodiest day of the Civil War. The Massachusetts author seems to have spent several days in and around Frederick, but never wrote a single word about Barbara Frietchie.

The niece and adopted daughter of Barbara Frietchie, a Mrs. Handschue, eventually entered the fray. She had inherited a silk flag from her aunt, but described it as "not rent with seam and gash from a rifle-blast; torn—only this and nothing more." The flag was among Handschue's most prized possessions, but it showed no evidence of having been the flag Frietchie allegedly waved.

Many people, considering themselves peacemakers, tried to find an explanation for the popularity of the famous story. Some of them uncovered what they judged to be good evidence that two little girls who lived in Middletown ran out with ribbons in their hair and waved tiny Union flags at Jackson. Since Middletown was only six miles from Frederick, the children could have been the actual flag-wavers. According to a number of Frederick residents, Mrs. Mary Quantrell, who lived on the same street as Frietchie, was the real heroine who waved the Stars and Stripes as Confederates rode by her home.

John Greenleaf Whittier accepted a vivid story of courage without bothering to inquire into its authenticity.— DICTIONARY OF AMERICAN PORTRAITS

So many conflicting claims exist that it is impossible to unequivocally conclude what did or did not take place in September 1862. In light of this dilemma, several analysts later reached an agreement concerning a version of the story that they judged to have all the hallmarks of truth.

Union troops entered Frederick on the heels of their gray-clad opponents; ample documentary evidence supports this assertion. Analysts speculate that as they rode past Barbara Frietchie's house on September 13, the aged widow raced upstairs with her prized silk flag to signal her joy at their arrival. This re-creation of the incident removes the stigma of her impunity, but preserves the tradition that a ninety-seven-year-old woman of German extraction was fiercely loyal to the Union. Regardless of whether the earlier version of the incident or this later redaction is true, Dame Barbara Frietchie lives on as the central character of this dramatic Civil War story.

29
Varina Davis
Relentless

Fort Monroe, Va., May 3, 1866

*I, Varina Davis, wife of Jefferson Davis, for the privilege of being
permitted to see my husband, do hereby give my parole of honor
that I will engage in or assent to no measures which shall lead to any
attempt to escape from confinement on the part of my husband or to
his being rescued or released from imprisonment without the sanc-
tion and order of the President of the United States, nor will I be the
means of conveying to my husband any deadly weapons of any kind.*

—VARINA DAVIS
Witness:
J. A. Fessenden, Second Lieutenant, Fifth Artillery

For more than a year the former first lady of the Confederacy had
fought for the privilege of signing such a pledge. She got it, not
because there was widespread sympathy for her in the North but
because she waged a nonstop campaign of writing letters to authorities
and newspapers. A postscript was attached to one of her letters to President Andrew Johnson. "Mr. President," she begged, "please decide this
matter for yourself. For the love of God and his merciful Son do not
refuse me. Let me go to him and admire and bless your name every hour
of my life." Late in April, Johnson personally directed that she be permitted to visit Davis after duly signing this pledge.

Nelson A. Miles, a major general of volunteers in command at
Fortress Monroe, forwarded the parole to Washington and assigned
quarters in a casemate to the wife of his most distinguished prisoner.
Grudgingly, he consented for her to oversee the preparation of her hus-

band's meals. He also sent to the capital a May 3 report by Surgeon George E. Cooper of the U.S. Army. "State prisoner Jefferson Davis is suffering from considerable derangement of the bowels with diarrhea," he said. Having made weekly reports about the health of Davis for nearly a year, the surgeon concluded that the prisoner "requires more exercise in the open air."

In a memorandum directed to Gen. E. D. Townsend late in May, Miles wrote that Davis had become "more cheerful and in better spirits since his wife has been here." At the same time, the commandant castigated Cooper, noting that "his wife is a secessionist and one of the F. F. V.'s of this state [First Families of Virginia]." The surgeon had been "exceedingly attentive to Mrs. Davis," he fumed and seemed to have come under her influence.

First lady of the Confederacy.— JOHN WOOD DODGE MINIATURE, NATIONAL PORTRAIT GALLERY, SMITHSONIAN INSTITUTION

Surgeon General J. K. Barnes visited the fortress to see for himself how the former president of the Confederate States of America was faring. He decided that Davis had "improved in all respects at least 50 per cent" since his report of the previous month. It would help, he believed, to permit the prisoner to walk about the courtyard "from guard mounting to guard mounting." Miles immediately acted on this recommendation, probably realizing that he could not successfully challenge the recommendation of the surgeon general.

After sending his wife and children southward earlier, Davis had left Richmond in 1865 on learning of Robert E. Lee's surrender at Appomattox. He initially planned to join Confederate forces in the West, which had not yet laid down their arms. When that course of action proved unfeasible, he decided to have his wife join this party and strike out for Mexico. They met on the Oconee River near Dublin, Georgia. Federal forces, which had been in hot pursuit for ten days, caught up with the fugitives on the following day and placed Davis under arrest. He was shipped northward under heavy twenty-four-hour guard, and officers in blue immediately began squabbling over what portion of the $100,000 reward offered for his capture should come to them and their men.

Taken to Macon, Georgia, and then sent to Richmond on May 22, the heavily ironed prisoner was assigned to a cell in Fortress Monroe. Initially charged with treason, Davis was now named as a coconspirator in the John Wilkes Booth plot to assassinate the president. Clement C. Clay Jr. of Alabama, a longtime friend of both Varina and Jefferson Davis, was soon brought to the fortress as a political prisoner. They so highly regarded him that he became the godfather of their son Joseph at Varina's request. The Alabaman who had withdrawn from the U.S. Senate on January 21, 1861, was at first charged only with treason—conviction of which would have meant an automatic death sentence. Soon he joined his friend in the ranks of former Confederates who were indicted and charged with being implicated in the assassination plot.

Both men were put into what today would be called solitary confinement. They were constantly shackled, and their cells were lighted around the clock. Guards shuffled back and forth at frequent intervals. The heavy iron manacles were later removed, but Davis was already suffering from a variety of ills, which grew steadily worse during nearly a year of imprisonment. He repeatedly begged to be put on trial, but authorities in Washington made no move to do so. In what she considered a dire situation, Varina won permission to visit Jefferson under stipulated conditions.

After fleeing from Richmond with her children, she had managed to spend a few days with Mary Boykin Chesnut (see Chapter 25) at her Chester, South Carolina, home. Soon after Jefferson was captured, Varina found refuge in Augusta, Georgia. Keenly aware that her presence in the city caused many of its citizens to be suspect, she went to Canada for a while. From there, she waged a ceaseless campaign on behalf of her husband.

As a result of her refusal to accept defeat, on May 24, 1866, the *New York World* published a lengthy article entitled "The Torture of Jefferson Davis." On the same day, editors of the *New York News* informed readers that the manner of his imprisonment had caused his life to hang by a thread. "The 'shriveled skin' and 'flaccid muscles' of the martyr of Fortress Monroe plead with irresistible eloquence in his behalf," the *News* reported. "Let us hope the plea will be heard."

It was no coincidence that Varina Davis reached Washington from Fortress Monroe on the very day that two New York newspapers published appeals on behalf of her husband. She had not yet seen a high official of the War Department, to say nothing of the president. But it was widely assumed that she had come to make an effort to get what one newspaper of the capital termed "some modification of the stringent orders in relation to her husband's confinement." What she accomplished during this visit, if anything, is unknown.

Returning to the South, she addressed an entreaty to Gen. Montgomery C. Meigs, asking him:

> Plead for me that I may be allowed to correspond with my husband. The reports harrow me so that under happier circumstances I should be unequal to bearing them. . . . If allowed to remain in the North until after my husband's trial, I will bind myself not to do anything prejudicial to your Government. Please answer by telegraph. I have been three weeks in suspense. Tell me what you know of Mr. Davis' health?

Though charged with treason and complicity in the assassination of Lincoln, Jefferson Davis was never put on trial. During the spring of 1867, Varina's ceaseless pleas, directed to every influential person she could identify, played an important role in bringing about a shift in public opinion. Horace Greeley, founder of the *New York Tribune*, agreed to become a cosigner of a bail bond for Davis in the sum of $100,000, even though he knew such a move would cost his newspapers tens of thousands of subscribers. When other influential Northerners took the same step, the ex-president of the Confederacy was released. Two years later a *nolle prosequi* plea was entered on behalf of the man who was still free on bail. This step made it clear that government attorneys had no intention of prosecuting him; thanks in large part to Varina he spent the rest of his life in relative tranquility.

It was the only lengthy period during their marriage in which he and his wife

Jefferson Davis soon after his release from Fortress Monroe.—Harper's Encyclopedia of U.S. History

Jefferson and Varina Davis early in their marriage.—MISSISSIPPI STATE ARCHIVES

were not in turmoil of one sort or another. Born into the wealthy plantation class of Mississippi in 1826, Varina Howell studied at a fashionable girls' academy in Philadelphia and under a private tutor. When wealthy widower Jefferson Davis met her at an 1843 Christmas party, he quickly realized that she was among the best-educated women of the period. Two years later, Davis took as his wife the unusually tall nineteen-year-old whose intimates considered her expressive eyes to be her prominent physical feature. He was nearly old enough to be her father, and very early on he made it clear that she would never be his equal in some significant respects.

Clearly with Jefferson's consent, his older brother took steps that barred the bride from ever inheriting any of the extensive Davis property. But some other fundamental differences between Jefferson and Varina were far more important than the disposition of property. He was accustomed to making all important decisions, and he had no intention of changing that practice. Even scheduled visits to her relatives could not be carried out until he gave his approval. Despite the fact that he was a man of means, he watched Varina's spending closely and accused her of being profligate. Virtually all mistresses of plantations liked ornamental and decorative things, which they called "household goods." Davis labeled such bric-a-brac "trumpery" and wanted none of it in his sight.

Varina often squirmed and sometimes protested, but always ended up yielding to her husband. She voiced no objection when, out of the blue, he astonished her by saying that he was going to Mexico to fight under Gen. Winfield Scott. Yet she was deeply offended that he had made potentially life-altering decisions without so much as asking her opinions. When he returned from the war in 1847, he quickly sensed that her anger had not subsided. Soon he was elected to the U.S. Senate. Knowing that Varina would love to plunge into Washington society, he punished her by keeping her in exile in Mississippi for many months.

Assessing the troubled, male-dominated marriage, historian Bruce Catton placed much of the blame squarely on the shoulders of Jefferson Davis. "He locked himself in behind a self-control so complete that it seemed to lock everyone else out," he concluded. That rigidity became more pronounced during Jefferson's tenure as U.S. Secretary of War. In that capacity he was one of the best (if not the very best) nineteenth-century secretary. He scrapped as many wooden gun carriages as possible and replaced them with iron. In a daring innovation, he brought camels from the near East and put them into the deserts of the American West. He dispatched survey crews to find good routes for a transcontinental railroad, and he boosted morale of officers and men in the U.S. Army with constant encouragement plus a pay raise.

After spending four years trying to make the nation's military force strong, he returned to the Senate and devoted some of his time and energy to extolling the benefits of the slavery

The four Davis children, with Joe sitting at the right.
—Embattled Confederates

system. At least as much as any other national leader, his insistence on the legitimacy of slavery helped split the Democratic party in 1860, a schism that virtually guaranteed the election of whomever the Republicans might pick as their candidate. By January 5, 1861, he had gone on record as an unequivocal advocate of Southern secession. As in previous matters of great importance, he did not bother to ask his wife for her views and perhaps did not know that from the beginning of the secession movement she predicted that it would lead to the ruin of the South.

By the time he resigned from the Senate and returned to Mississippi, hoping to lead the life of a plantation owner, Varina was caring for three children—Margaret, Joseph Evan, and Jefferson Jr. Both parents were surprised and shocked when a courier from the nearest telegraph office brought a message that Davis had been chosen as the first chief executive of the Confederation of seceded states that was being formed in Montgomery, Alabama. He left Mississippi immediately; Varina and the children soon followed. Jefferson assured his wife that though he'd much rather lead Confederate armies than serve as president, he would give his best to the new nation. Almost as an afterthought, he told her that he was confident she would be widely respected as the first lady of the Confederacy.

Despite this assurance, on her arrival at the new Confederate capital, Varina felt that Richmond society gave her the cold shoulder. Many of the ladies displayed what she called "a certain offishness in their manner." Though she didn't know it, one of her husband's top subordinates outside his cabinet scoffed at her as a squaw. Davis complained constantly about her extravagance, but the *Richmond Examiner* criticized the "parsimonious nature of her official entertainments."

A majority of men who became new acquaintances agreed that Mrs. Davis was still quite attractive at age thirty-five. Some of them spoke of her as "handsome." Newspaper correspondent William H. Russell of England was impressed with the wife of the Confederate president. To his readers Russell described her as being "a comely, sprightly woman of good figure and manners, well dressed and clever."

Some writers for newspapers much closer to home wondered whether or not her coal-black hair was inherited from a Native American. Others made fun of her height (5'10"), pointing out that few men were that tall when standing barefoot. A few unsigned newspaper comments described her as being "dowdy, and entirely too large for so young a matron." It's no wonder that later in life she characterized her four years in Richmond as the most miserable in her life.

President and Mrs. Jefferson Davis in postwar years.—NATIONAL ARCHIVES

A significant part of her misery stemmed from events that took place in the White House of the Confederacy. Davis tried valiantly to weather the storm that erupted from a series of military defeats and ceaseless opposition from governors wedded to the notion of states' rights. He worked so tirelessly that he often forgot to eat; early in 1864 Varina began taking him his lunch about 1 P.M. and staying long enough to see that he had at least begun to eat it.

On April 30, servants prepared the luncheon platter, and Varina glanced around her room to be sure that the children didn't need attention at the moment. When she saw that all was well, she moved into her husband's office and presented him with his meal. As she tells the story, she had barely uncovered the luncheon basket "when a servant came for me. The most beautiful and brightest of my children, Joseph Evan, had, in play, climbed over the connecting angle of a bannister and fallen to the brick pavement below. He died a few minutes after we reached his side."

In her early grief, Varina remembered news from about one hundred miles away in Washington. Another first lady had lost a son earlier. Newspaper accounts described Mary Todd Lincoln as "inconsolable" at the death of young William Wallace. Varina realized with a start that the Executive Mansion in Washington had more in common with her own home than she had imagined.

Shortly before the death of her beloved Joe, Varina had begun to squirrel away small amounts of cash. Most of it came not from her husband but from her sale of personal possessions, such as china and books. Though she never dared to breathe a word of such thoughts to Jefferson, she confided to Mary Chesnut and a few other close friends that she knew the Confederacy couldn't possibly survive.

In some respects, she was almost relieved when her husband saw the end coming and told her that she must go to North Carolina so she wouldn't be present during the fall of the capital. His actions on the day she headed for the lower South troubled her deeply, however. When he discovered that she had made plans to take along a few barrels of flour purchased from her own funds he became very stern. "You cannot remove anything in the shape of food from here; the people want it, and you must leave it here," he told her.

He later handed her a pistol and spent half an hour showing her how to use it. Knowing that partisans not under direct Confederate control roamed everywhere, he worried that a band of them might come across her and the children. If that should happen, he told her, "You can at least, if reduced to the last extremity, force your assailants to kill you." These worries were unfounded. Except for long delays caused by worn-out locomotives and railroad track, her journey was comparatively uneventful until she joined Jefferson for their planned escape. Florida was by then considered a more likely haven than Mexico.

She agonized when two bands of Federal soldiers who were competing for the honor and the cash of making the arrest fired into one another by accident. When her husband, who had a price on his head, was captured, she broke down and cried. Some of her post-war writings suggest that she experienced the low point of her adult life there, near Irwinville, Georgia.

Once Jefferson became what she termed "a most dreadfully abused prisoner," Varina became a different person. Working tirelessly with the announced goal of knocking on so many doors that at least one of them would open someday, she became one of the most indomitable crusaders of her century. Her *Memoirs* and her postwar critiques of Confederate blunders and mismanagement were largely forgotten as soon as they went into print. Her relentless pursuit of decency and justice for a husband whom she felt had been wronged beyond words made her a dynamic force whose boundless store of energy and ideas really did affect the course of events.

30
Anna Ella Carroll
Strategist

Be it enacted that the sum and emoluments given by the government to the major generals of the United States Army be paid to Anna Ella Carroll from November 1861, the date of her service to the country to the time of the passage of this act, and further payments of the same amount as the pay and emoluments of a major general in the United States Army be paid her in quarterly installments to the end of her life, as a partial measure of recognition of her services to the nation.

R eputedly identified by its author as H.R. 7256 and printed in full at his expense, the measure whose key paragraph appears here was drawn up twenty years after the fall of Fort Sumter. Democratic Congressman Edward Bragg of Wisconsin, credited with authorship, had once served as commander of the Civil War's famous Iron Brigade. The beneficiary of Bragg's bill, who was then living in a Washington hotel, was a member of one of Maryland's most distinguished families.

Months later, lawmakers were presented with another bill whose number was also 7256. This time, the proposed measure stipulated:

Be it enacted that the Secretary of the Interior be and is hereby authorized and directed to place upon the pension rolls of the United States the name of Anna Ella Carroll and to pay her a pension of $25 a month from and after the passage of this act during her life, for the important military service rendered the country by her during the late war.

Carroll and her large coterie of friends and acquaintances, some of whom held high offices, denounced the second bill as fraudulent. They immediately renewed an earlier campaign whose goal was to secure for her a lump-sum payment of $50,000 for "invaluable work done for the Union cause" from 1861 to 1862. Critics of Carroll, most of whom preferred to remain anonymous, said the earlier version of H.R. 7256 was bogus and vowed never to act favorably on such a preposterous piece of legislation. The woman from Maryland, some of them said, deserved nothing at all. Bragg remained on the sidelines during the growing fray and said nothing on the record.

Anna Ella Carroll was widely credited with having framed plans that led to the first significant Union victories of the Civil War. Controversy over what was due to a noted woman said to have been Abraham Lincoln's most trusted advisor flared just as the feminist movement was becoming politically potent. Women who called themselves suffragettes, plus a gaggle of nationally known men, screamed with indignation that if the second version of H.R. 7256 passed, a great injustice would be done. An occasional challenge of Carroll's claims was voiced, but most political leaders shook their heads in bewilderment and issued no statements about her or her Civil War work.

Decades later, Carroll and her claims were still being debated. In a 1952 study, *Lincoln and His Generals*, T. Harry Williams devoted an appendix to refuting claims that Carroll was responsible for U. S. Grant's great victory at Vicksburg. Twenty years later, Allan Nevins felt compelled to echo that verdict. In 1975 E. B. Long, noted author of *The Civil War Day by Day*, spoke his mind about the woman widely credited with having helped split the Confederacy. Writing for *Civil War Times Illustrated*, he offered a blow-by-blow refutation of practically all claims made by and on behalf of Anna Ella Carroll. Later, waving all questions and objections aside, Clara C. Jensen studied the complex issue and concluded that Carroll had enormous impact on the outcome of the sectional struggle. Published in the March 1995 issue of *America's Civil War*, the headline above her analysis lauded Carroll as "Abraham Lincoln's secret strategic weapon."

It is difficult to determine just what the Maryland woman did, but easy to learn some details of her early life. Anna was born at Kingston Hall in Somerset County on August 25, 1815. Her father, Thomas K. Carroll, was a genteel and cultured planter whose slaves made plantation life easy for him. All accounts stress that the girl was unusually precocious. By age eleven she was already reading books not published for children. Though she attended a boarding school near Annapolis for a while, she showed very little interest in music, dancing, or sewing.

Anna Ella Carroll frequently wore low cut gowns that were then in vogue.—J. C. BUTTRE ENGRAVING

An influential member of the legislature, her father became chief executive of his state in 1829. Anna, age fourteen, was thrilled at her father's political success, but became disconsolate and a bit withdrawn when his new position required him to be away from Kingston Hall a lot of the time. She seems to have turned her energy inward at about the same time politics became her absorbing interest. Soon she began submitting short political and legal writings to newspapers, using a pseudonym because she didn't think an editor would take anything written by an adolescent girl seriously.

If she was ever interested in marriage, she concealed her views with care. Sitting with pen in hand much of the time, at age forty she set out to help Thomas Hicks become the governor of Maryland. He faced what seemed to be an uphill battle because he was an outspoken adherent of the new American Party that the long-entrenched Whigs and Democrats despised and feared.

Many members of this political party called themselves Sons of '76 and took an oath not to reveal anything about their objectives. Since "I don't know" became the standard answer of these folk when questioned, they were popularly labeled as Know-Nothings. They opposed immigration into the United States and the growing power of the Roman Catholic Church, claiming that their aim was for Americans to rule America.

As a full-time volunteer worker for the Hicks campaign, Carroll proved herself to be highly skilled. When she claimed credit for his win at the polls, he went on record as being grateful to her. Though she later insisted that her candidate was the only Know-Nothing to win an important office at that time, a glance at the records reveals a different story. In 1855 the secret party swept to power in California, Connecticut, Kentucky, New York, and New Hampshire. It also made inroads into Alabama, Georgia, Louisiana, Mississippi, Texas, and Virginia. When Hicks took his oath of office, one-fourth of the nation's thirty-two governors were Know-Nothings.

Carroll's boast that she was responsible for making a Know-Nothing the governor of Maryland was a sign of things to come. Despite her failure to block the election of James Buchanan to the presidency, according to her devotees, she was involved in or was responsible for an amazing number of accomplishments that were concealed because she was a woman.

She allegedly had a secret meeting with President Lincoln shortly after the president-elect reached the capital. Soon afterward he was confronted by the Maryland dilemma: About half of the state's citizens were pro-Southerners. Secession of this crucial border state would seriously weaken the Union's war effort, so decisive action was needed. Carroll supposedly told the president that he could deal with the matter easily. By arresting legislators and preventing them from holding a scheduled session, it would be impossible for them to take their state out of the Union. Lincoln did precisely that, and his actions are widely believed to have "saved Maryland for the grand old flag."

More than two years later, Lincoln reached an agonizing decision. Though he would have liked to see all freed slaves sent to overseas colonies, he drafted and signed the Emancipation Proclamation in the presence of his assembled cabinet. Executive Mansion artist Francis B. Carpenter's famous painting of the January 1, 1863, ceremony depicts the president, pen in hand, flanked by all of his top advisors. In the painting, an empty chair sits in front of the table Lincoln is using. It was put there, say many Carroll devotees, to symbolize the fact that she was his invisible cabinet member. According to this interpretation of the painting, for months she had been secretly giving him the best and most important advice he received.

Anna Carroll advanced none of these claims herself, but she made it easy for her followers to do so. Her startling declarations about behind-the-scenes involvement in the 1862 Federal military move into the heart of the South set Washington agog. To lawmakers, generals, and members of the public she convincingly asserted that she had developed "the Tennessee Plan." She insisted that she had first carefully studied the course of major rivers, which in the 1860s played crucial roles. Once she had learned all she could about the rivers, Carroll publicly declared, it was clear to her that strategic plans made in Washington needed to be modified. Instead of seeking to master the mighty Mississippi, Union gunboats and troops should open the Tennessee and Cumberland Rivers, she suggested. They could then reach Nashville, Tennessee, with ease, and the lower South would be effectively divided into two segments.

This sequence of events would require no military victories except the reduction of Fort Henry and Fort Donelson, both of which had recently been erected by Confederates as defensive works. U. S. Grant and Andrew H. Foote could combine their forces and the resulting powerful army/navy expedition would make short work of Rebel installations that guarded the vital rivers.

Most people with an established interest in the Civil War know that Grant and Foote followed precisely this course of action. River boats were hastily constructed especially for joint operations, and the two commanders and their forces moved against the smaller of the Confederate forts early in February 1862. Built on a flood plain adjacent to the Tennessee River, Fort Henry was defended by only sixteen or eighteen guns, which were served by about a hundred men in gray. The attacking force consisted of nearly 15,000 men, plus four ironclad gunboats and their crews. Overwhelming Federal strength led to a quick and easy victory, during which the combined casualty list of Union and Rebel commands reached a total of only 125 men.

Fort Donelson on the Cumberland River, with an estimated 20,000 defenders, was much larger and stronger than Fort Henry. Yet Grant's men, who marched overland to reach it, were confidently deployed before the fort just six days after Fort Henry surrendered. Some Confederate officers later said they believed though they were outnumbered two to one, they could have dealt with the Federal soldiers had it been a land operation only. Knowing that Foote's gunboats were too powerful to resist, many men in gray fled to avoid capture. The fall of Fort Donelson on February 16 was celebrated throughout the North. Grant had informed his rival who commanded the installation that he would accept no terms except unconditional surrender.

There was no question about the actual sequence of significant events. Informed folk throughout the North and the South knew what had taken place, when it happened, and what it was likely to mean to the warring sections. Most of those who gave the question of strategic planning a second thought took it for granted that Grant, Foote, Gen. Henry W. Halleck, and Abraham Lincoln were the brains behind the campaign.

Outraged by this assumption, which was widely aired in the press, Anna Carroll offered an account of her own earlier activities. More than a decade later, she prepared a detailed summary that was published in *The North American Review* as "Plan of the Tennessee Campaign."

The famous Francis B. Carpenter painting of the signing of the Emancipation Proclamation; the empty chair is said to represent Anna Ella Carroll.—LIBRARY OF CONGRESS

She wrote that in the fall of 1861, she visited Col. Thomas A. Scott and reached an understanding with him. The assistant secretary of war, she declared, presented her proposal to the president and secured his endorsement. She continued her story:

> I concluded to go west and inform myself as to the military and political situation in that quarter. I promised to write anything valuable I obtained, and also to submit my writing for the Government to the Department (meaning Mr. Lincoln), in advance of their publication; which was done. I soon found that in the West, the cause of the Union was deemed hopeless, even by its strongest adherents.

With military aide Lemuel D. Evans accompanying her, the genteel lady who had spent much of her life on an immense plantation made her way to brawling, sprawling St. Louis. There she found Unionists of the city gripped in despair. This mood stemmed from the fact that everyone was sure that Union forces would be defeated when they tried to move down the Mississippi River. To Carroll's regret, Gen. John Charles

Fremont was too far away to see her. Hence, she spent several days researching in the city's big Mercantile Library.

Carroll's belief that the Mississippi River was impregnable was greatly strengthened by research, and she said her "apprehension of danger grew daily more intense." At the same time, this determined woman became more vigorous than ever in her effort "to find some solution for the difficulties." Almost as though given inspiration from above, Carroll wrote in her summary of those eventful days that "a conviction fastened upon me that there was a way of escape; that either the Tennessee or Cumberland River might afford the needed depth of water for the passage of the gun-boats into the heart of the South."

Her conviction was reassuring, but Washington would demand proof. Accompanied by a military aide and an experienced river pilot, she went down the Tennessee River for many miles. Returning to St. Louis, she sent a detailed report to Scott before setting out on her return journey to the capital. By late November she was back in Washington and had put her voluminous papers in order. She called at the War Department on the last day of the month and was elated to learn from Scott that Lincoln had already seen her letter. The president was eager to see her, Carroll claimed, and Scott said that her plan would both save the Union and cover her with glory.

Careful to avoid "in conversation generally" any mention of what she had done, she rejoiced inwardly that her plan was "the first and only idea of such an action that had ever been presented." In retrospect, she was convinced "of the fact there never was, and never can be, the shadow of a doubt" that she originated the Fort Donelson campaign.

Already a celebrity as a result of two books on political action that were published earlier, Carroll found it easy to gain access to prominent men. Her acquaintances, some of whom became friends, included Senator Benjamin F. Wade, presidential aspirant Stephen A. Douglas, Mayor Fernando Wood of New York City, U.S. Attorney General Edward Bates, distinguished orator Edward Everett, Secretary of War Edwin M. Stanton, and Senator Orville Browning of Illinois. She corresponded with or had interviews with many other nationally known leaders. Senator Wade seems to have gone on record as saying that Lincoln, with whom he sparred ceaselessly, had told him that "the merit of the Tennessee Plan was due to Miss Carroll."

Fiery abolitionist Thaddeus Stevens was an implacable foe of the South and everything Southern. Later he won lasting notoriety for managing the impeachment trial of Tennessee-born President Andrew Johnson. At the moment, he was fully occupied with Congressional business and with accusations directed toward Lincoln because of a series of Federal military defeats. Stevens reputedly took Carroll's claims seriously on the heels of smashing victories at Forts Henry and Donelson. Hence, he is said to have been the author of a plan to pay Carroll $50,000 as reimbursement of her travel expenses, plus the cost of printing booklets in defense of war against the South. He was quoted as having said that in addition to expense money, she should receive "a small token of gratitude for the vast sums she has saved the Union."

This proposal got nowhere in Congress, but it triggered rumors that Carroll "had tried to hold up Abraham Lincoln for fifty thousand dollars." Furious at being the subject of such gossip, she wrote and published "An Address to Maryland." Almost simultaneously, on August 14, 1862, she penned an eight-page letter to the president in which she explained and defended her activities since his nomination in Chicago in 1860. At the same time, she pressed her claim for compensation.

Measured against the immense holdings of later presidential libraries, the eight-volume *Collected Works of Abraham Lincoln* is comparatively small. It includes a single letter to Anna Carroll that is two sentences in length. Dated just five days after her lengthy epistle directed to him, it makes no mention of her claims concerning "the Tennessee Plan." Instead, it commends her for having framed and publicized her "Address to Maryland."

The proposal that she should receive a cash payment of $50,000 was never seriously considered. During his eight years a chief executive, U. S. Grant did not reply to charges by Carroll's supporters that she had made the plans that led to some of his spectacular victories. Undeterred by silence and by "Congressional apathy," her advocates submitted memorials and resolutions for a full generation after the beginning of her wartime activity.

The alleged suppression of "the original version of H.R. 7256" followed by "the substitution of a plea for a pittance of a pension" was a crushing blow to them and their heroine. When she heard that she might be offered $25 a month in lieu of a major general's pay, Anna Carroll was rendered prostrate. It was weeks before she resumed any of her customary activities; she never fully recovered from repudiation of her claim that she rendered invaluable military service.

Today, firm believers in Carroll's authorship of "the Tennessee Plan" seem almost resigned to the fact that "justice cannot be done to a woman who died long ago." Some of them take a bit of solace in frequently viewing and meditating on the mysterious empty chair that is shown in Carpenter's painting of the signing of the Emancipation Proclamation.

Many of her detractors are aware that standard reference works identify the vocation of the indomitable Maryland woman as simply "strategist." The most articulate challengers to her claims do not question the validity of that identification. They simply suggest that she was audacious and courageous as a political rather than as a military planner. Whether that assessment is accurate or not, if Anna Ella Carroll were a registered lobbyist today, Capitol Hill would be buzzing with word of her ceaseless and courageous work.

Conclusion

The women depicted in these pages represent millions about whom we know little or nothing. No book, nor lengthy series of books, will ever capture in its entirety the achievments of all the amazing women of the Civil War. Practically anyone who has studied the events of the mid-nineteenth century knows that Harriet Beecher Stowe, Julia Ward Howe, and Clara Barton had tremendous influence upon the war and the American way of life. Varina Davis, Mary Todd Lincoln, and Julia Dent Grant profoundly affected the careers and wartime actions of their husbands. Less known are Elizabeth Van Lew, Phoebe Pember, and Rose Greenhow, who helped shape the course and outcome of the war in various ways. Though they are so obscure that their names aren't even known, the adventures—or misadventures—of the Roswell women tell us a great deal about the intensity and savagery of the war fought almost exclusively by males. Harriet Tubman directly influenced only a small fraction of the men who went to war, but her impact upon these persons and upon the attitudes of the greater public was enormous.

Women of this period were still a long way from being liberated by today's standards, but some of them were anything but passive in their interactions with the male-dominated society. Dr. Mary Walker, Pauline Cushman, Nancy Hart, and Anna Ella Carroll not only made themselves known, but feared; even the men who considered them a nuisance were not always immune.

Only a tiny fraction of the colorful and sometimes influential women of the Civil War could be included in these pages. But you'll find immense amounts of material about these women and their contemporaries on the Internet. After browsing the sites of the Library of

Congress, Amazon.com, or Barnes & Noble, you'll no doubt find a wealth of other titles to buy or borrow from your local library. If very old books and magazines are of special interest to you, by all means get acquainted with the University of Michigan website entitled *The Making of America*. Funded by the Andrew W. Mellon Foundation, at last count this electronic library was offering nearly 700,000 pages of nineteenth-century books and magazines. A subject-matter search on this site is simple and very, very fast. The story of Princess Salm-Salm is one example of the riches that can be found there. Very little has been written about her during the present century, but at *The Making of America,* you'll find her name in at least forty-seven places.

Here's hoping that you've enjoyed acquainting yourself with the amazing women, if only a handful, of the Civil War.

Index

286 • Amazing Women of the Civil War